AUGUSTINE

DE DIALECTICA

SYNTHESE HISTORICAL LIBRARY

TEXTS AND STUDIES IN THE HISTORY OF
LOGIC AND PHILOSOPHY

VOLUME 16

AUGUSTINE

DE DIALECTICA

Translated with Introduction and Notes by

B. DARRELL JACKSON

University of Missouri - Columbia

from the Text newly Edited by

JAN PINBORG

University of Copenhagen

D. REIDEL PUBLISHING COMPANY

DORDRECHT-HOLLAND / BOSTON-U.S.A.

Library of Congress Cataloging in Publication Data

Augustinus, Aurelius, Saint, Bp. of Hippo. Spurious
    and doubtful works.
    De dialectica.

    (Synthese historical library ; v. 16)
    Latin and English.
    Bibliography: p.
    Includes index.
    1. Dialectic. 2. Logic – Early works to 1800.
I. Jackson, Belford Darrell, 1938–   tr. II. Pinborg,
Jan, ed. III. Title. IV. Series.
B655.D42E54   1975   160   74–28325
ISBN 90–277–0538–0

Published by D. Reidel Publishing Company,
P.O. Box 17, Dordrecht, Holland

Sold and distributed in the U.S.A., Canada, and Mexico
by D. Reidel Publishing Company, Inc.
306 Dartmouth Street, Boston,
Mass. 02116, U.S.A.

Printed in The Netherlands by D. Reidel, Dordrecht

To My Parents,

Mildred L. Jackson
Belford G. Jackson

TABLE OF CONTENTS

TRANSLATOR'S PREFACE

I first became interested in *De dialectica* in 1966, while I was doing research on Augustine's knowledge of logic. At the time I made a translation of the Maurist text and included it as an appendix to my doctoral dissertation (Yale, 1967). In 1971 I thoroughly revised the translation on the basis of the critical text of Wilhelm Crecelius (1857) and I have recently revised it again to conform to Professor Jan Pinborg's new edition. The only previously published translation of the whole of *De dialectica* is N. H. Barreau's French translation in the *Oeuvres complètes de Saint Augustin* (1873). Thomas Stanley translated parts of Chapters Six and Nine into English as part of the account of Stoic logic in his *History of Philosophy* (Pt. VIII, 1656). I offer *De dialectica* in English in the hope that it will be of some interest to historians of logic and of the liberal arts tradition and to students of the thought of Augustine. In translating I have for the most part been as literal as is consistent with English usage. Although inclusion of the Latin text might have justified a freer translation, for example, the use of modern technical terms, it seemed better to stay close to the Latin. One of the values in studying a work such as *De dialectica* is to see familiar topics discussed in a terminology not so familiar. In the translation I follow these conventions. Single quotation marks ordinarily indicate that a word is mentioned not used; in some cases they set off direct speech, for example, questions spoken in some of the illustrations. Double quotation marks are used only when another author is being quoted. To make the meaning clearer I have in a few instances inserted English words that are not strictly justified by the Latin. Such words are enclosed in brackets.

The Introduction and Notes which accompany the translation have limited purposes which it is well to state. Neither gives anything like a comprehensive interpretation of *De dialectica*. In the Introduction I consider the authorship of the treatise, first, in the context of its history and, second, by examining selected quantifiable aspects of its language. In the Notes I discuss points of translation, give references to the writings of antiquity that are most helpful in interpreting the treatise, and in some cases interpret or note interpretations of passages. A more complete commentary on *De dialectica* hardly seems required, given the existence of several expositions of its contents. The two most comprehensive accounts are Balduin Fischer's *De Augustini Disciplinarum Libro Qui Est De Dialectica* (1912) and Karl Barwick's *Probleme der Stoischen Sprachlehre und Rhetorik*, Chapters I and II (1957). Both Fischer and Barwick are concerned mainly with the sources of *De dialectica*, particularly with its relation to Stoic theory and to the writings of Varro. Similar interests control the shorter accounts by R. Reitzenstein, Georg Pfligersdorffer, and Jan Pinborg (see the Bibliography). Interpretation of the work in the context of Augustine's thought is found in Ulrich Duchrow's *Sprachverständnis und Biblisches Hören bei Augustin* (1965, pp. 42–62) and, with special interest in Chapter Five of the treatise, in my article, 'The Theory of Signs in St. Augustine's *De Doctrina Christiana*' (1969). Together these books and articles cover most aspects of the content and sources of *De dialectica* and should be consulted for interpretation of the work.

The stylistic study of *De dialectica* that is reported in the second part of the Introduction was done in 1969 and 1970 and so was based on the text of Crecelius. Professor Pinborg's text differs from Crecelius's in some ways that are relevant for my stylistic study. He changes some of the vocabulary and the length of some words (e.g., '*conpraehendo*' to '*comprehendo*'). His changes are, however, surprisingly few in number and so should not significantly affect the data from which I draw conclusions about the quantitative features of the style of the treatise.

During the eight years off and on that I have worked on *De dialectica* I have had much help, which I here gratefully acknowledge. My first translation of the work was thoroughly and profitably criticized by Eugene TeSelle, who supervised my doctoral research. The retranslation from Crecelius's text was immeasurably assisted by Norman Kretzmann. I have made the decisions about how precisely to translate Augustine's work, but the translation has been a truly joint effort. Investigating the authorship of *De dialectica* has led me into fields of research outside my training. I took up the use of computer techniques as a complete novice and but for the expert advice and assistance of Betsy Little, Lloyd Davis, and B. A. Fusaro I am sure that I would have met with total frustration. Ivor Francis helped me with the statistical interpretation of the quantitative data. For advice in matters of paleography I went to James John. Professor Pinborg has shared with me much information about the manuscripts. I have also incurred a large number of debts to institutions. I have received generous and timely financial support from the colleges where I have taught – Queens College (North Carolina), Wesleyan University, and the College of Wooster. The Board of Higher Education of the Presbyterian Church, U.S., and the Piedmont Universities Center of North Carolina supported my computer project with major grants. Several libraries have copied books and manuscripts for me and have allowed me to use their holdings. The Newberry Library, the Beinecke Library at Yale, the Bodleian Library, the University of Pennsylvania Library, and the Cornell University Library deserve to be singled out for mention. The Institut de Recherche et d'Histoire des Textes of Paris has loaned me copies of several manuscripts. Above all I acknowledge my debt to the Society for the Humanities at Cornell University. The bulk of the work on this book was done during my tenure as a Junior Fellow in the Society during 1970–71. Betty Tamminen of the Society typed hundreds of pages of drafts for me, patiently tolerant of the complicated requirements of my manuscript. Henry Guerlac, the director of the Society, did everything in his power to facilitate my work. I am especially grateful to him and the Society for giving me the opportunity to live and work in the vigorous intellectual climate of Cornell University, and particularly for introducing me to an extraordinary group of medievalists.

June 1974

ABBREVIATIONS AND METHOD OF REFERENCE

AL   *Aristoteles Latinus, Codices Descripsit.* Vol. I and II ed. by Lacombe; Vol. III ed. by Minio-Paluello.

CSEL *Corpus Scriptorum Ecclesiasticorum Latinorum.*

LCL Loeb Classical Library.

PL   *Patrologiae Cursus Completus, Series Latina.*

RLM *Rhetores Latini Minores.* Ed. by Halm.

References to the text of *De dialectica* are made by chapter, page, and line numbers in Crecelius's edition. Hence VII, 12, 15 refers to Chapter VII, page 12, line 15. Crecelius's page numbers and the numbers for every fifth line are printed in the margins of Pinborg's text below. They are indicated in the text by a slash mark (/). The endings of intervening lines are indicated by a vertical stroke (ˡ) in the text.

    Books and articles listed in the Bibliography are referred to merely by author or title in the notes. For full information consult the Bibliography.

INTRODUCTION

I. THE HISTORY OF *DE DIALECTICA*

Although *De dialectica* has been regarded as the work of Augustine of Hippo since at least the ninth century, neither the manuscript tradition nor the tradition of printed editions is unanimous in this attribution. Since the seventeenth century, when the Benedictines of St. Maur relegated it to an appendix of *spuria* in their great edition of Augustine's works, its authenticity has been in serious doubt. In the last one hundred years there have been, as we shall see, advocates of its authenticity. But the standard reference work *Clavis Patrum Latinorum* still lists *De dialectica* among the Augustinian *spuria*.[1] In the first part of this introduction I shall consider the issue of authorship from two directions. Because the main hypothesis is that Augustine wrote our treatise, I shall first present the evidence from Augustine's own writings which shows that he wrote a book on dialectic as part of a series of books on the liberal arts. This will lead me to an examination of how well our *De dialectica* fits Augustine's description of the book he says he wrote. The basic case for Augustinian authorship will thus be presented first. I shall then approach the question from what can be known about the history of the work itself, both in the medieval period when indisputable evidence of its existence first appears and in the modern period when its authorship is first carefully debated. In this history I shall concentrate my attention on the matter of authorship, but I shall also draw some conclusions about the distribution and use of *De dialectica*. To my knowledge no one has given careful attention to the history of the work. I shall, therefore, give a more detailed account of that history than I will give of Augustine's interests in the liberal arts. The latter subject has been more thoroughly discussed by others, notably by H.-I. Marrou.[2]

A. AUGUSTINE'S *Disciplinarum libri*

Augustine's *Retractationes* (written in 426–427) give us invaluable infor-

mation on the chronology, purpose, and authenticity of his treatises.[3] At
some point, probably after he became bishop of Hippo, he began
keeping a careful record of his writings.[4] This record or catalogue was
the basis for the *Retractationes*. In an early chapter of this work
Augustine says that at one time he proposed to write a series of books
on the liberal arts. Because this passage is so important for the question
of the authorship of *De dialectica* I quote it here in full.

> At the very time that I was about to receive baptism in Milan, I also attempted to write
> books on the liberal arts, questioning those who were with me and who were not averse to
> studies of this nature, and desiring by definite steps, so to speak, to reach things incorporeal
> through things corporeal and to lead others to them. But I was able to complete only the
> book on grammar – which I lost later from our library – and six books, *On Music*, pertaining
> to that part which is called rhythm. I wrote these six books, however, only after I was
> baptized and had returned to Africa from Italy, for I had only begun this art at Milan. Of
> the other five arts likewise begun there – dialectic, rhetoric, geometry, arithmetic, and
> philosophy – the beginnings alone remained and I lost even these. However, I think that
> some people have them.[5]

In undertaking such a project Augustine placed himself in a tradition
going back at least as far as Varro.[6] Indeed, his title for the series –
Disciplinarum libri – was also used by Varro for his now lost nine books
on the liberal arts and sciences. Although Augustine never mentions
Varro's work, there is evidence that he drew heavily on it.[7] By his own
testimony we do know that he had read many books on the liberal arts
from the time he was around twenty years old. This reading was part of
a program of self-education which Augustine undertook at the inspira-
tion of Cicero's *Hortensius*.[8] It took him beyond grammar and rhetoric,
subjects his formal education had already given him a thorough knowledge of. The only work Augustine mentions by author or title is Aristotle's *Categories*, but he says that he read books on rhetoric, logic,
geometry, music, and arithmetic.[9] Several years later and a few months
after his conversion we find that Augustine still had a strong interest in
the liberal arts. He proposed to use them to further his own education
and that of his student compatriots. As Augustine puts it in the *Retractationes*, he was attempting to use corporeal things as a means to ascend
to incorporeal things (*per corporalia ... ad incorporalia*).[10] It is clear that
this is not a later construction placed on the project as he looked back
over forty years, for in *De musica*, the one book of the series both
completed and definitely extant, he says that the purpose of the sixth
book is to pass from corporeal to incorporeal things.[11] The first five

books of *De musica* are a study of the vestiges of numbers in sounds, that is, of meter. This is a preparation for the sixth book, which describes a hierarchy of numbers that leads from numbers in bodies to numbers in the understanding and eventually to the contemplation of the source of wisdom and number, God. In Augustine's own intellectual development one of the major stumbling blocks to his acceptance of Christian doctrines had been that he could not conceive of anything incorporeal.[12] Right after his conversion he seems to have thought that the liberal arts could be useful in training the mind to conceive of the incorporeal and hence of God.[13]

How much of his project did Augustine accomplish? From the passage quoted earlier we can see that he worked only a short time on the books. They were written in 387, between early March, when he returned from Cassiciacum to Milan, and late April, when he was baptized.[14] During these six or seven weeks he also wrote *De immortalitate animae*. Augustine says that he finished the book on grammar; the others he only began. Of the latter he finished *De musica* after he returned to Africa late the same year. The remaining five were never again taken up and, along with *De grammatica*, were lost by Augustine.[15] In 426, however, he believes that someone still has them, a tantalizing bit of information, which he unfortunately does not expand upon. He could have left them in Milan or Rome or Thagaste. It seems more likely that they would have been read in Italy, where there were Christians interested in such things.[16] Whatever the particulars, there is a strong likelihood that the books on grammar, dialectic, rhetoric, and the other arts did not perish immediately and were extant in 426 when the Bishop of Hippo was a famous man.

Did Augustine's *disciplinarum libri* survive beyond his lifetime? *De musica* has, of course, come to us intact. In addition to *De dialectica* we also have from the manuscripts brief treatises attributed to Augustine on grammar and rhetoric. I shall not enter the debate on the authenticity of these treatises on grammar and rhetoric. I believe that they and *De dialectica* can be considered separately and that any one or two of them can be found to be authentic without requiring the same conclusion about the others.[17]

In the *Retractationes* Augustine says one thing quite plainly about the *De dialectica* he wrote: it was not finished. Our *De dialectica* fits this description. From its Chapter Four we see that a four-part work was planned. Furthermore, at the end of Chapter Five the first part is divided into four topics and at the opening of Chapter Six the first of these topics is itself said to have four sub-topics. The work ends abruptly, however, while considering the force of words, which is only the second of the four sub-topics. Augustine tells us nothing else quite so clearly about his *De dialectica* that can be used as a criterion of authenticity for the one we have.[18]

There are some other kinds of evidence that support the authenticity of our treatise. Perhaps the most striking is that in Chapter Seven (13, 6–7) the author gives his name as 'Augustinus.' Two conclusions have been drawn from this. Heinrich Keil says that it does not prove that Augustine of Hippo wrote *De dialectica* but it does disprove the earliest attribution given by the manuscript tradition, to Chirius Fortunatianus.[19] Jan Pinborg goes further and argues that since only one Augustine is known from the later classical period it is easier to attribute the treatise to him than to suppose that there was another writer on logic with the same name.[20] Keil's conclusion seems warranted, since 'Augustinus' occurs as the author's name even in the manuscript which attributes the work to Fortunatianus.[21] Pinborg's conclusion is harder to assess, but it seems to me acceptable, since the name is apparently rare and we know of no other Augustine who had an interest in logic.[22] We could, of course, have a case of forgery, though the name is not used ostentatiously, as we might expect if someone were hoping to capitalize on the fame of the Bishop of Hippo. By itself, the occurrence of the name is not convincing. But since there are other indications that Augustine wrote our *De dialectica*, it takes on considerable weight.

Canonical studies often cite as evidence parallels between a disputed work and an author's known works. There are such parallels between *De dialectica* and several of Augustine's undisputed works, especially *De magistro*, which was written in 389 and deals with some of the topics discussed in *De dialectica*. The parallels which can be cited concern similar or identical definitions,[23] etymologies,[24] examples,[25] and such relatively complex notions as the relation between written and spoken words, the distinction between self-referential and non-self-referential words, and the distinction between obscurity and ambiguity.[26] The demonstrative force of these parallels is weakened by the fact that many of the definitions, examples, and so on can also be found in other authors.[27] They were the common stock of late antiquity and their use in two writings by no means establishes identity of authorship. In the case under discussion now, we can say only that the parallels show that *De dialectica* contains language and ideas known to have been used and held by Augustine.

A far more convincing parallelism, because it involves a complex set of ideas, is one found between the semantic theory of *De dialectica* and the theory developed in *De doctrina christiana* and *De Trinitate*. The same general structure is found: signs, their apprehension, the *cogitatio* of what is apprehended, and the expression of the *cogitatio* by the further giving of signs. The most interesting and important point of contact is at the stage of *cogitatio*, which in *De dialectica V* is denoted by the technical term '*dicibile*' and is described there as "*verbi in mente conceptio.*" If the work is authentic, this could be an early stage of Augustine's reflection on what he eventually termed the "*verbum in corde*" in his mature Trinitarian thought.[28] This sort of parallelism allows us to say that the authenticity of *De dialectica* is credible not only because the treatise contains language and ideas known to have been a part of Augustine's stock but also because it fits well into what we know about the development of his thought.

Finally, it is worth pointing out that from Augustine's works we can see that he had some technical knowledge of logic. In 386 he wrote that he knew more about logic than about the other parts of philosophy.[29] Then and later he showed that he knew the elements of Stoic theories of propositions and of deduction.[30] It is for the most part Stoic theory that we find in *De dialectica*.[31] It is possible that Augustine had read some of the *libri Stoicorum* which he mentions in *Contra Cresconium* I.xix.24. In any case, accepting *De dialectica* as authentic does not require us to assume that Augustine had more technical knowledge than independent evidence allows us to attribute to him.

This is the basic case for Augustine's authorship of our *De dialectica*. He did write a *De dialectica*, which, like ours, was incomplete. Our work was written by someone named 'Augustine,' and it fits very well into the thought of Augustine of Hippo. I will present further arguments when I consider the Maurists' objections to authenticity.

B. THE MEDIEVAL AND RENAISSANCE TRADITION OF
De dialectica

A survey of medieval logical writings leads me to believe that direct references to or quotations from *De dialectica* are rare.[32] They are notably absent from two works which had great influence in the earlier Middle Ages, the *Institutiones* of Cassiodorus (c. 485–c. 580) and the *Etymologiae* of Isidore (c. 560–636). Cassiodorus does know a work by Augustine on grammar and he knows *De musica*,[33] but in their accounts of dialectic neither Cassiodorus nor Isidore so much as mentions Augustine.[34] The earliest clear reference to *De dialectica* I know of is in the *Metalogicon* of John of Salisbury (c. 1115–1180). John quotes the definition of dialectic as *bene disputandi scientia* from Chapter One and he comments on the *dictio*, *dicibile*, and *res*, which are discussed by Augustine in Chapter Five.[35] But John sees Augustine's work through Aristotelian spectacles. He takes 'dialectic' in the sense of the science of probable demonstration, following Aristotle, whereas Augustine takes it in the sense of the whole of logic, following the Stoics.[36] And he says that Augustine gets his notions of the *dictio*, *dicibile*, and *res* from Aristotle, whereas Chapter Five fits more closely into the Stoic tradition. More important, John leaves out the *verbum* and defines the other three in a way quite different from Augustine.[37] Nevertheless, *De dialectica* was apparently being read by some in the twelfth century, perhaps at Paris where John had been a student of Abelard, one of the great logicians of the age. Further evidence that *De dialectica* had some influence in the twelfth century has been cited by L. Minio-Paluello and L. M. de Rijk, who believe that Adam of Balsham (died c. 1159) was influenced by it in the views on ambiguity and equivocation expressed in his *Ars disserendi*.[38] As to earlier use of *De dialectica*, there is one case of probable use in another important period in medieval intellectual history, the Carolingian renaissance. The author or authors of the *Libri Carolini* appear to have adapted a passage in Chapter Ten for use in the argument against the iconoclasts of the East.[39] Some scholars believe that Alcuin is the author of this work.[40] If so, this would show that he not only knew the Pseudo-Augustinian *Categoriae decem*, which he made into a popular work, but also may have been responsible for the considerable use of *De dialectica* in the ninth century.

These few instances of definite or probable use of *De dialectica* afford us only a very sketchy picture of the medieval tradition of the work. In the remainder of this section I shall adopt another method for filling in the picture. From catalogues of medieval and renaissance libraries and from the surviving manuscripts of the treatise I shall glean what can be learned about its history to 1500, that is, to about the time of its first appearance in printed form. Analysis of this kind of evidence will, in my opinion, lay a foundation for further study of the influence of *De dialectica*.

1. *Catalogue Listings and Extant Manuscripts*

For ease of reference I present two lists and a table containing the basic information which I have been able to gather. The list of library catalogues mentioning the treatise is in chronological order and gives place, date, kind of library, exact listing, the works among which it is listed, and the sources of my information. Though I have consulted standard sources and have done some searching of my own, this list is probably far from exhaustive.[41] Also, one cannot be sure that every '*dialectica Augustini*' is our treatise. I know of one instance where that title refers to the *Categoriae decem*.[42] The second list presents in alphabetical order (by place of present housing) the extant manuscripts of *De dialectica*. The shelf mark, folio numbers of *De dialectica*, date, provenance, and sources consulted are given. I believe that this list is close to being complete. It contains far more manuscripts than any of the earlier editions have used. The table presents the manuscripts in chronological order (alphabetical within a century). In the table I have given the information on the basis of which I shall draw conclusions about the attribution, distribution, and use of *De dialectica* in the Middle Ages and the early Renaissance.

De dialectica in Library Catalogues to 1500

REICHENAU (S. Germany), s. IX, Benedictine abbey, "Dialectica Augustini et Boecii geometria", listed among liberal arts books, including Aug. mus. and Ar. cat.[43] (Lehmann, *Mittelalt. Bibliothekskat. Deutschlands und der Schweiz*, I, p. 266, 7f.)

TOUL (E. France), s. XI (before 1084), Benedictine abbey, "item dialectica Aug[ustini] cum epistola Alexandri vol. I", listed among a large collection of liberal arts books, including Ps.-Aug. cat. x, Ar. cat. and peri., Porph. is., Apul. peri., Boeth. in is., in cat., in peri., de syll. cat., syll. hyp., Alcuin dial., and M. Cap. dial. (Becker, *Catalogi*, no. 68, item 244)

GORZE (N. E. France), s. XI (ca. 1032), Benedictine, "Dialectica eiusdem Augustini," listed among miscellaneous works sent from Gorze to Amel, including a number of liberal arts books, and specifically Ps.-Aug. cat. x, Ar. cat. and peri., Porph. is., Boeth. in cat., in peri., in is. (Morin, "Le Catalogue... de Gorze," p. 9, line 161; Manitius, *HSS in Mittelalt. Bibl.*, p. 224)

TRIER (W. Germany), s. XI or XII, cathedral church of St. Maximus, two copies: "dialectica Aug. cum ysagogis Porphirii", listed among books of Augustine ("Augustiniani libri"), including mus.; and "Fortunacianus [sic] de rhetorica cum dialectica Augustini", listed among various works, including Boeth. in is. (?) as well as Fortun. rhet., with which it is bound. (Becker no. 76, 45 and 140. The second MS is Berlin 687, described below.)

ROUEN (N. France), s. XII (1111–28), cathedral, "liber beati Augustini de dialectica", in a brief miscellaneous list, mainly of liberal arts books, including Apul. peri. and probably Ar. peri. and Boeth. in cat. and cat. syll. (Becker 82, 27)

ANCHIN (N. France), s. XII, Benedictine abbey, "dialectica Augustini", in a long list of liberal arts books, which includes Ps.-Aug. cat. x, Ar. cat. and peri., Porph. is., Apul. peri., Boeth. in peri., in is. prim. et sec., in cat., M. Cap. dial., Alcuin dial. (Becker 121, 24)

ARRAS (N. France), s. XII, Benedictine abbey of St. Vedast, "dialectica Augustini et decem praedicamenta et Arator in uno volumine", listed among liberal arts books ("Libri philosophice artis et auctores"), including cat. x (?), which it is bound with and Ar. cat., Boeth. in cat., in peri., and in is. (Becker 125, 13)

SALZBURG (Austria), s. XII, Benedictine abbey of St. Peter, "Dialectica Augustini", listed among literary and liberal arts books, including Boeth. in cat. (Möser-Mersky, *Mittelalt. Bibliothekskat. Österreichs*, IV, 72, 18)

ENGLAND and SCOTLAND, s. XIII (before 1278), at Exeter, Durham, St. Andrews, and Gede(s)worth,[44] as "Dialectica eiusdem [Augustini]" in a long list of the works of Augustine. (*Registrum Angliae de libris doctorum et auctorum veterum*, Oxford Bodl. MS Tanner 165, folio 104v. See also Henry of Kirkstede (?), Rouse, p. 37, for the same listing made in the fourteenth century.)

AVIGNON (S. France), s. XIV (1375), the papal library at the time of Gregory XI, two copies: "dialetica [sic] Augustini," and "dialectica" listed among "libri beati Augustini" and in both cases bound with Ps.-Aug. cat. x; the library also has four copies of Aug. mus. (Ehrle, *Historia*, v. I, pp. 459 and 462)

PEÑISCOLA (N. E. Spain), s. XV (1408–1429), in the papal library which was moved here ca. 1408 from Avignon, two copies, which may be the same as those listed above at Avignon, both titled "dialectica Augustini": one is listed among the works of Augustine and is bound with several works including cat. x; the other is listed with misc. works but bound with Augustine writings including Ps.-Aug. cat. x. (Faucon, *Librairie*, II, pp. 73, no. 301, and 148f., no. 1068)

URBINO (Italy), s. XV (ca. 1485), the Library of Urbino, "Augustini Logica, sive Dialetica [sic]", listed with the works of Augustine; this library also has Fortun. rhet. (*Giornale Storico degli Archivi Toscani*, VI, no. 2, p. 138.)

NÜRNBERG (Germany), s.XV (ca. 1500), private library of Hartmann Schedel (1440–1516), "Dialectica et rhetorica Fortunatiani," may be *De dial.*, which is attributed to Fortunatianus in Cologne MS 166 and in other manuscripts. (Ruf, *Mittelalt. Bibliothekskat. Deutschlands und der Schweiz* III, 808, 34f.)

Extant Manuscripts of *De dialectica*

BERLIN, Deutsche Staatsbibliothek (until Second World War, when it was lost), Lat. Qu. 687 (Görres 67), foll. 16r–20r. s. IX, from St. Maximus, Trier. (*AL* no. 2089, III, p. 107;

Schillmann, *Verzeichnis*, III, 64–66. P. Gehring and W. Gebhardt, *Scriptorium* 13 (1959), 127–131, list the Berlin MSS which were moved to Marburg and Tübingen, but Lat. Qu. 687 is not included in their list.)

BERLIN, Staatsbibl., Phillipps, 176 (1780), foll. 1r–6r. s. X, from the Benedictine abbey of St. Benoit-sur-Loire at Fleury. (*AL* 2090, III, 107; Rose, *Verzeichniss*, I, 391–3; A. van de Vyver, "Les Étapes de Développment Philosophique de Haut Moyen-Age," p. 438.)

BERN, Stadtbibliothek, 363, foll. 153v–160v. s. IX, from the Benedictine abbey of St. Benoit-sur-Loire, at Fleury, written under Irish influence. (*AL* 2121, III, 120; Hagen, *Catalogus*, 347–350; Ogilvy, *Books Known*, 2nd edn., p. 95; Kenney, *Sources*, pp. 556–560; facs. of entire MS in Hagen, *Codices Graeci et Latini*, II. This is B in Pinborg's edn.)

BERN, Stadtbibl., 548, foll. 1r–8r. s. X–XI. (*AL* 2122, III, 120; Hagen, *Cat.*, p. 452.)

BERN, Stadtbibl., A92, no. 35, fragment (VI, 10, 18 to VII, 12, 16). s. X. (Hagen, *Cat.*, p. 133.)

BRUSSELS, Bibliothèque Royale, 1117 (49–62), foll. 147v–151v. s. XIV. (*AL* 2029, III, 64f.; van den Gheyn, *Catalogue*, II, 148–150.)

CAMBRIDGE, Corpus Christi College, 206, foll. 120r–131v. s. IX or X. (*AL* 2036, III, 70; James, *Catalogue*, I, 495–498; van de Vyver, p. 439.)

CHARLEVILLE, Bibliothèque Municipale, 187, foll. 24r–35r. s. XII, from a monastery at Signy. (*AL* 2056, III, 86; *Cat. Gén.* (Quarto Series), V, 626f.)

COLOGNE, Dombibliothek, 166, or Darmstadt 2191, foll. 62r–74v, incomplete (lacking X, 19, 18 to the end). s. VIII (or perhaps VII), at Cologne since the ninth century, except from 1794 to 1867 when it was at Darmstadt. (Jaffé and Wattenbach, *Col. Codices*, 65–68; Lowe, *Cod. Lat. Ant.* VIII, no. 1160, p. 39, and "A List of the Oldest Extant MSS of St. Augustine," p. 247. This MS is designated by D in Pinborg's edn.)

EINSIEDELN, Stiftsbibliothek (Benedictine), 324, pp. 54–72. s. X or XI. (*AL* 1157, II, 816f.; Meier, *Cat.* I, 295f.; personal examination of a microfilm copy of the MS obtained through the Institut de Recherche et d'Histoire des Textes, Paris.)

ETON, College Library, 120, foll. 1r–3r. s. XIVin. (*AL* 2042, III, 73; James, *Catalogue*, 52f.)

FLORENCE, Biblioteca Medicea Laurenziana, aed. Flor. eccl. 168, foll. 200r–204r. s. XV, written in Ferrara in 1438, based on a copy of Cologne 166 made by Giovanni Aurispa in 1433. (Bandini, *Bibl. Leopoldina Laurentia*, I, col. 475–480; Leonardi, "Il Codici di Marziano Capella," 43–45; Billanovich, "Il Petrarca e i Retori Latini Minori," 141, 145f.)

FLORENCE, Bibl. Med. Laur., S. Marco, 113, foll. 100r–104r. s. XII, from the Dominican convent of St. Mark, Florence. (*AL* 1383, II, 951; information from Jan Pinborg.)

FLORENCE, Bibl. Med. Laur., S. Marco, 264, foll. 37v–40v. s. XV, written by Giorgio Antonio Vespucci (O. P.) of Florence in blank folia of a 14th century MS once owned by Coluccio Salutati (1331–1406); given by Vespucci to the convent of St. Mark, Florence, in 1499; based on Aurispa's copy of Cologne 166. (Leonardi, "Codici," 48f.; Billanovich, "Petrarca," 141, 145f.; Ullman, "The Humanism of Collucio Salutati," 154.)

FLORENCE, Biblioteca Riccardiana, 709, foll. 52r–64r. s. XV, written by Marsilio Ficino of Florence in 1456. (Oberleitner, *Die Handschriftliche Überlieferung*, I/2, 118.)

LEIDEN, Bibliotheek der Rijksuniversiteit, Vossius 8° 88, foll. 26r–39v. s. X. (Information from Inst. de Recherche, Paris, and from Jan Pinborg.)

LENINGRAD, Publichnaia Biblioteka, F. v. class. lat. n. 7, foll. 10v–18v. s. IXex., from the Benedictine abbey of Corbie, then Saint-Germain-des-Prés, where it had the number 613. (*AL* 1698, II, 1151 and III, 173; Staerk, *Manuscrits*, I, 127f.; Dobiaš-Roždestvenskaïa, *Histoire*, 160f.; van de Vyver, p. 438.)

ORLÉANS, Bibliothèque Municipale, 263, pp. 139–144, incomplete (ends following 'asperitate concordat' at VI, 10, 11; see on Paris BN lat. 6638). s. X–XI, from the Benedictine abbey at Fleury. (*AL* 2054, III, 84; *Cat. Gén.* (Octavo), XII, 127f.; van de Vyver, p. 438;

personal examination of a photo-copy of the MS obtained from the Inst. de Rech., Paris. This plus Paris BN lat. 6638 is O in Pinborg's edn.)

OXFORD, Bodleian Library, Bodl. 587 (2359), foll. 46r–57r. s. XV, first section (apparently to fol. 26v, but 39r–57r in same hand) written by John Free (d. 1465) in Ferrara between 1456 and 1458; then to John Gunthorpe, dean of Wells (d. 1498); based on the copy of Cologne 166 made by Aurispa. (Madan and Craster, *Summ. Cat.*, II, pt. I, p. 328; Billanovich, "Petrarca," 142, 145f.; personal examination of the MS.)

PARIS, Bibl. Arsenale, 350, foll. 253r–257r. s. XIV–XV, from the library of St. Victor, Paris. (*AL* 2058, III, 87; Martin, *Catalogue*, I, 215–218.)

PARIS, Bibl. Arsenale, 351, foll. 75r–82v. s. XII, from the Cistercian abbey of Chaalis, then the library of St. Martin des Champs, Paris. (*AL* 2059, III, 87f.; Martin, *Cat.*, I, 219f.)

PARIS, Bibl. Mazarine, 632, foll. 56v–58v. s. XIII, used by the Maurists. (*AL* 2060, III, 88; Molinier, *Catalogue*, I, 278–280.)

PARIS, Bibl. Nationale, Lat. 2083, foll. 52v–55v. s. XIII. (*AL* 2064, III, 90; Bibl. Nat., *Cat. gén.* II, 311f.)

PARIS, Bibl. Nat., Lat. 6638, foll. 17r–21v, a fragment (from '*crura tamen,*' VI, 10, 12 to the end, the missing part of Orléans 263; it begins precisely at the point where the latter ends). s. X–XI, from Fleury. (*AL* 2067, III, 92; Vernet, "Notes de Dom André Wilmart," p. 15; Lowe, "A New List of Beneventan Manuscripts," p. 213. Wilmart dates this fragment as s. IX–X, but notes its resemblance in contents to Orléans 263. Lowe, apparently following Bernhard Bischoff, regards Orléans 263 + Paris 6638, foll. 17–32, as one MS. They are O in Pinborg's edn.)

PARIS, Bibl. Nat., Lat. 7581, foll. 14r–22r. s. X. (*Catalogus* (1744), T. IV, p. 376; information from Jan Pinborg, who uses this MS in his edn. as Q.)

PARIS, Bibl. Nat., Lat. 7730, foll. 15v–19v. s. IX–X, from the Benedictine abbey at Fleury. (*AL* 2068, III, 93; *Catalogus* (1744), IV, 388f.; van de Vyver, p. 439; personal examination of a microfilm copy of the MS obtained from the Inst. de Rech., Paris. This is P in Pinborg's edn.)

PARIS, Bibl. Nat., Lat. 12949, foll. 12r–21v. s. IX, from Auxerre, Corbie, and Saint-Germain-des-Prés (where it was numbered 1108). (*AL* 621, I, 535f. and III, 94; Delisle, "Inventaire de Saint-Germain-des-Prés," p. 545; van de Vyver, p. 438; Hauréau, *Histoire*, I (1872), 184ff.; Cousin, *Ouvrages inédits d'Abélard*, 618–624; personal examination of microfilm copy obtained from the Inst. de Rech., Paris. This is G in Pinborg's edn.)

PARIS, Bibl. Nat., Lat. 16598, foll. 60r–70r. s. XIII, from the Sorbonne. (*AL* 2077, III, 99; Delisle, "Inventaire de la Sorbonne," pp. 152f.)

PHILADELPHIA, University of Pennsylvania, Lat. 63, foll. 79r–87r. s. XII, from the Phillipps collection (no. 11901). (*AL* 2195, III, 185; Bond and Faye, *Supplement*, 492; Zacour and Hirsch, *Catalogue*, p. 14; personal examination.)

TROYES, Bibl. Mun., 40 (vol. X), foll. 83r–88v. s. XII, from the Cistercian abbey at Clairvaux; this is the tenth volume of the famous *opera omnia Augustini* assembled during the lifetime of Bernard. (*AL* 2082, III, 101; *Cat. gén.* (Quarto), II, 33–42; de Ghellinck, "Une edition," pp. 63–82; personal examination of a photo-copy of the MS obtained from the Inst. de Rech., Paris.)

TROYES, Bibl. Mun., 70, foll. 155v–160r. s. XIII, from the monastery of St. Mary, Auxerre. (*AL* 2083, III, 102; *Cat. gen.* (Quarto), II, 51.)

VATICAN, Biblioteca Apostolica, Chigiano H VI 186, foll. 134r–146r. s. XV, owned by Francesco Piccolomini of Siena, 1467; based on the copy of Cologne 166 by Aurispa. (Billanovich, "Petrarca,". 142f., 145f.)

VATICAN, Bibl. Apost., Palatina Lat. 1588, foll. 31r–38v. s. IX, from the monastery of St.

Nazarius at Lorsch; a direct copy of Cologne 166. (Billanovich, "Petrarca," 111f.; information from Jan Pinborg, who uses it as d in his edn.)

VATICAN, Bibl. Apost., Reginensis, 233, foll. 28r–38v. s. XI, from France. (*AL* 2187, III, 179; Wilmart, *Codices*, I, 554f.)

VATICAN, Bibl. Apost., Urbinas, Lat. 393, foll. 37r–42r. s. XII–XIII. (Stornajolo, *Codices*, I, 373–5; information from Jan Pinborg.)

VATICAN, Bibl. Apost., Urb. Lat. 1180, foll. 52r–64r. s. XV, written in 1446 in Ferrara by Nicolo Perotti (1430–1480); based on the copy of Cologne 166 by Aurispa. (Stornajolo, *Codices*, III, 192f.; Leonardi, "Codici," 474; Billanovich, "Petrarca," 143, 145f.)

VATICAN, Bibl. Apost., Vaticana Lat. 1485, foll. 79v–90r. s. XV, a copy of Vat. Urb. lat. 1180; owned by Jean Jouffroy (c. 1412–1473). (Nogara, *Codices*, III, 17f.; Leonardi, "Codici," 476; Billanovich, "Petrarca," 143, 145f.)

VENICE, Biblioteca Nazionale Marciana, Lat. VI, 68, foll. 85r–87v. s. XII, from Padua (1440). (*AL* 1615, II, 1105f.; Valentinelli, *Manuscripta*, T. IV, 17.)

VERCELLI, Archivio Capitolare Eusebiano, 138 (143), foll. 27r–32v. s. X. (*AL* 1653, II, 1126f.; Mazzatinti, *Inventari*, 31, p. 111.)

2. *Title and Attribution*

From the titles and colophons accompanying *De dialectica* we can see how it was entitled and to whom it was attributed by copyists.[45] Little need be said about how the work was entitled. In most of the thirty-two manuscripts for which I have this information, the work is called either '*De dialectica*' or '*Dialectica*.' The majority of the catalogue listings concur in this. In six manuscripts the work has no title. Four manuscripts simply lengthen the title to '*Tractatus in dialectica*' or '*De arte dialectica*.'[46] The only really deviant title is found in Florence, B. Laur., S. Marco 113: '*Augustinus de vi verborum*.' This is apparently derived from the topic of what is now Chapter VII in the editions. The Cambridge and Brussels manuscripts say in their titles that the work was written by Augustine for the education of Adeodatus, his son. There is no evidence that Augustine wrote his books on the liberal arts exclusively or even primarily for Adeodatus. We may conclude that the manuscripts generally conform to the title indicated by Augustine in the *Retractationes*, namely, '*De dialectica*,' and provide no basis for the title '*Principia dialecticae*,' which was used in the Augustine editions of the sixteenth and seventeenth centuries.

The attributions given in the manuscripts are of more interest than the titles because of their bearing on the question of the authenticity of the work. I have information on thirty-two manuscripts. In twenty Augustine is regarded as the author, in six Fortunatianus, and in six the

Summary of Information on the Manuscripts

Date	MS	Provenance	Author	Title	Type	Augustine disc. lib.	Logica vetus	Other logic and liberal arts
VIII	Cologne 166	Cologne (IX)	Fortun.	De dial.	Liberal arts	rhet.	–	Fortun. rhet. Victor. in Cic. rhet. Censorinus
IX	Berlin 687	Trier (IX)	Anon.?ª	None?	Liberal arts	rhet. cat. x	Porph. is. Ap. peri. Boeth. in peri.	Alcuin dial. (excerpts) Fortun. rhet.
	Bern 363	Fleury	Aug.	De dial.	Liberal arts	rhet.	Boeth. in cat. (fragment)	Fortun. rhet. Servius, Ovid, Horace, Bede
	Leningrad 7	Corbie, St.-Germ.-des-Prés	Aug.	Tractatus in dial.	Logic	–	Boeth. in cat., in is.	–
	Paris 12949	Auxerre, Corbie, St.-Germ.	Aug.	De dial.	Logic	cat. x	Ar. peri. Porph. is. Ap. peri. Boeth. in peri. (part)	–
	Vatican Pal. 1588	Lorsch	Fortun.	De dial.	Liberal arts	rhet.	–	Fortun. rhet. Victor. in Cic. rhet.
	Vercelli 138	?	Aug.	Tractatus in dial.	Liberal arts	mus. cat. x	Ar. cat. Porph. is.	Boeth. arith. Bede nat. rer. Alcuin dial.
IX–X	Paris 7730	Fleury	Anon.	None contemporary	Liberal arts	rhet. cat. x	Porph. is. Ap. peri.	Fortun. rhet. Isidore etym. Servius and others
	Cambridge 206	?	Aug.	De dial.	Misc.	cat. x	Porph. is. Ap. peri.	M. Cap. dial. Alcuin dial.

Cent.	Manuscript	Place				cat.		
X	Berlin 176	Fleury	Aug.	Dial.	Liberal arts	cat. x	—	Cassiod. inst. II.1–2 (gramm. and rhet.) Alcuin dial. and rhet. Glossae in Boeth. inst. arith. Isidore de diff. verb. Remigius exp. in Prisc.
	Leiden Voss. 88	?	Aug.	De dial.	Misc.	—	—	—
	Paris 7581	?	Anon.	None	Liberal arts	—	—	—
X–XI	Bern 548	?	Aug.	Tractatus in dial.	Logic	—	Ar. cat. (fr.)	—
	Orléans 263 + Paris 6638	Fleury	Aug.	De dial.	Logic	cat. x	Ar. peri[b] Ap. peri[b]	M. Cap. dial. (excerpts) Cassiod. inst. (ex.) Alcuin dial. Abbo Flor. syll. hyp.[b]
	Einsied. 324	?	Anon.	None	Liberal arts	—	Ar. cat., peri.	Cic. top. Boeth. in Cic. top.
XI	Vatican Reg. 233	?	Aug.	Dial.	Logic	cat. x	—	—
XII	Charleville 187	Signy	Aug.	De dial.	Logic	cat. x	Boeth. top.	Victor. def.
	Florence S. M. 113	Florence (XV)	Aug.	De vi verborum	Logic	—	Ar. cat. Boeth. in is. sec., in peri. sec.	—
	Paris Ars. 351	Chaalis	Aug.	De dial.	Misc.	cat. x	—	—
	Philad. 63	?	Aug.	De dial.	Misc.	cat. x	—	—
	Troyes 40	Clairvaux	Aug.	De dial.	Aug. 17 works	cat. x	—	—
	Venice VI, 68	Padua (XV)	Anon.	None	Logic	—	Boeth. in peri. sec.	—

Date	MS	Provenance	Author	Title	Type	Augustine disc. lib.	Logica vetus	Other logic and liberal arts
XII–XIII	Vatican Urb. 393	Urbino?	Aug.	Dial.	Misc.	–	–	–
XIII	Paris Maz. 632	?	Aug.	Dyaletica	Aug. 14 works	cat. x	–	–
	Paris 2083	?	?	?	Misc.	cat. x	–	Cic. top. John Dam. dial.
	Paris 16598	Sorbonne	?	?	Liberal arts	cat. x	Porph. is.	–
	Troyes 70	Auxerre	Aug.	De arte dialectica	Aug. 17 works	cat. x	–	John Dam. dial.
XIV	Eton 120	?	?	?	Misc.	cat. x	–	John Dam. dial.
	Brussels 1117	?	Aug.	De dyal.	Aug. 14 works	mus.	–	–
XIV–XV	Paris Ars. 350	Paris, St. Victor	Aug.	Dyaletica	Aug. 44 works	mus.	–	–
XV	Florence aed. 168	Ferrara	Fortun.	De dyal.	Liberal arts	rhet. mus. (ex.)	–	Fortun. rhet.[c] M. Cap. rhet. 31–38 Priscian gramm. Diomedes gramm.
	Florence S. M. 264	Florence	?	?	Liberal arts	rhet.	–	Fortun. rhet. M. Cap. rhet. 31–38 Priscian de fig. num. Cic. part. orat.
	Florence Ricc. 709	Florence	(no further information)					
	Oxford 587	Ferrara, England	Anon.	None	Liberal arts	rhet.	–	Fortun. rhet. M. Cap. rhet. 31–38
	Vatican Chig. H VI 186	Siena	Fortun.	De dial.	Liberal arts?	rhet.	–	Fortun. rhet. M. Cap. rhet. 31–38 F. Patricius epitome of Quintilian

				Liberal arts			
Vatican Urb. 1180	Ferrara	Fortun.	Dial.?	Liberal arts	rhet.	–	Fortun. rhet. M. Cap. rhet. 31–38 Priscian gramm. Servius de cent. metris
Vatican Vat. 1485	Italy, France	Fortun.	De dial.	Liberal arts	rhet.	–	Fortun. rhet. M. Cap. rhet. 31–38

a A question mark following an entry means that the item is doubtful. A question mark in a blank means that I do not have the information.

b In a part of the MS written later and joined with *De dial.* at an unknown date.

c This is a 14th-century MS to which *De dial.* was added in the 15th century.

work is anonymous. There is no simple chronological pattern to the attributions; all three occur in both earlier and later manuscripts. Nevertheless a rough outline emerges when we realize that all of the later
manuscripts that attribute *De dialectica* to Fortunatianus are derived
directly (Vat. Pal. 1588) or indirectly (Flor. aed. 168, Vat. Chig. H VI
186, Vat. Urb. 1180, Vat. Vat. 1485) from the Cologne manuscript.[47]
Thus the Fortunatianus attribution goes back to one manuscript, the
oldest one extant. Most of the manuscripts in which it is anonymous
are relatively early. Several Augustine manuscripts are just as early as
the anonymous ones, but there are more Augustine manuscripts in the
twelfth, thirteenth, and fourteenth centuries. These facts can be plausibly
interpreted as an instance of the process that Bernhard Blumenkranz
has observed in the case of most of the Augustinian apocrypha: a work
either was anonymous originally or it became anonymous and then was
assigned to Augustine because of his fame and authority.[48] The great
periods for faulty attributions of anonymous works were the Carolingian
renaissance and the twelfth century, when libraries were being built and
manuscripts needed to be classified.[49] *De dialectica* fits into this chronology well, for several manuscripts from the Carolingian period give
the author as Augustine. It is possible, therefore, that the original attribution of the treatise was to Fortunatianus, that this name was dropped
or there were other anonymous copies, and that in the first great period
of library building the name of Augustine was attached to the work.
This account must be tested, particularly the attribution to Fortunatianus.

Whether or not the attribution to Fortunatianus is original, it is certainly the oldest we have. The Cologne codex is dated no later than the
eighth century.[50] Very little is known about Chirius Fortunatianus.[51]
The only work certainly attributed to him is an *Ars rhetoricae* in three
books. This work seems to have had some popularity in the early Middle
Ages, due probably to its recommendation by Cassiodorus as a good
brief account of the art of rhetoric.[52] There are six manuscripts of it from
the ninth century or earlier. Five of these also include *De dialectica*.[53]
But of these five only the Cologne manuscript and the Vatican manuscript
copied from it attribute *De dialectica* to Fortunatianus. Is this attribution sound? Aside from the fact that it does not fit with the passage in
Chapter Seven where the author names himself 'Augustinus,' there are

other reasons why we need give this attribution little credence. In the first place, the way the attribution is given indicates that the scribe may have been uncertain. The titles and colophons to Books One, Two, and Three of the *Ars rhetoricae* clearly give Fortunatianus as the author. The title for *De dialectica*, on the other hand, states merely that it is Book Four: INCPIT DEDIALECTICA LIB IIII.[54] Of course, it could be that the scribe had wearied of writing out the name. But if that were so, one might expect at least an '*eiusdem.*' A second reason for doubting the attribution is that the earliest evidence is that Fortunatianus's work contained only three books.[55] Though the scribe could still be correct about the author, his treating of *De dialectica* as the fourth book of Fortunatianus's rhetoric casts doubt on the soundness of the attribution he inherited or invented. Finally, the credibility of the attribution is further weakened by another error in the Cologne manuscript. It includes as the latter part of Book Three of Fortunatianus (foll. 50–62) the little treatise on rhetoric later attributed to Augustine. One need not accept the Augustinian authorship of *De rhetorica* to see that it fits poorly as a part of Book Three of Fortunatianus's work. The major consideration here is that it takes up many of the topics covered by the *Ars* and so would be a repetition, not a continuation, of that work.[56] It seems to me, therefore, that the Cologne manuscript does not give the original attribution of *De dialectica*. It is more likely that this manuscript was transcribed from a copy in which *De dialectica* was anonymous. It would then represent an early attempt to determine the author. This line of argument leads us to suppose that there were anonymous copies of *De dialectica* in the seventh or eighth century. That there were such seems to be supported by the existence of two ninth or tenth-century manuscripts (Berlin 687, Paris BN lat. 7730) that contain the same three works as Cologne 166 (*Ars, De rhet., De dial.*), but with *De dialectica* as anonymous.[57] If these two later manuscripts are independent of Cologne 166, then they show that an anonymous tradition may predate that manuscript. If they are dependent on Cologne 166, and this is very unlikely in the case of one of them,[58] then they at least give evidence of an uneasiness with the Fortunatianus attribution.

A conjectural reconstruction of the history of the manuscript attribution of *De dialectica* might follow along some such line as this. There were anonymous copies of the work dating from before the Carolingian renaissance. It is even probable that the copy that came from Augustine's hand had no name on it, since it was not completed by him and was only a draft. The work was grouped with the *Ars rhetoricae* of Fortunatianus, perhaps because of the use of the same form of definition in the opening of both works.[59] At least one scribe thought both works to be by the same author. In the ninth century someone drew the obvious conclusion that the author was named 'Augustine' and assigned the work to the best-known Augustine, perhaps on the basis of the *Retractationes* passage.[60] This is conjectural, of course. The probability of the truth of this account is limited by the selective process by which manuscripts survive. For example, a different account might be required if we had a manuscript that Bartolomeo Capra, archbishop of Milan, reported he found in 1423 in a monastery of his diocese. According to Capra the manuscript included Fortunatianus's *Ars rhetoricae* and "*Aurelius Augustus de rhetorica et de dyalectica*." Giuseppe Billanovich argues that this manuscript pre-dated the Cologne manuscript and was the basis for the Augustine attribution found in Bern 363.[61] The Bern manuscript may have been written in Milan, where Capra could also have found his manuscript.[62] This is an intriguing combination of circumstances, since Augustine wrote his *De dialectica* in Milan. If Capra's manuscript survived (apparently it does not), we might be able to say that the attribution of the work to Augustine is much older than we can now say it is. Indeed, we might be able to say that this attribution occurs in the Milanese tradition of the work, a tradition that could easily be closest to the first copies of Augustine's *De dialectica*.

3. *Distribution and Use*

Regardless of whom they thought to be the author of *De dialectica*, scribes throughout the Middle Ages and early Renaissance found reason to copy it. There are extant manuscripts dated in each century from the eighth onward. And from catalogue listings and what is known about the provenance of some manuscripts it is clear that *De dialectica* had a varied and fairly widespread circulation.[63] The earliest precise information is from the ninth century, when the work is found in four of the great monastic centers of the Carolingian renaissance – Reichenau, Lorsch, Corbie, and Auxerre – as well as at Cologne, Trier, and Fleury. In the tenth, eleventh, and twelfth centuries it is found at other locations in the same general area of north and central France and west and south Germany (Anchin, Arras, Chaalis, Clairvaux, Fleury, Gorze, Rouen, Salzburg, Signy, Toul). There is no unmistakable evidence that *De dialectica* circulated outside this general area until the thirteenth century,[64] when it is listed at four English and Scottish libraries. In the fourteenth and fifteenth centuries we find it in southern Europe at Avignon, Peñiscola, Florence, Padua, Urbino, Siena, and Ferrara. At these locations *De dialectica* was found in various kinds of libraries. The largest number are monastic libraries, with several orders being represented.[65] It was also in cathedral libraries.[66] In addition, a thirteenth-century copy was in the possession of the Sorbonne (Paris 16598) and the papal library at Avignon had two copies in 1375. It is reasonable to suppose that *De dialectica* was used in both monastic and cathedral schools and eventually in the universities. With the fifteenth-century Italian manuscripts there is a new trend – manuscripts owned by individuals. I shall discuss these manuscripts after I look at the strictly medieval tradition of the work.

How was *De dialectica* used in the schools of the Middle Ages? A partial answer to this question can be inferred from the kinds of works the treatise is associated with in manuscripts and catalogues. In the table given above I have characterized the kind of work which is dominant in each of the manuscripts. On the basis of this characterization, three periods can be discerned. In the earlier manuscripts (through the ninth century) the dominant type is liberal arts. During these centuries *De dialectica* is found with treatises on the parts of both the *trivium* and the *quadrivium*. This association with liberal arts books is found also in the library listings, continuing there even in the twelfth century. The tenth, eleventh, and twelfth-century manuscripts, on the other hand, seem to reflect a change. Half of the manuscripts from these centuries contain only logical works. A third period is discernible in the manuscripts from the thirteenth and fourteenth centuries. There *De dialectica* is most often placed with works of Augustine. This holds as well for the later catalogues. These three periods – association with writings on the liberal arts, then with logical treatises, and then with works of Augustine – are not clear cut, for there are liberal arts manuscripts in all three periods and an Augustine *opera* from the twelfth century (Troyes 40) and two logical manuscripts from the ninth century (Leningrad 7 and Paris 12949).

Nevertheless, in these three periods there are tendencies which fit well with what is known about the general course of medieval thought and education. *De dialectica* would seem to have been used first in the liberal arts curriculum, that is, as part of general education. Then it appears to have been used for a more specialized study of logic.[67] Finally, in the thirteenth and fourteenth centuries it probably ceased to be of interest as a work on logic and was copied and perhaps read largely because it bore the name of Augustine. This waning of topical interest in *De dialectica* is contemporaneous with the advent of the *logica nova*, the rediscovery of the greater part of Aristotle's *Organon*.[68] As the major logical writings of Aristotle became available there was less need for the more elementary works on logic – the Pseudo-Augustinian *Categoriae decem*, Apuleius's *Peri hermeneias*, as well as Augustine's *De dialectica*. Well into the twelfth century these lesser works seem to have been read along with translations of Aristotle's *Categories* and *Peri hermeneias*, Porphyry's *Isagoge*, and Boethius's commentaries on these works by Aristotle and Porphyry. *De dialectica* is joined with these works of Aristotle, Porphyry, Boethius, and Apuleius especially in the manuscripts of the ninth century, but also in some from the tenth, eleventh, and twelfth centuries. The library catalogues of the eleventh and twelfth centuries also list it among these works. But after the twelfth century *De dialectica* is rarely associated with these writings which are commonly known as the '*logica vetus*.'[69] The only logical work which it continues to be associated with is the *Categoriae decem*, which was regarded as one of Augustine's *disciplinarum libri*.[70] But whatever its fate in the later period, its association with the major works of the *logica vetus* in earlier centuries suggests that *De dialectica* could have had more influence than historians of medieval logic have generally recognized. Further research is needed in this area.

There is one case of direct use of *De dialectica* which indicates a direction that such research could take. The ninth-century manuscript Paris, Bibl. Nat. lat. 12949 contains marginal and interlinear glossing on *De dialectica* as well as on *Categoriae decem*.[71] This indicates that *De dialectica* was probably used as a textbook.[72] An inscription on folio 24v identifies the author of the glosses as "*Heiricus, magister Remigii.*" Although this inscription occurs with the *Categoriae*, Hauréau has argued that it is meant to apply to the glosses on *De dialectica* as well.[73] He identifies this Heiric as Heiric of Auxerre (840–876), educated at Fulda and Ferrières and teacher in the monastic school of Saint-Germain d'Auxerre, where one of his students was Remigius of Auxerre.[74] On the basis of excerpts given by Cousin,[75] of what Hauréau says about the glosses on the *Categoriae*,[76] and of my own preliminary reading of some of the glosses I believe that this manuscript is worth studying. It might reveal some influence of *De dialectica* on the discussion of logic and its place in the *trivium*[77] and on the early course of the controversy on universals. Heiric is usually said to have held a conceptualist position or at least to have been primarily interested in the psychological formation of universal concepts.[78] It seems likely, therefore, that he would have found interesting Augustine's notion of the *dicibile* as a *verbi in mente conceptio* (V, 8, 7). Whether that notion was the basis for Heiric's position can be determined only by further research.[79] At this point we can say only that in the Middle Ages *De dialectica* had early and fairly widespread circulation, was read along with the major works of the old logic in the liberal arts curriculum, and had some intensive school use which could have been important for such matters as the discussion of universals.

We have much more precise information about the fifteenth-century manuscripts of *De dialectica* than we have about the earlier manuscripts. Not only dates and places but names of individuals are attached to all but one of them. The following list summarizes the information I have on the provenance of the seven fifteenth-century manuscripts.[80]

Florence aed. 168: written in Ferrara in 1438 (fol. 192ra).

Vatican Urb. 1180: written by Nicolo Perotti in Ferrara in 1446 while he was in the household of William Grey (fol. 63v). Vatican Vat. 1485 is a copy of this MS (fol. 34v); it was owned by Cardinal Jean Jouffroy, and thus was written before 1473, the year of Jouffroy's death.

Florence Ricc. 709: written by Marsilio Ficino of Florence in 1456 (fol. 190r).

Oxford Bodl. 587: written by John Free in Ferrara between 1456 and 1458. To John Gunthorpe in 1465 at the death of Free.[81] Gunthorpe took it to England.

Vatican Chig. H VI 186: owned by Cardinal Francesco Piccolomini of Siena, 1467 (fol. 1r).

Florence S. Marco 264: written and owned by Giorgio Antonio Vespucci of Florence before 1499.

Billanovich discusses all of these manuscripts but one (Flor. Ricc. 709) and argues that they are derived from a copy of Cologne 166 that Giovanni Aurispa made in 1433 while he was attending the council of Basel.[82] Sometime after that Aurispa must have taken his manuscript to Ferrara, for several of the extant manuscripts were written in that city. Since 1429 it had been the home of Guarino da Verona (1370–1460), one of the major humanistic teachers of the Italian Renaissance.[83] Two of the manuscripts have rather direct connections with Guarino. Vatican Urb. 1180 was written by Perotti while his education was being financed by William Grey, a wealthy Englishman who was attending Guarino's lectures in Ferrara during 1445–1446.[84] And Oxford Bodl. 587 was written by John Free, an Englishman, who was sent to Ferrara to study with Guarino by the same William Grey.[85] The Oxford manuscript eventually came into the hands of John Gunthorpe, yet another Englishman who studied under Guarino.[86] We may assume that the copying of these manuscripts, as well perhaps as that of some of the others, was stimulated by the teaching of Guarino. Why would De dialectica have been of interest to him and his students?

Guarino's curriculum was essentially literary and rhetorical. The rhetorical part drew mainly on Cicero and Quintilian.[87] This humanistic interest in classical rhetoric is enough to explain why Aurispa copied the Cologne codex and why his copy generated further manuscripts, for the work of Fortunatianus on rhetoric is the main treatise in the Cologne, Oxford, and Vatican manuscripts. Indeed De dialectica, as well as the De rhetorica assigned to Augustine and excerpts from Martianus Capella's book on rhetoric, was regarded as part of Fortunatianus's work in the manuscripts written in Italy in the fifteenth century.[88] It is unlikely that the humanists would have copied De dialectica if it had not been attached to these rhetorical works, for they were much more interested in rhetoric than in dialectic, a discipline which they regarded as typically scholastic.[89] On the other hand, De dialectica would not have been completely outside of their range of interests. Following the advice of Cicero and Quintilian, they did give the study of logic a certain limited place in their educational scheme.[90] De dialectica could have supplied some of the knowledge of dialectic believed necessary though secondary to an education in grammar (literature) and rhetoric. Thus in the early Renaissance the use of the treatise returned full circle, albeit in new circumstances, to the liberal arts tradition that dominated the early Middle Ages.

C. PRINTED EDITIONS OF *De dialectica*

1. *The First Edition*

As in the manuscript tradition, so in the tradition of printed editions of *De dialectica* various opinions are exhibited on the authorship of the treatise. *De dialectica* has been printed most often in the several editions of the complete works of Augustine, but the first edition, in agreement with the earliest surviving manuscript, printed it under the heading '*Chirii Consulti Fortunatiani Dialectica*.' It was included as the last work in a book which also contains the *Ars rhetoricae* of Fortunatianus and translations of several short works of Dionysus of Halicarnasus. There are several things puzzling about the earliest printing of *De dialectica*. Cataloguers of incunabula have listed two books containing the treatise. In neither of the books is there indication of place and date of publication or of the printer's name. There is agreement that both books were printed in Venice sometime during the last three years of the fifteenth century (1498–1500). One has been tentatively attributed to the press of Christophoro de Pensis, the other has been tentatively assigned to Joannes Tacuinus.[91] Several libraries have copies of the books. I have studied two copies attributed to de Pensis and one copy attributed to Tacuinus.[92] From this study I conclude, on the one hand, that in the strict sense of the term these two books are the same edition. Each contains precisely the same works, the same titles and colophons, and, as far as I have checked them, the same text. It is also clear, on the other hand, that they were printed separately, that is, that they are two printings of the same edition.[93] This state of affairs admits of three possible explanations. Either one printer re-issued a book printed earlier by himself, or one printer reprinted a book published first by another printer,[94] or two printers at about the same time independently printed the same work from the manuscript(s) of the same editor. The third explanation seems most unlikely, for it does not account for the very great similarity in appearance between the two printings. I see no compelling reason for choosing between the other two explanations, although the incunabula experts are inclined to assign the two printings to two different printers. For my purposes a decision on this is not required. Both the supposed de Pensis book and the supposed Tacuinus book are the same edition of *De dialectica*. I shall refer to this edition as the Venice edition, and because the two printings were issued at about the same time I shall include both under the label 'first edition.'

In the Venice edition there is no information given on how the printing of *De dialectica* came about, who edited it, what manuscript(s) he used, and so on. The book is prefaced by a dedicatory letter by Francesco Puteolano from which it is clear that he is the editor of Fortunatianus's *Ars Rhetoricae*. He devotes three pages to the praise of the *Rhetorica*, but he does not mention the *Dialectica*.[95] If he were the editor of the latter as well as of the former, it seems likely that he would have said something about it. Two other considerations count against the hypothesis that Puteolano edited *De dialectica*. First, there is a book consisting only of Puteolano's edition of the *Rhetorica* that may be earlier than the edition containing *De dialectica*. It may have been printed by de Pensis.[96] And second, the *Dialectica* in the de Pensis and Tacuinus printings is separated from the *Rhetorica* (by the works of Dionysus) and has a new set of signatures.[97] The most plausible explanation of these facts is given by Billanovich. According to him Puteolano edited Fortunatianus's *Ars rhetoricae* about 1484 and had it published by itself. Then someone, probably the Venice printer who originally published the rhetoric (de Pensis?), later reprinted the rhetoric with the added works.[98] Puteolano probably used a manuscript that did not contain *De dialectica*. But his manuscript of Fortunatianus must have included Augustine's *De rhetorica* and the excerpts from Martianus Capella's book on rhetoric as undifferentiated parts of Book Three of Fortunatianus, for his edition includes them in this way.[99] There are Italian manuscripts that include just these works.[100] There are other Italian manuscripts that in addition include *De dialectica* as Book Four of Fortunatianus, as we have seen.[101] Probably on the basis of one of these manuscripts Puteolano's original edition was expanded to include *De dialectica*. Whatever the exact source or sources of the Venice edition, it prints a good text, a text superior to that of any other edition before Crecelius.[102] It is very close but not identical to the text of the best old manuscripts, Cologne 166 and Bern 363.[103] It is, therefore, almost certainly based on one of the manuscripts that derive from Aurispa's copy of the Cologne manuscript.[104] The Venice edition of *De dialectica* was apparently reprinted several times in the sixteenth century, the best known reprints appearing at Basel in 1542 and 1558.[105] To my knowledge, *De dialectica* was not issued under the name of Fortunatianus after the sixteenth century.

2. *Editions of the Sixteenth Century*

During the sixteenth century three editions of all the works of Augustine were published. *De dialectica* appeared in all three editions. Unlike the *De grammatica*, *De rhetorica*, and *Categoriae decem* it was not one of the fairly numerous *opuscula* of Augustine which were printed in the fifteenth century.[106] A *Logica Beati Augustini*, published in Florence (1479, 1480) and Venice (1500?), was in fact the *De dialectica* of Alcuin.[107] Johannes Amerbach was the first to print *De dialectica* under the name of Augustine. Amerbach placed it in the first volume of his 1506 Basel edition of the works of Augustine.[108] This location and the heading under which he grouped the work with the treatises on grammar, rhetoric, and the ten categories – '*De libris disciplinarum*' – were based on the *Retractationes* passage quoted above.[109] Amerbach does not say which manuscripts he used for his edition of *De dialectica*, though his surviving correspondence witnesses to the search for manuscripts which he says he made in France, Germany, and Italy.[110] His edition set precedents for subsequent editors on at least three matters, the title, chapter divisions, and text. As far as I can determine, Amerbach was the first to call the treatise '*Principia dialecticae.*' We have seen that there is no basis for this in the manuscripts now extant. The source of this title may be Augustine's statement that only the beginnings (*principia*) survived of most of his projected books on the liberal arts.[111] However it is to be explained, the title has been used by all subsequent editors except Crecelius and is the one commonly used by scholars. Amerbach was apparently also the originator of the chapter divisions and titles used by the later editions.[112] Finally, Amerbach's text was followed closely until Crecelius. He may be said to be the first printer of the Augustine *textus receptus*. This text is inferior to the one printed in the first edition. It is, therefore, probably based on a more corrupt manuscript than the first edition used.[113] In the light of the influence of Amerbach's edition, it is regrettable that it is not a better edition.

Two more editions of the complete works of Augustine were printed in the sixteenth century, one edited by Erasmus and published at Basel in 1528–29,[114] the other edited by members of the theological faculty of the University of Louvain and published at Antwerp in 1577.[115] Both editions improved upon Amerbach in distinguishing authentic from inauthentic works and in investigating manuscripts,[116] but neither raised any doubts about the authenticity of *De dialectica*.[117] These editions introduced two innovations. The first is minor, but the second is of some importance. Erasmus added brief marginal scholia explaining some points and giving classical references.[118] Both Erasmus and the Louvain editors made the more momentous change of adding to the end of the *Retractationes* passage on the *disciplinarum libri* the sentence: "*Hoc opus sic incipit: Omnia nomina tredecim.*" Throughout the *Retractationes* Augustine usually gives the first words of each work he describes. "*Omnia nomina tredecim*" are the first words of the *De grammatica* attributed to Augustine in the manuscripts. Amerbach had not included this sentence in his text of the *Retractationes*. Thus the editions of Augustine which superseded Amerbach's strengthened the appearance of authenticity of the books on grammar, dialectic, and rhetoric regarded as Augustine's by Amerbach, Erasmus, and the Louvain editors.[119]

3. *The Edition of the Benedictines of St. Maur*

With the 1679 publication of the first volume of the Maurist edition of Augustine's works the standing of our treatise in the Augustinian corpus changed. The Maurists concluded that *De dialectica*, *De grammatica*, *De rhetorica*, and *Categoriae decem* are certainly spurious.[120] They gave four reasons in support of their conclusion.[121]

(1) According to *Retractationes* I. v (the Maurists apparently have in mind the phrase "*interrogans eos, qui mecum erant*") Augustine wrote the books on the liberal arts in dialogue form. But none of the four are dialogues.

(2) In addition, Augustine said that his purpose was "to reach things incorporeal through things corporeal and to lead others to them." But these works do not move the soul to consider incorporeal things.

(3) Furthermore, the books are of mediocre quality. They abound in trite commonplaces, showing none of the skill with which Augustine treated similar subjects in *De ordine* and *De musica*.

(4) As to the sentence printed by earlier editions identifying the first words of *De grammatica*, examination of the manuscripts of the *Retractationes* shows this to be an interpolation.

Three of these objections to authenticity concern the *Retractationes* passage on the *disciplinarum libri*; the other is about the quality of the works. I shall consider these objections only in their application to *De dialectica*.

The objection that the treatise is mediocre can be met in two ways. In the first place, judgments of quality are highly subjective and though some scholars concur in the Maurists' evaluation,[122] not all do.[123] That there is disagreement on the quality of *De dialectica* weakens the force of this objection to the authenticity of the treatise. But, in the second place, even if it be granted that *De dialectica* is mediocre or at least is below the level of most of Augustine's writings, it need not follow that Augustine could not have written it. The treatise is probably a first draft and would have been improved by subsequent revision. Moreover, it is in a genre, the school handbook, which does not easily lend itself to brilliance. And there is no reason why a good writer, particularly a young one still seeking his proper subject matter and style, cannot occasionally do poor work. Indeed, recognition of this by an author could be a reason for stopping a project, as Augustine did in the case of most of the liberal arts books.

As far as I know, no one doubts the accuracy of the Maurist emenda- tion of *Retractationes* I. v. The latest critical edition is in agreement with their excision of the *incipit* for *De grammatica*,[124] and it is clearly implausible to believe that Augustine would remember the opening words of a treatise written forty years earlier and since lost. Even if the sentence were authentic, it would be relevant mainly to the authenticity of *De grammatica*. Acceptance of the emendation of the *Retractationes* has no direct bearing on the question of the authenticity of *De dialectica*.

The Maurists' objections that *De dialectica* agrees in neither form nor purpose with Augustine's description of his books on the liberal arts have been argued against strongly by later scholars. Crecelius was the first to oppose the Maurists' objections on the basis of the incomplete- ness of the work.[125] Marrou and Pinborg have repeated Crecelius's argument.[126] All point out that the elevation of the mind to incorporeal things becomes an explicit purpose in *De musica* only after five long books have discussed rhythm in a strictly technical and decidedly prosaic manner. If Augustine intended *explicitly* in *each* of the works to reach and lead others to incorporeals by means of corporeals, and it is by no means clear that he intended this, then it is likely that he would have done this towards the end of each work. In *De dialectica* he simply never got that far. Similar reasoning applies to the lack of dialogue form. Crecelius, Marrou, and Pinborg say that Augustine would have made *De dialectica* into a dialogue, probably between *magister* and *discipulus* as in *De musica*, if he had finished and revised it.[127] These scholars

believe they see harbingers of this plan in some passages where *De dialectica* contains statements in the second person singular, as if the author
were already thinking ahead to the form his work was eventually going
to take.[128] It may be, however, that the evidence here is more ambiguous
than either the Maurists or their critics have supposed. It is not clear
from the *Retractationes* that the books were to be dialogues. Heinrich
Keil believes that Augustine's "*interrogans eos, qui mecum erant*" refers
only to how he intended to use the books and not to the form in which
he wrote them.[129] Keil argues that the straight prose form of *De dialectica* is evidence in favor of its authenticity. In my opinion, the Maurists'
view that the *disciplinarum libri* were to be dialogues is correct. The form
of *De musica* supports this view. Moreover, in the early part of the *Retractationes* Augustine seems to use such language as the *interrogans*
phrase only in connection with his dialogues.[130] The uses of the second
person singular cited by Crecelius and others may indicate eventual dialogue form for *De dialectica* or they may be interpreted in other ways.[131]
But commitment to any one view on this matter or on the intended final
form of the work does not require us to reject the work's authenticity,
for whatever our view the unfinished state of *De dialectica* would render
indecisive any criteria based on that view.

Thus the Maurists' arguments fail to sustain their conclusion that *De
dialectica* was not written by Augustine. It is noteworthy that the
Maurists did not object to authenticity on the grounds of the manuscript
tradition. As I have shown above, this tradition is not uniform in its attribution of *De dialectica*. The Maurists knew of the 1558 publication
of the treatise under the name of Fortunatianus, but they say that the
five manuscripts which they used for their edition all attributed the work
to Augustine.[132] They named only two of these five manuscripts, a
Corbeiensis and a *Germanensis*,[133] probably Leningrad 7 and Paris 12949,
which were in the Maurists' library at Saint-Germain-des-Près.[134] Whatever the manuscripts used by the Maurists,[135] the text of their edition is
basically what I have called the Augustine *textus receptus*.[136] A thorough
revision of the text was not carried out until the nineteenth century. In
the meantime the Benedictine *Opera omnia* superseded all earlier editions
of the works of Augustine, and their edition of *De dialectica* became
the one by which the work was known.

4. *The Edition of Wilhelm Crecelius*

In 1857 the question of the authenticity of *De dialectica* was reopened by Crecelius (1828–1889) in an edition of the treatise published as a Programm of the Gymnasium in Elberfeld.[137] In this pamphlet-sized edition, Crecelius both challenged the Maurists' arguments and criticized the text of the earlier Augustine editions.[138] He used the two Bern manuscripts, but relied mainly on the Cologne manuscript, which he compared closely with the Maurist text.[139] His inclusion of a critical apparatus was a major improvement over earlier editions. Philological scholars recognized the superiority of Crecelius's edition, though one, Hermann Hagen, argued that it requires improvement.[140] Hagen's major criticism was that Crecelius did not give sufficient weight to Bern 363. This was because Crecelius believed that the manuscript is to be dated in the twelfth century, whereas its correct dating is ninth century.[141] Also Crecelius failed to see that Bern 363 is not derived from the Cologne codex, even though it closely resembles the latter, and to evaluate carefully the readings of Bern 548, which resembles the *textus receptus* more than the other two manuscripts do.[142] Hagen's critique of Crecelius is based on an investigation of the manuscripts that Crecelius used, though he also draws some conclusions from the fragmentary Bern A 92. Now Professor Pinborg has carried out a much wider investigation of the manuscript tradition. His new text, on which my translation is based, makes changes in Crecelius in about three dozen passages, with fewer than a third of these being major as to the substance of the work.[143] Pinborg's research thus makes it clear that Crecelius gave scholars a basically sound text. Since this text differs significantly from the *textus receptus*, arguments about degree of sophistication and about Augustinian style should henceforth be based only on the basic text that Crecelius and now Pinborg have given us.

D. SUMMARY

The history of *De dialectica* and of the debate on its authorship presents us with two traditions, both appearing in the early Middle Ages and continuing well into the Renaissance. One attributes the little book to Chirius Fortunatianus. It begins with the Cologne codex and flourishes in Italy in the fifteenth century. The other tradition attributes *De dialectica* to Augustine of Hippo. This tradition moves more forcefully through the centuries, beginning with several ninth-century manuscripts. It is attested by numerous library listings and later manuscripts, with evidence of use of the work (intensively in some cases) as a logic text in the liberal arts tradition. And it appears in all of the sixteenth-century editions of Augustine's works. This second tradition suffered a setback with the Maurists' critique, but it has been revived by recent scholars. The other tradition seems to have expired in the sixteenth century.

Is the revived Augustinian tradition sound? I believe that it is. The Maurists' critique has been rejected, no serious alternative attribution has been proposed, nothing about the treatise keeps it from being Augustine's, and there are positive indications that he wrote it. Complete certainly eludes us, of course, but we can say that it is more probable that it is Augustine's than that it is not his. In the second part of this introduction I shall attempt to assess the probability in another way.

NOTES

[1] In *Sacris Erudiri* **3** (1951), p. 65, under the title *'Principia dialecticae.'* See also Palemon Glorieux, "Pour revaloriser Migne," *Mélanges de Science Religieux* **9** (1952), Suppl., p. 22.

[2] In *Saint Augustin et la Fin de la Culture Antique*, 1938.

[3] He intended to cover his sermons and letters but did not manage to do so. See *Retr*. II. 93.

[4] See *Retr*. II.67 (*CSEL* 36, p. 179, 15–16): *"opusculorum meorum indiculo."* Also, Possidius, *Vita Augustini* 18. On Augustine's library see Berthold Altaner, "Die Bibliothek Augustins," pp. 174–178 in his *Kleine Patristische Schriften* (Berlin, 1967).

[5] *Retr*. I.5, trans. by Mary Bogan, *The Retractations*, pp. 21f. In older editions this paragraph is treated as a separate chapter and is given the number 6. The full Latin text is (*CSEL* 36, p. 27, 12ff.):

> Per idem tempus, quo Mediolani fui baptismum percepturus, etiam disciplinarum libros conatus sum scribere interrogans eos, qui mecum erant atque ab huius modi studiis non abhorrebant, per corporalia cupiens ad incorporalia quibusdam quasi passibus certis vel pervenire vel ducere. sed earum solum de grammatica librum absolvere potui, quem postea de armario nostro perdidi, et de musica sex volumina, quantum adtinet ad eandem partem, quae rythmus vocatur. sed eosdem sex libros iam baptizatus iamque ex Italia regressus in Africam scripsi: incoaveram quippe tantummodo istam apud Mediolanium disciplinam. de aliis vero quinque disciplinis illic similiter incoatis, de dialectica, de rhetorica, de geometrica, de arithmetica, de philosophia, sola principia remanserunt, quae tamen etiam ipsa perdidimus, sed haberi ab aliquibus existimo.

The liberal arts books are also included in the catalogue which Possidius appended to his life of Augustine. Listed there under *'diversi libri'* are: *De grammatica liber unus, De musica libri sex*, and *Ceterarum disciplinarum principia: libri quinque, idest de dialectica, de retorica, de geometria, de aritmetica, de philosophia* (Wilmart's edition of Possidius' *Operum S. Augustini Elenchus*, p. 175). Possidius' list may not be an independent witness for these books, as Wilmart notes (p. 159). But he provides another source from which future readers of Augustine could learn that Augustine wrote such books.

⁶ On the liberal arts tradition see Marrou, pp. 211–235.
⁷ Harald Hagendahl, *Augustine and the Latin Classics*, II, pp. 590 and 592f. Several editors of Varro have regarded most of the first six chapters of *De dialectica* as fragments of Varro. See notes on the translation, Ch. I, n. 3, Ch. II, n. 1, and Ch. VI, n. 3.
⁸ See Marrou, pp. 161–186.
⁹ *Confessiones* IV. xvi. 28 and 30.
¹⁰ In *Retr.* I.3 Augustine uses the same language to explain why he discussed the liberal arts in *De ordine*, a work he wrote just a short time before he began the *disciplinarum libri:* "... de ordine studiendi..., cum a corporalibus ad incorporalia potest profici" (p. 19, 14–15).
¹¹ "... a corporeis ad incorporea transeamus ...." (*De mus.* VI.ii.2, *PL* 32, col. 1163). Marrou, pp. 580–583, argues that Augustine revised Book Six, but in his opinion the major revision was the addition of Chapter One. I have quoted from the beginning of Chapter Two, which was probably the original opening of the book. See also *Epistle* 101.3, where, writing in 409 about *De musica*, Augustine says that the study of rhythm "... quasi gradatis itineribus nititur ad superna intima veritatis ...." (*LCL* edn., p. 194).
¹² *Conf.* VII.i, v, x, and xx.
¹³ It may be that the corporeal-incorporeal rubric is found in Varro and is taken over by Augustine from him. B. Fischer, *De Augustini Disciplinarum Libro qui est De Dialectica*, pp. 54–61, argues that Augustine's *Epistle* 26 and the poem of Licentius appended to it show that at Cassiciacum Augustine had used Varro's *Disciplinarum libri* and that his own books on the liberal arts were intended to be an exposition of Varro's teachings. Even several years later (around 395) Licentius, one of the young men at Cassiciacum with Augustine, was still asking Augustine to help him understand the *"arcanum Varronis iter"* (*CSEL* 34.1, p. 89, 1), perhaps, Fischer believes, even urging Augustine to complete the *disciplinarum libri* begun in Milan. We need not accept all of Fischer's interpretation of the letter and poem to see that even a pagan (Licentius was never converted to Christianity as far as is known) placed a religious or quasi-religious interpretation upon study of the arts and sciences. This interpretation has its source in Plato and, ultimately, in Pythagoras. Augustine would come to a different view of the liberal arts, continuing to affirm the value of studying them but under the more prosaic notion that they aid the interpreter of Scripture. (See esp. *De doctrina christiana* II.xxxi.48–x1.61.) His earlier view, that the liberal arts aid directly in passing to incorporeal things, was closer to the Pythagorean, Platonic, and, it seems, Varronian outlook.
¹⁴ *Retr.* I.5, p. 25, 19. Peter Brown, *Augustine of Hippo*, pp. 74 and 124, gives these dates for the return to Milan and the baptism. The latter was on the night of April 24–25, to be precise.
¹⁵ Later he seems to have lost the first five books of *De musica*. See *Epistle* 101.
¹⁶ Memorius, a bishop in Italy, whose chief claim to fame is that he is the father of Julian of Eclanum, wrote to Augustine asking for a copy of *De musica*. Augustine's reply is *Epistle* 101. Licentius may have had copies of the books. (See note 13 above.) He resided in Thagaste, Augustine's home town, but was a frequent visitor to Rome. See Brown, pp. 126 and 381.
¹⁷ There seem to be few reasons for accepting the *De rhetorica* as authentic. Marrou, p. 578, the Maurists, *PL* 32, col. 1439, note a, and J. Zurek, *De S. Aurelii Augustini praeceptis rhetoricis*, in *Dissertationes Philologae Vindobonenses* 8, pt. 2 (1905), pp. 96ff., all argue against its authenticity. It is viewed as authentic by A. Reuter, "Zu dem Augustinischen Fragment De arte rhetoricae," in *Kirchengeschichtliche Studien*, ed. by T. Brieger (Leipzig, 1890), pp. 321–351, by B. Riposati, "Agostino o Pseudo-Agostino?" in *Studi in onore di Gino Funaioli* (Rome, 1955), pp. 378–393, and by Karl Barwick, "Augustins Schrift De rhetorica und Hermagoras von Temnos," *Philologus* 105 (1961), p. 97, n. 1. *De rhetorica* is printed in *PL* 32, cols. 1439–1443 and Halm, *RLM*, pp. 135–151. – Marrou, pp. 571–576,

has argued that we may have two abridgements made of Augustine's *De grammatica* by later grammarians. The Maurists argue against it. *PL* 32, col. 1385–6. It is printed in *PL* 32, cols. 1385–1408 and H. Keil, *Grammatici Latini* V (Leipzig, 1923), pp. 496–524 for the long form, pp. 494–496 for the short form. A work often grouped with *De dialectica* is the *Categoriae decem*, which is universally regarded as spurious. See L. Minio-Paluello, "The Texts of the *Categoriae*: The Latin Tradition." *The Classical Quarterly* **39** (1945), 63–74.

[18] See below, section C.3, on the Maurists' attempt to derive other criteria from *Retr.* I.5.

[19] In his review of Crecelius's edition, p. 155.

[20] Pinborg, "Das Sprachdenken der Stoa und Augustins Dialektik," p. 149.

[21] This is Cologne 166, discussed below.

[22] Pauly-Wissowa-Kroll list no other writer in antiquity with the name 'Augustine' in the *Real-Encyclopädie der Klassischen Altertumswissenschaft*. J.-P. Migne speculated that this Augustine might be the seventh-century Irish author of *De mirabilibus sacrae Scripturae* who bore the name (*PL* 32, col. 1414, note a). But the seventh century seems late for *De dialectica*, nothing is known about this Irish Augustine beyond what can be learned from *De mirabilibus*, and in particular there is no evidence that he was interested in logic. See James F. Kenney, *Sources for Early History of Ireland*, pp. 275–277. The other famous Augustine is the saint of Canterbury (d. 604 or 605) who had no interest in logic that we know of and wrote very little.

[23] In *De musica* I.2 Augustine defines music as the *'scientia bene modulandi,'* showing that he knows the form of definition used in *De dial.*, where dialectic is the *'bene disputandi scientia'* (I, 5, 2). In *De mag.* VIII.24 he gives the standard definition of *'homo'* as *'animal rationale mortale'* which is also in *De dial.* IX (p. 16, 25). Pinborg, pp. 150f., sees the somewhat more elaborate definition of 'to speak' in *De mag.* I.2 *(Qui enim loquitur suae voluntatis signum foras dat per articulatum sonum.)* as similar to *De dial.* V (7, 8): *Loqui est articulata voce signum dare.*

[24] *'Verbum'* from *'verberando'* (*De dial.* VI, 9, 6ff.) is given in *De mag.* V.12; *'lucus'* from *'quod minime luceat'* (*De dial.* VI, 10, 22) is given in *De doctrina christiana* III.xxix.41; and *'piscina'* is given the same explanation as it is given in *De dial.* (10, 17–19) in *De doctrina* III.xxix.40).

[25] For instance, *'pone'* as having two meanings depending on where the accent is placed is used in *De dial.* X (20, 11–13) and in *De musica* I.1.

[26] For the notion that written words are signs of spoken words (*De dial.* V, 7, 11) see *De mag.* IV.8. Pinborg, pp. 150f., cites parallels on the discussion of self-reference between *De dial.* X (p. 17, 17–20 and p. 18, 16 and 20f.) and *De mag.* V.16, VI.18, and VIII.22. Marrou, p. 577, n. 6, notes the general parallelism between the discussions of obscurity and ambiguity in *De dialectica* VIII and *De doctrina christiana* II.x.15.

[27] For example, Fortunatianus uses the same form of definition for rhetoric: *'bene dicendi scientia'* (*Ars rhetoricae* I, *RLM* 81, 4). Crecelius, pp. 10 and 20, notes fourth-century references to *'piscina', 'lucus',* and *'pone'* in the grammarians Donatus and Servius.

[28] *De trin.* XV.x.19. I have discussed the semantic theories of *De dial.*, *De doctr. chr.*, and *De trin.* in detail in my article, "The Theory of Signs in St. Augustine's *De Doctrina Christiana*," pp. 15–26.

[29] *Contra Academicos* III.xiii.29.

[30] On this see my article, "The Theory of Signs," pp. 33–36 and 39–41.

[31] See the article by Pinborg and the first chapter of Karl Barwick's *Probleme der Stoischen Sprachlehre und Rhetorik*.

[32] Norman Kretzmann, "History of Semantics," p. 367, says that Augustine's semantic discussions, of which *De dial.* V is a major instance, had very little influence on medieval

logic. William and Martha Kneale, *The Development of Logic*, p. 188, say that Chapter Five may have stimulated medieval logicians, but they give no references to support this view.

[33] *Inst.* II.i.1 (Mynors, p. 94, 13–17); II.v.10 (p. 149, 21). Pierre Courcelle, *Late Latin Writers and Their Greek Sources*, pp. 340 and 349, notes that Augustine had little influence on Cassiodorus's views of the liberal arts.

[34] *Inst.* II.iii.1–20 and *Etym.* II.xxii-xxxi.

[35] *Meta.* II.4 (Webb, p. 65, 22ff.): *"Est autem dialectica, ut Augustino placet, bene disputandi scientia...."* III.5 (p. 142, 16ff.): *"Eo spectat, illud Augustini, tractum quidem ab Aristotile, quoniam de fonte isto hauserunt omnes, quia in omni enuntiatione spectanda sunt tria, dictio, dicibile, et res."*

[36] That John's view of dialectic is the narrower Aristotelian view is clear from *Metalogicon* II.3.

[37] He says that the *res* is that concerning which *(de quo)* a statement is made, the *dicibile* is what is said about the thing *(quod de aliquo)* and the *dictio* is the way in which it is said *(quo dicitur hoc de illo)*. According to John the *res* and the *dicibile* are natural and the *dictio* is arbitrary.

[38] Minio-Paluello, "The *Ars Disserendi* of Adam of Balsham 'Parvipontanus',", *Medieval and Renaissance Studies* III (1954), p. 128, note 1 compares *Ars diss.* I.xxxi (pp. 19f. of edn. by Minio-Paluello in *Twelfth Century Logic* I, Rome, 1956) with *De dial.* VIII, 14, 4–7, and *Ars* I.xlii (pp. 26f.) with *De dial.* X, 17, 14ff. De Rijk, *Logica Modernorum* I (Assen, 1962), pp. 64, n. 2 and 66, n. 1, agrees that the passages cited by Minio-Paluello from *De dialectica* are the basis for Adam's views.

[39] As an example of the equivocal use of a name, the *Libri Carolini*, composed around 790, gives the following (I.2, *Mon. Germ. Hist.* edn., p. 13, 23–25):

    Augustinus fuit summus philosophus,
    et: Augustinus legendus est,
    et: Augustinus pictus in ecclesia stat,
    et: Augustinus illo loco sepultus est....

This is strikingly parallel to *De dial.* X, 18, 1–6, with changes appropriate to the different names used:

    ... (Tullius) fuit summus orator...
    et Tullius inauratus in Capitolio stat
    et Tullius totus tibi legendus est
    et Tullius hoc loco sepultus est.

I came upon this parallel independently, before I discovered that Luitpold Wallach, "The *Libri Carolini* and Patristics, Latin and Greek: Prolegomena to a Critical Edition," in *The Classical Tradition*, ed. by Wallach (Ithaca, 1966), p. 464, also believes that *De dial.* is the source of this passage.

[40] Wallach, pp. 497f. For the view that it was written by Theodulf of Orleans, see Ann Freeman, "Theodulf of Orleans and the *Libri Carolini*," *Speculum* 32 (1957), 663–705.

[41] My major source, Gustav Becker's *Catalogi Bibliothecarum Antiqui*, covers only the period through the twelfth century. I have not checked the sources he gives for later centuries.

[42] In Durham Cathedral MS B.IV.6, fol. 144. See Thomas Rud, *Codicum manuscriptorum ecclesiae Cathedralis Dunelmensis catalogus classicus* (Durham, 1825), p. 179, and R. A. B. Mynors, *Durham Cathedral Manuscripts to the End of the Twelfth Century* (Oxford, 1939), p. 57. This could be the MS listed as at Durham in the thirteenth century by the *Registrum Angliae*. See below, the listing for England and Scotland.

[43] Works listed frequently in the catalogues and manuscripts have been abbreviated as

follows:

Aug. mus.	Augustine, *De musica*
„ gram.	„ ?, *De grammatica*
„ rhet.	„ ?, *De rhetorica*
Ps.-Aug. cat. x	Pseudo-Augustine, *Categoriae decem*
Ar. cat.	Aristotle, *Categoriae*
„ peri	„ , *Peri hermeneias*
Ap. peri	Apuleius?, *Peri hermeneias*
Porph. is.	Porphyry, *Isagoge*
Boeth. in cat.	Boethius, Comm. on Ar. cat.
„ in peri	„ , „ „ Ar. peri ⎫
„ in is.	„ , „ „ Porph. is. ⎬ edd. not usually distinguished
„ syll. cat.	„ , *De syllogismo categorico*
„ syll. hyp.	„ , *De syllogismo hypothetico*
M. Cap. dial., rhet.	Martianus Capella, *Dialectica, Rhetorica*
Fortun. rhet.	Fortunatianus, *Ars rhetoricae*
Victor·	Marius Victorinus, various works

Other abbreviations for works which occur less often should be obvious.

[44] These are presumably Franciscan houses, since the *Registrum Angliae* is organized along the lines of the Franciscan custodies in effect before 1278. There were Franciscan houses at Exeter, Durham, and St. Andrews. See David Knowles, *Medieval Religious Houses in England and Wales* (London, 1953), index for Exeter and Durham, and A. G. Little, *Franciscan Papers, Lists, and Documents* (Manchester, 1943), pp. 225f., for St. Andrews and for the *Registrum* as a source. Gede(s)worth is probably Jedworth in Scotland, the present Jedburgh (see George Smith Pryde, *The Burghs of Scotland*, Oxford, 1945, p. 9). There was an Augustinian monastery, there before 1209 according to L. H. Cottineau, *Répertoire Topo-Bibliographique des Abbayes et Prieurés* (Macon, 1939), Vol. I, col. 1262.

[45] Manuscripts ordinarily give the author and title of a work in standardized formulas at the beginning or end of the work. A manuscript of *De dialectica* which does both is Philadelphia lat. 63, which I have personally examined. Its title is: *Incipit liber aurelii augustini episcopi de dialectica* (f. 79r). The colophon is: *Explicit liber sancti augustini episcopi de dialectica* (f. 87r). (I have expanded the abbreviated words.)

[46] One would expect *'dialecticam'* and *'dialecticae'* in these titles, but I report them as given in my sources. I have not seen copies or photos of any of the MSS with these two titles.

[47] Billanovich, pp. 111f., 145f.

[48] Blumenkranz, "La survie médiévale de saint Augustin à travers ses apocryphes," pp. 1008f. and 1017.

[49] *Ibid.*, p. 1014.

[50] Lowe, *Cod. Lat. Ant.* VIII, p. 39, dates it eighth century; Jaffé and Wattenbach, p. 65, say that it is seventh century. Lowe is more likely to be correct.

[51] See the article on Fortunatianus by Münscher in Pauly's *Realencyclopädie*, Vol. VII, cols. 44–55. He is usually dated as late fourth or early fifth century.

[52] *Inst.* II.ii.1, 4, 10, and 16.

[53] Cologne 166, Bern 363, Berlin 687, Paris 7730, and Vat. Pal. 1588. The early MS without *De dial.* is Paris BN lat. 7530. Halm, *RLM*, p. 80, lists two later MSS of Fortun. *Ars rhet.* that do not include *De dial.*: Munich lat. 14649 and 6406. The several fifteenth-century MSS that include both the *Ars rhet.* and *De dial.* will be discussed in the next section.

[54] Jaffé and Wattenbach, p. 67.

[55] This is all that Cassiodorus knew. *Inst.* II.ii.10 (p. 104, 8–9): *"Fortunatianum... tribus voluminibus...."*

[56] Examples of topics discussed in both works: *officia oratoris* in *Ars* I.1 (p. 81, 6) and in *De rhet.* 1 (*RLM*, p. 137, 4); *finis* in I.1 (81, 7–8) and in 2 (138, 3ff.); and *civiles quaestiones* in I.1 (81, 9–11) and in 4 (138, 34ff.).

[57] The descriptive catalogue for the Berlin MS (Schillmann) lists no attribution. Since it gives attributions for other works, I assume that *De dial.* has none. In the Paris MS, which I have examined in microfilm form, there is no author given for *De dial.* The title *'Dialectica'* is given but in a modern hand. No author or title is given for Fortunatianus's work either, except in the same later hand.

[58] Paris 7730. Since the *Ars rhet.* was originally anonymous and untitled in the Paris MS (see note 57 above), supposing that the MS is dependent on Cologne 166 requires us to assume that the scribe for the Paris MS eliminated all of the titles and colophons he would have found in his exemplar. This seems unlikely.

[59] Fortunatianus opens his work with: *"Quid est rhetorica? bene dicendi scientia."* (*RLM*, p. 81, 4)

[60] Two MSS, one early and one late, show evidence of reflection on the identity of the author of the treatise. A gloss in Paris BN lat. 12949 (fol. 12r), probably by Heiric of Auxerre, says that the author of *De dial.* was the bishop of Hippo, not the Augustine who was a teacher in England (presumably Augustine of Canterbury). This gloss is printed by Cousin, *Ouvrages inédits d'Abélard*, p. 619. For further discussion of this MS see the next section. – In Florence, aed. 168 there is a gloss by someone other than the scribe on VII, 13, 6 (*cum Augustino nominato*): *"Ex hoc videtur quod Augustinus nuncuparetur auctor."* On the basis of this the title, originally *'quartus* [of Fortun. rhet.] *de dyalectica,'* is changed to *'Dialectica Augustini.'* Billanovich, p. 145.

[61] Billanovich, pp. 138–140.

[62] Billanovich, p. 140; Kenney, p. 560.

[63] All of the conclusions drawn in this section about the distribution and use of *De dial.* are subject to the partial and sometimes uncertain information upon which they are based. Even if research were exhaustive, one cannot know how many manuscripts have perished or how many library catalogues are lost or, perhaps more important, how many libraries were never catalogued adequately or at all. Courcelle, pp. 393f., notes, for example, that there are no catalogues for the Lateran library, which played such a major role in the dispersion of books in the early Middle Ages. See Mark Sullivan, *Apuleian Logic* (Amsterdam, 1967), p. 203, for a statement, similar to mine here, regarding his study of the influence of Apuleius' *Peri hermeneias*.

[64] The only possible exception is Bern 363 (ninth century), which Kenney, p. 560, tentatively says was written in Northern Italy, perhaps at Milan. See above, p. 18.

[65] Benedictines at Reichenau, Fleury, Auxerre, Corbie, Gorze (and Amel), Anchin, Toul, Arras, and Salzburg; Cistercians at Clairvaux and Chaalis; Franciscans at Durham, Exeter, and St. Andrews (see note 44 above); Dominicans at Florence.

[66] At Cologne, Rouen, and Trier.

[67] Van de Vyver, p. 437, notes that the later the period the more treatises on logic became isolated from books on the other liberal arts.

[68] See van de Vyver, p. 450.

[69] The label *'logica vetus'* is variously applied by scholars. Some mean by it only the *Categories* and *Peri hermeneias* of Aristotle and the *Isagoge* of Porphyry. See J. Isaac, *Le Peri Hermeneias en occident de Boèce à Saint Thomas* (Paris, 1953), pp. 38f. Others expand the coverage to include all of Boethius's logical works (see M. Grabmann, "Aristoteles im

zwölften Jahrhundert," *Medieval Studies* **12** (1950), pp. 123f.) and Apuleius's *Periherme-neias* and the *Categoriae decem* (see van de Vyver, p. 446, and Sullivan, *Apuleian Logic*, pp. 229–232). To my knowledge *De dialectica* has not been included on the list, but if *'logica vetus'* is to be used for writings on logic read before the recovery of all of Aristotle, then *De dialectica* should clearly be on the list. Van de Vyver, p. 450, says that *De dial.* is important in the ninth and tenth centuries, but he does not list it in the *logica vetus*.

[70] *Categoriae decem* is in twenty of the MSS which contain *De dial.* Alcuin wrote introductory verses to the *Cat. dec.*, used it in his own *De dial.* (chapters III–XI on the categories; *PL* 101, cols. 949ff.), and may be responsible for its attribution to Augustine. (van de Vyver, pp. 431 and 435) The oldest MS of the work, Rome Bibl. Patrum Maristarum, sine num. (*AL* 2163, III, 147ff.), dates from around 814 and already contains Alcuin's verses. See Lowe, *Cod. Lat. Ant.*, IV, p. 4, no. 417.

[71] Van de Vyver, p. 438, gives the provenance of this MS as Auxerre, then Corbie, and then Saint-Germain-des-Prés, where it had the number 1108 and, according to Cousin, p. LXXXI, was used by the Maurists (see below, section C.3). On the basis of information given by their cataloguers, I would conjecture that two extant, later MSS are dependent on this MS. The first scholium of Vatican Cod. Urbinas lat. 393, given by Stornajolo, I, p. 375, begins with the words of the prologue found in the Paris MS (with a few differences: Vat. adds *'noster'* after *'dominus'* and for *'item propter'* reads *'interpretatur'*). And the title line of Charleville 187, given by *Cat. Gén.*, V, p. 626, contains the verse *"Ingeniti geniti flantis sic nomine fungor,"* which is also in the title of the Paris MS.

[72] Van de Vyver, p. 437.

[73] Hauréau, *Histoire de la Philosophie Scholastique* I, pp. 185f. Hauréau notes that Cousin, p. 621, misread when he gave the name as 'Henricus.' Other scholars are not so certain that the inscription is meant to apply to *De dial.* See van de Vyver, p. 438, Prantl, *Geschichte der Logik im Abendlande*, II, p. 41, and Manitius, *Geschichte der lateinische Literatur des Mittelalters* (1911), I, pp. 502f. I have examined this MS in microfilm form and the hand for the glossing of the two works appears to be the same.

[74] Hauréau, p. 181.

[75] Cousin, p. 619.

[76] See note 78, below. Hauréau's own opinion about the glosses is that they are of little interest. But this opinion is based in part on his view that *De dial.* itself is a grammatical and not a logical work (p. 186). This view clearly does injustice to *De dial.*

[77] In the prologue, which Cousin, p. 619, prints, Heiric says that *'dialectica'* means either speech between two persons or refers to logic as being on speech (*de dictione*). He also states the Varronian view that dialectic and rhetoric are related to each other as the closed fist and the open palm.

[78] Hauréau, pp. 188–196, on the *Cat. dec.* glosses. See also Frederick Copleston, *A History of Philosophy*, vol. II (Westminster, Md., 1960), pp. 141f.

[79] In fact, there is little glossing of Chapter Five. *'Dicibile'* is glossed as *'quod dici potest'* (fol. 13v). But all of the glossing needs to be read and interpreted.

[80] Based on sources given in the manuscript list above.

[81] Roberto Weiss, *Humanism in England*, p. 123.

[82] Billanovich, pp. 145f. For a short sketch of Aurispa's life see John E. Sandys, *A History of Classical Scholarship*, Vol. II, pp. 36f.

[83] William H. Woodward, *Studies in Education during the Age of the Renaissance, 1400–1600*, pp. 26–45; Weiss, pp. 84f.

[84] On Grey see Weiss, pp. 86–95. Stornajolo and Leonardi give the date of the MS as 1448, but Grey was not in Ferrara then. Aurispa left Ferrara with Grey in 1446. Weiss, p. 89.

85 On Free see Weiss, pp. 106–111. Weiss, pp. 123 and 126, says that Free wrote only the Fortun. rhet. in this MS, but the hand for foll. 39r–57r (including *De dial.*) seems to me the same as the hand for the first part of the MS (to fol. 26v).

86 On Gunthorpe see Weiss, pp. 122–126.

87 Woodward, *Studies*, pp. 38–45, and *Vittorino da Feltre and Other Humanist Educators*, pp. 161–178. The latter is a translation of *De ordine docendi et studendi* by Battista Guarino, the son of Guarino da Verona. Battista summarizes the educational views of his father.

88 Cologne 166 does not have the Capella excerpt. This entered our manuscripts apparently via another tradition. See Billanovich, pp. 140f.

89 Woodward, *Vittorino*, pp. 36 and 60.

90 Woodward, *Vittorino*, pp. 107, 155, and 172. Had *De dialectica* been widely recognized as Augustinian by Guarino and other humanists, it might have been more important to them, since the authority of Augustine was still very high for the earlier humanists. See Woodward, *Vittorino*, pp. 227, 149, 165, and 170. Battista Guarino mentions Augustine's *De musica* in his treatise on education (Woodward, p. 165).

91 For the copy attributed to de Pensis (P) see M. Pellechet, *Catalogue Général des Incunables des Bibliothèques Publiques de France*, Vol. III (Paris, 1909), no. 4889; Robert Proctor, *An Index to the Early Printed Books in the British Museum*, Vol. II (London, 1898), no. 5256; *Catalogue of Books Printed in the Fifteenth Century Now in the British Museum*, Pt. V (London, 1924), p. 475; and Frederick Goff, *Incunabula in American Libraries*, Third Census (New York, 1964), no. F–273, p. 249. For the copy attributed to Tacuinus (T) see Pellechet, no. 4890; Goff, no. F–274; and J. C. T. Oates, *A Catalogue of the Fifteenth Century Printed Books in the University Library Cambridge* (Cambridge, 1954), no. 2123. One catalogue, the *Indice generale degli incunaboli delle biblioteche d'Italia*, Vol. II (Rome, 1948), p. 237, attributes both copies to de Pensis. Neither P nor T has a title page. They are listed in the catalogues by the first words of their table of contents page: *Hoc in volumine aurea haec opuscula continentur. Chirii consulti Fortunatiani Rhetoricorum libri tres....* For information on de Pensis and Tacuinus and for lists of books printed by them, see the British Museum catalogue (1924) cited above, pp. xlii and 467–476 on de Pensis and pp. xlix and 526–535 on Tacuinus. Both printed mostly classical authors and modern Italian authors.

92 I obtained a microfilm copy of P from the Newberry Library in Chicago and a microfilm copy of T from the Beinecke Rare Book and Manuscript Library at Yale University. Eventually I directly inspected the Yale copy of T as well as a copy of P in the Bodleian Library, Oxford.

93 The evidence for separate printings is as follows: (1) The signatures differ. P has aa, a-o, A-C; T has a, A-O, A-C. (2) T seems to use abbreviations more frequently than P and uses two that are not found in P ('9' for '-us' and 'p̄' for '*prae*'). (3) T, unlike P, has decorative initials at the beginning of books and chapters. There is, however, space in P for these to be added by hand. This could be a difference in the two copies I have examined, not in the two printings. (4) The location of words on the page is not always the same. T seems to separate the words more distinctly. In some cases this makes for a difference in pagination, e.g., n in P and N in T are different. (5) T prints more running titles, prints them more often in capital letters, and has some unique errors, e.g., on A verso and A ii recto of the *Dialectica* the running title is 'EPISTOLA.' As far as I can tell, the type is the same for P and T. Konrad Haebler, who has made a major study of type, notes in *The Study of Incunabula* (New York, 1933), pp. 107–110, the difficulties in trying to identify Italian printers by types. – Minor differences between the Newberry and Bodleian copies of P may raise some doubt as to whether there were only *two* printings. The Bodleian copy lacks a signature that the New-

berry copy has on aa recto and in the Bodleian copy page a iv verso, which is blank in the Newberry copy, is printed. In addition the Bodleian copy places *De dialectica* early in the book instead of at the end, where it is located in both Newberry's P and Yale's T. I should further note that the Bodleian (P) and Yale (T) copies have the same watermarks, a balance very close to no. 2541 in C. M. Briquet, *Les Filigranes* (Amsterdam, 1968), vol. I, p. 187. According to Briquet this watermark was very common in Venice up to 1550.

[94] Haebler, p. 191, says that printers in the fifteenth century saw nothing objectionable in reprinting from editions by other printers. Just as in the manuscript period it was a service to copy a manuscript, so in the early period of printing to copy by reprinting was a service to the literate public.

[95] The letter is printed on folios 1b–2b (aa verso to aa ii verso by the signatures in P, the only form of numbering printed in the books). Puteolano ranks Fortunatianus below Isocrates, Aristotle, Cicero and others, but praises him for summarizing so well the teachings of the great writers on rhetoric. In this he seems to be following Cassiodorus, whose praise of Fortunatianus is quoted without credit on the first page of the edition (*Inst.* II.ii.10, Mynors, p. 104, 8–15, is quoted). According to F. A. Eckstein, *Nomenclator philologorum* (Leipzig, 1871), p. 449, Puteolano was a professor of law in Milan during the second half of the fifteenth century. Theodore of Gaza (d. 1478) translated the Dionysus pieces included in the latter part of the book. There is no reason to believe that he had anything to do with the editing of *De dialectica*.

[96] Described by Pellechet, no. 4888 (Hain-Copinger 7306). I have examined a copy of this book in the Beinecke Library at Yale. It is the same edition of Fortunatianus's rhetoric as P and T, but not the same printing.

[97] Fortunatianus's *Ars rhet.* ends on fol. 54b and is followed by the translations of Dionysus on foll. 55a–59b. *De dialectica* then follows on foll. 61a–72a, even though it is listed right after the *Ars rhet.* in the table of contents on the first page. The signatures begin anew with A for *De dial.* This was common practice when all of the letters of the alphabet had been used earlier in a book, but the earlier part of the book had only reached the letter O (in T, o in P). Oates, no. 2124, describes a little book consisting of the *Dial.* only. It may be, therefore, that *De dial.* was first intended to be published separately and was then added to the other book as an afterthought.

[98] Billanovich, "Petrarca," p. 144.

[99] Augustine's *De rhet.* is on foll. 37a–51a in P (by signatures, k recto to m iii recto; it begins on f iv recto in the supposedly earlier edition). The excerpts from Capella, chaps. 31–38 of Book V, are on foll. 51a–54b in P (m iii recto to n ii verso; h viii recto in the earlier edition). Where the *Ars rhet.* ends the Venice edition prints *'FINIT'* and then *'DE OFFICIO ORATORIS INCIPIT.'* Throughout the rest of the book *'finis'* and *'incipit'* are used only between works or books of a work. Their use here makes it appear that a new work is beginning, but the colophon on 54b (n ii verso) makes it clear that everything included since the colophon at the end of Book Two is regarded as part of Book Three of Fortunatianus.

[100] For example, Florence, Bibl. Med. Laur., Plut. LII, Cod. XXXI, described by A. M. Bandini, *Catalogus codicum latinorum Bibliothecae Mediceae Laurentianae*, II (Florence, 1775), cols. 569–571. Bandini identifies foll. 1–40 as Fortunatianus and 40–52 as Augustine; I have identified foll. 52v–57v as Capella on the basis of the *incipit* and *explicit* which Bandini gives. The edition begins at the same point as the MS. Both omit the first few words of the sentence which begins chapter 31 of the Capella. The latter begins: *"Duabus his officii partibus absolutis elocutionis cura"* (*RLM*, p. 478, line 18). The edition and the Flor. MS begin: *"Nunc elocutionis cura."*

[101] Vat. Chig. H VI 186, Vat. Urb. lat. 1180, and Vat. Vat. lat. 1485. Also Flor. Laur. aed.

168, although its annotations on the authorship of the various parts of Fortunatianus, if they are older than the Venice edition, would seem to rule it out as the source of that edition. See above, note 60.

[102] I base my judgment of superiority on a close check of the variant readings given by Crecelius for the first five chapters. On the fifty or so variant readings Crecelius gives, the Venice edition agrees with the manuscripts (Cologne 166, Bern 363 and 548) over against the editions (Amerbach, Erasmus, Louvain, Maurists) in all but five instances.

[103] On readings unique to one manuscript in the first five chapters, the edition follows Cologne 166 in only four of fifteen readings, Bern 363 in two of four, and Bern 548 in none of four. I did my research on the text of the Venice edn. before I had Pinborg's edition.

[104] See above, p. 21f.

[105] I have seen the Bodleian Library's copy of the 1558 edition. A spot check of several passages in which the Venice edition has readings not found in other editions turned up no differences in the Basel edition. The 1542 and the 1558 editions are described in *Catalogue Général de Livres de la Bibliothèque Nationale, Auteurs*, Vol. 53, col. 797, and Vol. 124, col. 193. The edition of 1558 was known to the Maurists (*PL* 32, 1409, note a) and many sources follow them in citing it. Marrou, p. 576, n. 2, even says that it is the first edition of *De dialectica*. Prantl, Vol. I, p. 666, n. 28, is one of the few earlier writers on *De dial.* who know of the Venice edition. *De dial.* may be in some of the other editions of Fortunatianus (see Pauly-Wissowa, VII, col. 53, for these). I have not looked into that question.

[106] *Gesamtkatalog der Wiegendrucke*, III (Leipzig, 1928), nos. 2867 and 2869.

[107] *Gesamtkatalog*, nos. 2957–9. See Minio-Paluello, "The Text of the *Categoriae*: the Latin Tradition," p. 68, note 1, for a conjecture on the source of this attribution of Alcuin's little work.

[108] The volume has the title '*Prima pars librorum divi Aurelii Augustini quos edidit cathecumenus*' and is one of the eleven making up the edition published by Amerbach in partnership with Johannes Petri and Johannes Froben. I have used the copy in the Beinecke Rare Book and Manuscript Library at Yale. There is no page numbering, so I shall not give exact references. For an account of Amerbach's edition see, Joseph de Ghellinck, *Patristique et Moyen Age*, III, pp. 371ff.

[109] Section A. Amerbach quotes this passage in full preceding *De grammatica*. He states his principle of following the order of the *Retractationes* in the prefatory epistle to Volume One. This epistle is no. 293 in Hartmann (ed.), *Die Amerbachkorrespondenz*, vol. I, pp. 275–277. Some medieval MSS follow the *Retr.* order for the works they include and quote the relevant *Retr.* passage. Brussels 1117 is a striking case of this for the works reviewed by Augustine in *Retr.* I.i–xii. Amerbach probably had access to similar MSS.

[110] He mentions his search in the Preface (Letter 293, Hartmann, p. 276, lines 19f.). See also letters 37, 48, 50, 56, 61, 211, 234, 238, and 246. Only two of the *disciplinarum libri* are mentioned in this correspondence: *De musica* is sent from Paris by Amerbach's son, Bruno (no. 238, 33f.), and *De rhetorica* is discussed by Reuchlin in reply to questions put to him by Amerbach about Greek technical terms in the treatise (no. 261).

[111] *Retr.* I.v. See Crecelius, p. 5.

[112] De Ghellinck, pp. 375f., notes that Amerbach had a strong interest in dividing the works into chapters. Some of the divisions may have already been in MSS he used, but in the eight MSS which I have had access to there are only a few divisions. In both Troyes 40 (fol. 83v) and Philadelphia 63 (fol. 79r) what is now regarded as the second chapter is set off by a decorative initial and the gloss "*De simplicibus locutus est; nunc de compositis dicet.*" Amerbach and subsequent editors have used "*De simplicibus verbis*" as the title for the first chapter; no one has used "*De compositis*" for the second chapter. In Orléans 263 what are

now regarded as the fourth and fifth chapters are set off by decorative initials (p. 141). Later editors adopted Amerbach's chapter divisions. Erasmus changed the titles for chapters II, III, IV, VIII, IX, and X and the Maurists followed him. The Louvain editors used slightly different titles for chapters IV, VIII, IX, and X.

[113] On the basis of Crecelius's critical apparatus for Chapters I–V I have determined that Amerbach is in agreement with the editions (Erasmus, Louvain, Maurists) far more often than he is in agreement with the three MSS used by Crecelius (Cologne 166, Bern 363, and Bern 548). These three MSS are from the eighth, ninth, and tenth centuries. I have had access to two later MSS. I have examined the first five chapters in the Philadelphia MS and find that it is closer to the Augustine editions than the first edition is (in fifteen readings, whereas the first edition agrees in only three readings). The Philadelphia MS is dated in the twelfth century and would seem to be moving toward the relatively corrupt state of the *textus receptus*. An example is the ten words in Chapter Three (p. 6, 15f.; see note 3 on this chapter): Crecelius's MSS and the first edition contain them; Phil. 63 and Amerbach do not. A check of some passages in Troyes 40, another twelfth-century MS, shows that it is in agreement with Phil. 63 on a number of readings. (The gloss referred to in note 112 above indicates that Phil. 63 and Troyes 40 are probably closely related.)

[114] I have used the copy of Erasmus's edition in the Bodleian Library. *De dial.* is in vol. I, pp. 187–195. On Erasmus see de Ghellinck, pp.379ff.

[115] I briefly examined a copy of this edition in the Divinity School Library at Yale. *De dial.* begins on page 111 of vol. I. On the Louvain edn. see de Ghellinck, pp. 392ff.

[116] De Ghellinck, pp. 387 and 393.

[117] Erasmus was particularly interested in the question of authenticity. In the preface to his edition he says that he has retained several inauthentic or doubtful works but has prefaced such works with a *censura*. (The preface is printed in P. S. and H. M. Allen, eds., *Opus Epistolarum Des. Erasmi Roterodami*, VIII (Oxford, 1934), no. 2157; see lines 460–481). There are no *censurae* for the liberal arts books.

[118] An example of each: In the margin of Chapter Three the term *'summa'* is explained by *"Summa, id est conclusio"*; in Chapter Six the sentence beginning *"Perspicis enim haec...."* (p. 10, 3) is said to be *"Ex Cratylo Platonis."* A gloss on VIII, 14, 5 – *"Differunt obscurum & ambiguum"* – is almost identical to a marginal gloss found in Einsiedeln 324, p. 64 – *"differentiam inter obscurum et ambiguum."* Erasmus may have used this MS, especially if its Swiss location dates from that early. For their edition the Louvain editors used a MS which they called *'Carthusianus.'* I have not been able to identify this MS with any of the extant MSS.

[119] Many MSS do not include the *incipit* for *De gramm.* See below, section C.3, for the Maurists' discussion of this.

[120] *PL* 32, cols. 579–580. I have used Migne's reprint of the Maurist edition, because it is more readily available than the 1679 edition. I have examined the Bodleian Library's copy of the latter. On the Maurist edition see de Ghellinck, pp. 413ff.

[121] *PL* 32, cols. 1385–1386. The *admonitio* containing these reasons precedes *De grammatica* but is explicitly applied to all four works.

[122] For example, Marrou, p. 578, and Hagendahl, *Augustine and the Latin Classics*, p. 557.

[123] For example, Hagen, "Zur Kritik und Erklärung der Dialektik des Augustinus," p. 757, Duchrow, *Sprachverständnis und Biblisches Hören*, p. 42, and Kretzmann, "History of Semantics," p. 366. Kretzmann claims that the level of sophistication reached in the semantic theory of *De dialectica* V was not reached again for at least eight hundred years.

[124] *CSEL* 36, p. 28. The editor (Knöll) cites MSS both with and without the sentence, including some rather old ones with it. I have not gone into this question on my own.

[125] Crecelius, p. 2.

[126] Marrou, p. 577; Pinborg, pp. 149f.

[127] Crecelius, p. 2; Marrou, p. 577; and Pinborg, pp. 149f. Pinborg believes that the interlocutors would have been Augustine and Adeodatus, his son. He says that *"ingenio ... tuo"* at X, 19, 24 refers to the brilliant Adeodatus.

[128] Crecelius, p. 2, refers to *"nunc quod instat, accipe intentus"* (V, 7, 10f.), *"tu iudicabis"* (X, 17, 14), and *"ingenio praesertim tuo"* (X, 19, 24). Pinborg adds *"nec mireris"* (I, 5, 4) and Marrou gives *"ad te"* (VI, 9, 15) and *"accipias"* (VI, 9, 18). To these can be added *"a te"* (VI, 10, 1) and numerous uses of the second person singular, e.g., in Chapter Ten, *"vide"* (17, 28 and 19, 24), *"constitue"* (17, 30), and *"vides"* (19, 4).

[129] Keil, Review of Crecelius, p. 155.

[130] Speaking of the dialogues *De beata vita, De ordine,* and *De libero arbitrio,* he uses forms of *'disputatio'* and *'disputo'* (*CSEL* 36, pp. 18, line 7; 19, 14; 36, 16f.). He calls *De animae quantitate* a *dialogus* (p. 34, 10). More significantly for the interpretation of I.v, he says that he wrote the *Soliloquia "me interrogans mihique respondens"* (p. 22, 8). The chapter on *De musica* (I.x) says nothing of its form. Possibly Augustine thought he had specified that in the earlier chapter.

[131] There is no reason why a writer cannot address his audience in the singular. Or use of the singular could be characteristic of a first draft where one is more concerned with argument than with correct form.

[132] *PL* 32, 1409, note a.

[133] *PL* 32, 1410, note 1.

[134] The Saint-Germain numbers of these two MSS were 613 and 1108. The library at Saint-Germain had over six thousand manuscripts by 1733; many of these came from Corbie in 1638. (de Ghellinck, p. 436) Richard Kukula has made a major study of the correspondence and other documents connected with the Maurist edition. Part of his study deals with manuscripts used ("Die Mauriner Ausgabe des Augustinus" in *Sitzungsberichte der Kaiserlichen Akademie der Wissenschaften zu Wien,* Philosophisch-Historische Classe, Bd. 138 (1897), V, pp. 1–81). He lists a *Corbeiensis* and a *Germanensis* (pp. 14 and 16), but does not say which works they contain or give numbers for them. And his list of manuscripts used for particular works contains nothing for *De dialectica.* He does note (pp. 36–37) that for *De musica* and the *Categoriae decem* the Maurists used Vatican manuscripts and, for the latter, a 1586 Paris printing (presumably of the Louvain edn.).

[135] Molinier, *Catalogue,* I, p. 280, says that the thirteenth-century MS Paris Bibl. Maz. 632 was used by the Maurists.

[136] Again I have examined the variant readings for the first five chapters. The Maurist text agrees with the earlier Augustine editions (Erasmus, Louvain) in most instances. Four times it agrees with the Louvain edition over against Erasmus. It has five unique readings and sides with the Cologne and Bern MSS in only three or four variant readings. I have not thoroughly examined the text of Paris 12949, which the Maurists apparently used (see above, note 134), but in some passages which I have examined it diverges from the tradition represented by the Cologne and Bern MSS. It may, therefore, be close to the *textus receptus.* Professor Pinborg's study of the textual tradition supports this conclusion. One characteristic of the *textus receptus,* the Chapter Five interpolation, is not in Paris 12949. But a gloss in that MS may be a source of the interpolation. See note 2 on Chapter Five.

[137] *S. Aurelii Augustini De Dialectica Liber. Jahresbericht über das Gymnasium zu Elberfeld,* 1857. On Crecelius, see the brief entry in Eckstein, *Nomenclator Philologorum,* p. 104. Elberfeld is near Düsseldorf.

[138] In the introduction to the edition, pp. 1–4. Crecelius did not examine any of the

Fortunatianus editions of *De dial.* He knew of the 1558 Basel edition, but says that he did not see a copy of it (p. 3, n. 4).

[139] Crecelius, p. 3.

[140] Keil, reviewing the edition in the *Jahrbucher für classische Philologie* **5** (1859), 154–157, was complimentary. Hagen, writing for the same journal (**18**, 1872, pp. 757f.), recognized Crecelius's valuable work, but went on to give a critique which I have briefly summarized below.

[141] Crecelius, p. 3, derives his dating of Bern 363 from J. R. Sinner, *Catalogus Codicum MSS Bibliothecae Bernensis*, 3 vols. (Bern, 1760–1772), apparently from vol. I, p. 9, where the MS is said to be twelfth century. In vol. III, pp. 561f., however, Sinner dates Bern 363 as eighth or ninth century.

[142] Hagen, pp. 765f.

[143] Pinborg makes major changes in the following passages: II, 5, 18; V, 7, 17; VI, 10, 1; 10, 18; 11, 12; VIII, 14, 10; 14, 22–23; and X, 17, 17.

II. A QUANTITATIVE STUDY OF THE AUTHORSHIP OF
DE DIALECTICA

In the last thirty years several major authorship studies have been done using statistical techniques. Some of the more recent ones have also taken advantage of the great advances in data processing made possible by the electronic computer. Notable among these studies are the work of G. Udny Yule on the *De imitatione Christi*,[1] of Alvar Ellegård on the *Junius* letters,[2] of Frederick Mosteller and David Wallace on the *Federalist* papers,[3] and of Anthony Morton on Paul and Plato.[4] These researchers have had varying success and their particular methods and results have met with varying degrees of acceptance, but the validity of statistical study of authorship seems well established. Its fundamental goal is to discover objective ways to describe style and to assess differences among authors. In the following pages I shall report on my own attempt to apply quantitative methods to the question of the authorship of *De dialectica*. In this I shall be seeking to give some substance to the judgment of Wilhelm Thimme that the style of *De dialectica* is unmistakably that of the young Augustine.[5]

A. PRINCIPLES AND TECHNIQUES

The studies mentioned above have usually been regarded as investigations of style.[6] I shall not discuss the various meanings of "style," a notoriously ambiguous term, but the basic nature of what is being studied must be outlined.[7] A very general definition of style states that it is any pattern formed in the linguistic encoding of information.[8] For the purpose of distinguishing one writer from another not just any pattern will do, however, since many aspects of a given language are characteristic of all users of that language.[9] What we require are individual characteristics which are not shared by authors writing in the same language and which, in addition, cannot be explained by differences in date, place, subject, or genre of writing. The ideal discriminant stylistic characteristic is one which remains constant throughout an author's writings or at least a major segment of them. There is wide agreement on what sort of thing is likely to fit these criteria for idiosyncracy of style, namely, any aspect of composition which is largely unconscious, not a matter of deliberate choice.[10] In search of such unconscious aspects of style, researchers have investigated word and sentence length, the use of high frequency function words, the concentration of vocabulary, and various features of syntax. From these investigations data expressible in quantitative form are obtained and may be evaluated by means of statistical tests.

What can be inferred by such means? The basic inference pattern as it would be carried out in a situation similar to our problem is this:[11] If on a certain stylistic feature the works of author A differ among themselves less than they differ from the works of other authors writing in the same language, genre, and so on, then that feature can be regarded as characteristic of A. If a disputed work has that feature, it could have been written by A; if it does not have the feature, it very probably was not written by A. Two things should be noted about this reasoning. First, the conclusion is only probable, not certain. And second, a negative result is more certain than a positive one; it is easier to show who could not have written some work than to find the one person who did write it.[12] These limitations would seriously cripple statistical study of authorship if it were carried out in isolation from other knowledge. In practice, however, there are ordinarily other things known about a disputed work which incline us to one hypothesis or another. In conjunction with this knowledge quantitative analysis can be of considerable value in confirming or weakening a hypothesis.[13] In the case of *De dialectica* the evidence here presented should be considered in conjunction with the evidence presented in Part I. The latter establishes a prior probability for the hypothesis that Augustine wrote *De dialectica*. The quantitative analysis which I shall here report tends to support that hypothesis.

My research design was constructed with the principles just discussed in mind. The first task was, in statistical language, to define the population from which measurements would be taken. The population was defined by period, genre, and subject matter. Then authors were chosen who at least partly fit the definition. I chose to define the population as consisting of late fourth-century Latin prose authors who wrote on the liberal arts. Since Augustine is the primary candidate for author of *De dialectica*, he was an obvious choice. From his vast corpus only those works completed between his conversion (386) and his ordination (391) were chosen. This gives a period of some length and yet does not reach far into the time when Augustine's Latin was becoming increasingly Christianized.[14] Moreover, if Augustine wrote *De dialectica*, he did it during these years. As to genre, I chose to study both the dialogues and the strictly prose writings. This was necessary for two reasons. In the first place, the genre of *De dialectica* is mixed. It is now uninterrupted prose, but if completed it could have been a dialogue. In the second place, to ignore the dialogues would be to ignore most of Augustine's early writings. As to subject matter, I also collected several passages in Augustine's works in which logic or the liberal arts are discussed. Three other fourth-century authors were studied, Marius Victorinus (d. 362), Ambrose (d. 397), and Chirius Fortunatianus. Fortunatianus was chosen because he is the only other candidate for author of *De dialectica* and because his *Ars rhetoricae* is a late ancient treatise on one of the liberal arts. Victorinus was an African like Augustine and he wrote extensively on logic and rhetoric. Ambrose was chosen because of his possible influence on the young Augustine.[15] I should like to have obtained data on other fourth-century writers but was limited both by available funds and by the lack of research done by others on this period. I was able to draw upon some studies of Golden and Silver Age writers, particularly the work of Louis Delatte and Étienne Evrard on Seneca (d. 65).[16]

The second task was to decide on a method of sampling from the population. I chose to do stratified simple random sampling with proportional allocation.[17] The population was divided into strata by author and work. For Augustine the works were divided into two strata, dialogues and prose. Each work was divided into segments approximately one thousand words in length, the segments were numbered, and for each work the number of samples to be chosen (using a table of random numbers) was determined in accordance with its size relative to the other works in its authorship stratum.[18] Hence from a brief work such as *De beata vita* one sample was taken; from longer works more samples were selected. This method of sampling seemed most appropriate because it insured both that all works included in the population would be represented and that a work would be represented in proportion to its size. A total of fifty-eight samples were chosen by this method and the first

five hundred words of each sample were keypunched onto punch cards.
In addition the whole of *De dialectica* and selected passages of Augustine's writings on logic were keypunched. This gave the data sets listed
in Table I and more fully described in the Appendix.

TABLE I

Data Sets

		No. of samples
Augustine, Early Dialogues (EDIAL)		
Contra Academicos		4
De beata vita		1
De ordine		3
Soliloquiorum		2
De quantitate animae		3
De libero arbitrio I		1
De musica		8
De magistro		2
	Total	24 (13,000 words)[a]
Augustine, Early Prose (EPROSE)		
De immortalitate animae		1
De moribus ecclesiae Cath.		5
Epistulae 1–17		1
De Genesi contra Manichaeos		3
De vera religione		3
	Total	13 (6,600 words)[a]
Augustine, Logical Writings (LOGIC)		
Selections from *Contra Academicos*,		
De ordine, De doctrina christiana,		
and *Contra Cresconium*		
	Total	(3,700 words)
Marius Victorinus (VICTOR)		
Ars grammatica		3
De definitione		1
Explanationum in Ciceronis rhetoricam		3
	Total	7 (3,700 words)
Chirius Fortunatianus (FORTUN)		
Ars rhetoricae		5 (6,800 words)
Ambrose (AMBROS)		
De officiis ministrorum		2
De virginibus		1

De fide	2	
De spiritu sancto	1	
De incarnatione Dominicae sacramento	1	
De paenitentia	1	
Total	8	(3,600 words)

De dialectica (De dial.)	
Complete text	(5,700 words)

[a] Number of words rounded off to the nearest 100.

Once keypunched and verified the data were stored on disc packs in preparation for analysis. Five computer programs were developed to make the measurements desired. Two, called COUNT and COUNT 1, determined the mean and frequency distribution for word and sentence length. Three, called INDEX, SORT, and PRINT, produced an index of each data set giving the location and frequency of each word. Other programs were developed to aid in the statistical analysis of the measurements obtained by these five programs.

Before reporting the results of my study, I should indicate some of the weaknesses of the design. First, the size and number of samples may be inadequate. It would have been better to have included all one thousand words of each sample.[19] The total number could also have been higher. Some researchers believe that very large total samples are required as a sound basis for inference.[20] But available funds and time placed limitations on the total number of words to be put into machine-readable form. Perhaps, therefore, my study should be regarded as a rather large pilot study. A second weakness is the grouping of measurements into seven sets which cannot be broken down into measurements for each sample. This made it hard or impossible to measure the consistency of an author within a given stratum. This problem was anticipated but no solution was found short of greatly increasing the amount of computer time needed.

B. WORD LENGTH

The first kind of quantitative evidence I shall present has to do with the number of letters per word. For each data set I determined the mean number of letters (word length), the standard deviation from the mean, and the frequency distribution. These measures were made only for an author's own words; quoted material was excluded from the counting. I shall first discuss mean word length and then move on to the frequency distribution.

1. Mean Length

Table II gives the means and standard deviations for the various data

TABLE II

Word length: Mean and standard deviation

Data set	Total words	Mean length	Standard deviation
De dialectica	5,629	5.4308	2.6629
EDIAL	12,974	5.4277	2.6366
EPROSE	6,588	5.4488	2.7002
LOGIC	3,868	5.7784	2.9237
VICTOR	3,727	5.7606	2.8873
FORTUN	6,814	5.6517	2.9917
AMBROS	3,582	5.8048	2.7271

sets. By inspection we can see that there appear to be two rather clearly defined groups. Statistical testing of the differences between the means confirms this. One group is made up of the means for Augustine's early dialogues and early prose writings and for *De dialectica*. These three means (5.43, 5.45, 5.43) differ only slightly from each other in amounts not significant at the .05 level of significance.[21] A second group is made up of the means for the other data sets. The means in this group (5.78, 5.76, 5.65, and 5.80), though not as close together as the means of the first group, are not significantly different from each other at the .05 level but are all significantly different from all of the means of the first group at that level. Thus the homogeneity of the means within each group and the heterogeneity of the two groups is clearly established. What can we conclude from this?

In the first place, we can see that average word length does not distinguish all the authors tested from each other. Victorinus, Fortunatianus, and Ambrose cannot be distinguished from each other by this statistic, nor can Augustine's logical writings be distinguished from any of the three other authors. In the second place, however, we can see that

Augustine's earlier writings do have an average word length which distinguishes them from the other writings tested and that *De dialectica* has virtually the same average word length as those early writings. Statistically speaking, therefore, the data on average word length give us no reason to believe that it is not of the same population as the earlier writings studied. More simply put, Augustine could have written our *De dialectica* sometime during the early years of his authorship. It is something of a puzzle why the logical passages in Augustine (LOGIC) are so unlike the early writings and *De dialectica* on word length. It may be that this data set has a higher average word length because it is made up from later works (most of the material is from *De doctrina christiana* and *Contra Cresconium*, which were written in 397 and 406) or of passages dealing with a technical subject matter. Further study of Augustine's later writings would be helpful in evaluating the average word length of the logical writings. At this point we know enough only to suspect that the samples making up this data set are not representative of the early Augustine, who seems to have used shorter words on the average than his contemporaries. This latter may also be true when Augustine is compared with earlier Latin authors. In Table III I list the findings of Tore Janson[22] and Stephen Waite[23] for their studies of authors who wrote mainly in the first centuries B.C. and A.D. Their findings are in harmony with mine in showing that most authors have a higher average word length than the early Augustine. In addition, Janson found that a section of Augustine's *De civitate Dei* XIX, written in 427, has an average word length of 5.53, rather close to the figures for the early writings which I have studied. This suggests that time is not the important variable in the longer word length of the logical writings. It is interesting that the figure for *De civitate Dei* is closest to figures for two Ciceronian works and, in the light of the recognized Ciceronian character of Augustine's earliest writings,[24] that the mean word length for the early writings is closer only to Cato's *De agri cultura* than to these two works of Cicero.

2. *Frequency Distribution*

Although the mean and standard deviation of word length are apparently of some value in determining authorship, they measure only central tendency and variability from it. For a more precise description of word length I turn to the frequency distribution, the statistic used by T. C.

TABLE III

Word length: Means obtained by other researchers

Author, work(s)	Mean length	
Livy, Book 27 (Janson)	6.06	
Pliny the Younger, *Panegyricus* (J.)	5.97	
Sallust, *Catilina* and *Jugurtha*, sel. (Waite)	5.95	
Caesar, *De Bello Gallico* (J.)	5.91	
Cato, Fragments (W.)	5.91	
Livy, Selections (W.)	5.89	
Tacitus, *Dialogus de Oratoribus* (J.)	5.77	
Cato, *Orationes*, fragments (W.)	5.74	
Seneca, *Dialogi* 6 (J.)	5.67	
Vergil, *Aeneis* 4 (J.)	5.64	
Cicero, *De oratore* 3 (J.)	5.61	
Cicero, *Pro Roscio Amerino* (J.)	5.54	
Augustine, *De civitate Dei* 19 (J.)	5.53	
EPROSE		5.45
De dialectica		5.43
EDIAL		5.43
Cato, *De agri cultura* (W.)	5.39	
Plautus, *Rudens* (J.)	4.79	

Mendenhall in his pioneering authorship studies.[25] Having in mind the graphs in which he displayed his findings, Mendenhall named the frequency distribution for word length the "characteristic curve of composition." His investigations of sixteenth and nineteenth-century British authors convinced him that this curve remains constant throughout an author's works. He explained this constancy as due to the unconscious nature of the curve.[26] An author is most unlikely to give any thought to what proportion of his words are two letters in length, and so on. Mendenhall's method was to test for intra-author consistency and inter-author variance. He did this only by inspecting the graphs. Later studies of the frequency distribution have used the Chi-Square test to evaluate the data.[27] I follow them in using this test. But first I present the data for inspection.

Figures 1 and 2 represent graphically the data given in Table IV. The distributions are severely skewed right, as are most of the distributions discovered by other investigators.[28] Looking at the curves we can discern a greater degree of similarity of *De dialectica* to EDIAL and EPROSE. It is grouped with these early writings of Augustine both in being more

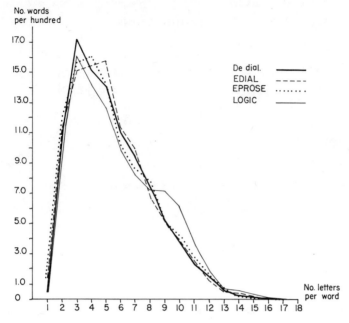

Fig. 1. Word length: *De dialectica* and Augustine's writings.

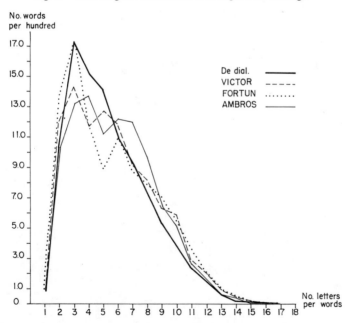

Fig. 2. Word length: *De dialectica* and other authors.

TABLE IV

Word length: Frequency distribution (number of words per hundred)

Data set	Number of letters																	
	1	2	3	4	5	6	7	8	9	10	11	12	13	14	15	16	17	18
De dial.	.6	10.7	17.2	15.2	14.1	11.0	9.4	7.5	5.3	3.8	2.3	1.5	.6	.2	.1	.03	0	0
EDIAL	.5	11.3	15.1	15.5	15.8	11.4	9.9	6.8	5.1	3.8	2.4	1.3	.5	.4	.2	.03	.02	.007
EPROSE	.4	12.0	15.6	16.0	14.1	10.3	8.7	7.8	5.1	4.3	2.8	1.5	.5	.2	.2	0	0	0
LOGIC	.4	10.5	16.1	14.2	12.7	9.9	8.2	7.2	7.2	6.1	3.6	1.9	.7	.6	.3	.02	.05	0
VICTOR	.7	12.1	14.3	11.8	12.8	11.8	9.2	8.1	6.3	5.9	3.0	2.0	.9	.4	.1	.08	.02	0
FORTUN	1.0	13.7	17.3	11.8	8.9	11.1	8.8	7.4	7.0	5.4	3.5	2.0	.9	.5	.2	.03	0	0
AMBROS	.5	10.3	13.2	13.7	11.2	12.2	12.0	9.6	6.4	5.1	2.6	1.6	.6	.4	0	.05	.02	0
	1	2	3	4	5	6	7	8	9	10	11	12	13	14	15	16	17	18

even than the other authors' curves and in having fewer long words. The relation of *De dialectica* to Augustine's logical writings is more ambiguous. LOGIC has a rather smooth curve, like *De dialectica*, but it has relatively more long words, unlike *De dialectica*.

The differences on word length could have been predicted on the basis of our knowledge of mean word length for the data sets, but the precise form of the distributions is a new kind of information which requires evaluation. The irregularities in the curves for VICTOR, FORTUN, and AMBROS could be due to inadequate sample size. Mendenhall found that curves of composition become somewhat smooth when the total sample is at least five thousand words.[29] Indeed he believed that a sample of around 100,000 words is needed to get an author's characteristic curve,[30] though he has been challenged on this.[31] Sample size could explain the unevenness of the Victorinus and Ambrose curves, since each is based on considerably fewer than five thousand words. It cannot explain the Fortunatianus curve, for the latter is based on the second largest total sample. To neutralize partially the possible effects of unevenness due to inadequate sample size I have grouped the data in cells of two (Table V, Figures 3–4). It is in this form that I shall evaluate the data first.

The statistical test which I have used is the Chi-Square test. It enables one to compare two or more distributions and is so constructed that χ^2 has a value of zero when the distributions are the same. The higher the value of χ^2 the less the similarity of the distributions compared. Since two distributions are rarely the same, one ordinarily adopts a level of significance by which to decide whether differences are great enough to warrant rejection of the null hypothesis concerning the populations sampled.[32] Adopting .05 as the significance level, I have found that for all but two comparisons of the various data sets the value of χ^2 is not only critical but very large.[33] Mosteller and Wallace had similar results when they used the Chi-Square test to evaluate the curves of composition for Hamilton and Madison.[34] Instead, therefore, of asking about level of significance, they sought to determine whether Madison papers had lower values when compared to other Madison papers than when compared to Hamilton papers, and similarly for Hamilton papers. In other words, they asked whether inter-author differences exceed intra-author differences. Their results showed that inter-author differences are not

TABLE V

Word length: Frequency distribution, grouped by cells of 2

Data Sets	1–2	3–4	5–6	7–8	9–10	11–12	13–14	15–	
De dial.	639	1819	1418	958	516	221	48	10	No. words
	(11.3)	(32.3)	(25.1)	(16.9)	(9.1)	(3.9)	(.9)	(.2)	No. per 100
EDIAL	1529	3970	3536	2157	1157	473	129	23	
	(11.8)	(30.6)	(27.2)	(16.6)	(8.9)	(3.7)	(1.0)	(.2)	
EPROSE	816	2087	1614	1095	627	285	51	13	
	(12.4)	(31.6)	(24.4)	(16.5)	(9.5)	(4.3)	(.8)	(.2)	
LOGIC	426	1173	875	597	518	215	50	14	
	(10.9)	(30.4)	(22.6)	(15.4)	(13.4)	(5.6)	(1.3)	(.4)	
VICTOR	481	973	921	647	457	188	51	9	
	(12.8)	(26.1)	(24.6)	(17.3)	(12.2)	(5.0)	(1.4)	(.2)	
FORTUN	1002	1984	1371	1110	851	378	100	18	
	(14.7)	(29.1)	(20.0)	(16.2)	(12.4)	(5.5)	(1.5)	(.3)	
AMBROS	389	968	840	777	413	154	38	3	
	(10.8)	(26.9)	(23.4)	(21.6)	(11.5)	(4.3)	(1.1)	(.1)	

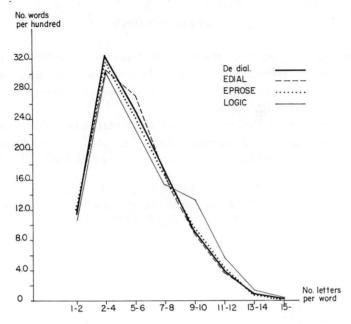

Fig. 3.   Word length: *De dialectica* and Augustine (grouped data).

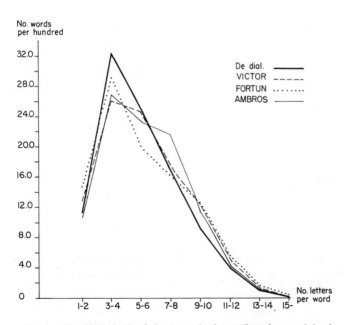

Fig. 4.   Word length: *De dialectica* and other authors (grouped data).

always greater and hence the curve of composition has little discrimi-natory value between Hamilton and Madison. I shall use an argument similar to Mosteller and Wallace's in evaluating my findings on χ^2 for the word length distribution.

The first step in the argument is to show that intra-author variation is less than inter-author variation. The values of χ^2 for comparisons of the six data sets of known authorship are given in Table VI. All are

TABLE VI

Word length: Frequency distribution, values of chi-square for comparison of data sets of known authorship (based on data given in Table V)

	EDIAL	EPROSE	LOGIC	VICTOR	FORTUN	AMBROS
EDIAL	–	24.9	122.4	82.9	229.0	95.2
EPROSE	24.9	–	61.5	54.7	101.4	68.0
LOGIC	122.4	61.5	–	29.3	37.7	65.4
VICTOR	82.9	54.7	29.3	–	39.8	33.0
FORTUN	229.0	101.4	37.7	39.8	–	95.2
AMBROS	95.2	68.0	65.4	33.0	95.2	–

(The table may be read horizontally or vertically. The values on each side of the diagonal formed by the blank spaces duplicate each other. The degrees of freedom for all comparisons is 7.)

significant at the .05 level and some are extremely high. If we average the values we can get some indication of the discriminating power of the word length distribution. The mean χ^2 for Augustine's three sets (24.9, 61.5, 122.4) is 69.6. The means for the various inter-author com-parisons are:

Augustine sets-VICTOR	55.3
Augustine sets-FORTUN	122.7
Augustine sets-AMBROS	76.2
VICTOR-FORTUN	39.8
VICTOR-AMBROS	33.0
AMBROS-FORTUN	95.2

These figures show Augustine's writings to be less similar to each other than they are to the writings of Victorinus and than Victorinus is to Fortunatianus or Ambrose. This result depends, however, on the odd values obtained when testing Augustine's logical writings. They have high values when compared to EDIAL or EPROSE but lower values when compared to the other authors. If these values are omitted from the averages, rather different results follow.

EDIAL-EPROSE	24.9
Aug.-VICTOR	68.8
Aug.-FORTUN	165.2
Aug.-AMBROS	81.6
VICTOR-FORTUN	39.8
VICTOR-AMBROS	33.0
AMBROS-FORTUN	95.2

Now the value of χ^2 (24.9) for Augustine's early writings, the only intra-author comparison, is lower than any of the inter-author comparisons and is, in particular, lower than the values for the comparisons of the early writings to the other authors. Hence, even though Augustine's early dialogues and prose differ significantly from each other, they are still more similar to each other than they are to writings by other authors. This conclusion depends on eliminating the logical writings from consideration. Can this be done without bias? I believe that it can on the grounds that most of the samples in this data set are from later writings. Of course, this now means that generalizations about Augustine apply only to the early period, an acceptable limitation, since it is the early period that most concerns discussion of *De dialectica*.

The final step in the argument is to show how *De dialectica* compares with all of the data sets. From Table VII we see that *De dialectica* has a much lower χ^2 value when compared with Augustine's early writings than when compared with the writings of Victorinus, Fortunatianus, or Ambrose.[35] To see if this result depends on the grouping of the data, I also computed χ^2 for the ungrouped data.[36] The results are given in

TABLE VII

Word length: Frequency distribution, values of chi-square for comparisons of *De dialectica* with other data sets (based on data given in Table V)

EDIAL	12.9	(P>.05)	Average=9.4
EPROSE	5.8	(P>.50)	
VICTOR	67.2	(P<.001)	
FORTUN	131.6	(P<.001)	Average=87.6
AMBROS	64.1	(P<.001)	

(Degrees of freedom=7. The formulas of the form 'P>n' give the probability that the value obtained is due to chance and not to differences in the populations sampled.)

Table VIII. The χ^2 values are higher, as would be expected for the increased number of degrees of freedom, but the same conclusion holds: *De dialectica* is much more similar to Augustine's early writings than to the writings of the other authors.[37] Thus analysis of the word length distribution yields evidence not incompatible with the view that Augustine wrote *De dialectica*.[38]

TABLE VIII

Word length: Frequency distribution, values of chi-square for comparisons
of *De dialectica* with other data sets (ungrouped data)

EDIAL	25.7	(P > .025)	Average = 23.0
EPROSE	20.3	(P > .10)	
VICTOR	79.2	(P < .001)	
FORTUN	184.7	(P < .001)	Average = 113.2
AMBROS	75.9	(P < .001)	

(Degrees of freedom = 14, except for comparison with AMBROS where = 13.)

C. VOCABULARY

In a second line of research I have investigated the rate of occurrence of selected words in the authors tested. Several investigators have studied vocabulary, but others have been critical of its value as an authorship discriminator. Notable among the critics is Louis Milic, who has argued that vocabulary is consciously chosen, easily imitable, and subject-bound.[39] Milic believes that syntax is the proper subject for study of an author's personal style.[40] If vocabulary studies are examined, however, it can be seen that Milic's critique is not entirely applicable to them. Ellegård, Mosteller and Wallace, and Morton have all studied function words, those words of a language which are necessary to the discussion of any subject and which, because they are so common, are used without much conscious deliberation.[41] Only Yule studied content words, namely, nouns; but he was interested in the relative richness of noun vocabulary, not in how often any particular nouns are used. In any case, the choice between syntax and vocabulary ought to be made on the basis of evidence. No aspect of either should be regarded as characteristic of an author unless investigation shows it to be so. This has been shown in several instances to be true of the use of function words.[42]

The techniques I have used in my study are an adaptation of Ellegård's method.[43] On the basis of the frequency rates for various authors' use of any given word, he calculates a distinctiveness ratio (D). For example, if author A uses 'not' at a rate of three words per hundred (.03) and the average rate for other authors of his period and genre is two per hundred (.02), A's use of 'not' has a D of .03/.02 = 1.5. Since the goal is to be able to distinguish one author from other authors, Ellegård looks for words on which an author has either a high or a low distinctiveness ratio. He regards a D below .7 or above 1.5 as critical. I have set .67 as the lower limit, since it is the precise inverse ratio of 1.5. The basic datum for this approach is the frequency rate, which is calculated by dividing the number of times a word occurs by the total number of occurrences in the data set. For the purposes of my computer analysis 'word' was defined as any unique alphabetic character string. Thus the various inflections of a dictionary word were treated as separate words. Likewise no distinction was made between homonyms or between the different grammatical uses of the same word (for example, 'ut' may be an adverb or a conjunction). This unorthodox definition of 'word' has little effect on my study of function words, for with one exception (id) the discriminator words I have discovered are uninflected and have no homonyms. As to the different uses of the same word, this is properly a matter of syntax and though it may be important in some instances I have not considered it.

My investigation of vocabulary had three stages. In the first stage, I examined the ten most frequent words and selected other words in both strata of Augustine's early writings, looking for words used by Augustine at a similar rate in both the dialogues and the prose writings. Initially I included the logical writings in the investigation, but they varied considerably from EDIAL and EPROSE. This in conjunction with the findings on word length convinced me that the logical writings should not be investigated further. Out of this first stage there emerged a number of words which Augustine uses at a consistent rate. The second stage of the research was to determine which of the words discovered in the first stage are used by Augustine in such a way as to distinguish him from Victorinus, Fortunatianus, Ambrose, and Seneca. Information on Seneca was taken from the indices compiled by Delatte and Evrard of four of Seneca's works.[44] The weighted mean[45] frequency rate for Augustine's early writings was compared with the rates for the individual data sets and with the weighted means for Victorinus, Fortunatianus, and Ambrose and for Seneca. Many words were eliminated by this comparison,[46] and few emerged with an unambiguous power to distinguish Augustine from the other authors. It became clear at this stage that only tendencies to differ and not clearcut differences were being discovered. The third stage was to compare *De dialectica* to the other data sets in order to determine the degree of its likeness to them, in particular to see if it resembles Augustine more than it does the other authors.

In Table IX are presented the frequency rates and mean rates for eighteen words in the various data sets.[47] I shall discuss these words in three groups. The first group consists in high frequency words and the second is made up of lower frequency words. I have kept them separate because there is disagreement on whether high or low frequency words are the best authorship discriminators.[48] A third group is rather small and concerns choice between words.

1. *High Frequency Words*

High frequency words are a good topic for study because variation due to the chance factors of sampling is not as likely to occur as with low frequency words.[49] As candidates for Augustine's characteristic high frequency words I studied the twelve words which rank in the first ten in the early dialogues and in the first ten in the early prose writings.[50] Among these twelve words seven are of potential value as discriminators. The data for these seven words are given in Table X. Five of the seven – ENIM, NON, SI, UT, SED – have a distinctiveness ratio very close to 1.0; that is, Augustine uses them at about the same rate in dialogues as in uninterrupted prose. The other two – ET and IN – have rather poor distinctiveness ratios, but have identical ranks in each kind of writing, ET ranking first and IN ranking fourth. When Augustine's use of these seven words is compared with the other authors' use, varying degrees of discriminating power are found. The best discriminators are the conjunction ENIM ('for') and the adverb NON ('not'), both of which are generally used more frequently by Augustine than by other authors. But neither is perfect. Ambrose uses ENIM at a rate similar to Augustine's ($D = .95$); and Seneca in *De constantia sapientis* uses NON at a rate similar to Augustine's ($D = .89$). The worst discriminator is the con-

TABLE IX

Vocabulary: Frequency rate (No. of words per 1,000)

	De dial.	EDIAL	EPROSE	EDP Mean[a]	VICTOR	FORTUN	AMBROS	VFA Mean	CP[b]	CH	CM	CS	SENECA Mean
A	5.2	4.6	3.8	4.2	6.2	9.2	3.6	7.1	4.0	3.1	2.7	4.1	3.4
AB	3.9	3.0	2.7	2.8	2.5	3.4	1.2	2.6	2.8	1.9	.7	1.9	1.7
AT	1.4	.76	.63	.72	.0	.29	.0	.15	.35	1.2	.84	.17	.99
AUT	11.7	6.9	6.2	6.7	6.5	18.3	2.4	11.5	5.5	2.1	3.8	5.9	4.1
AUTEM	5.3	5.6	6.3	5.8	2.8	1.3	2.7	2.0	1.2	1.0	.35	4.7	1.6
ENIM	8.7	9.0	7.9	8.7	5.2	4.0	9.2	5.6	4.2	2.9	3.5	5.9	4.0
ERGO	2.8	3.6	4.4	3.9	2.2	1.0	4.8	2.2	1.2	1.2	.84	2.8	1.4
ET	26.1	27.6	40.6	32.0	31.5	27.4	31.2	29.4	28.5	27.0	34.2	40.0	32.0
EX	6.6	3.3	2.2	2.9	7.1	5.9	2.1	5.2	5.6	5.8	5.9	3.8	5.3
ID	4.4	4.0	3.5	3.8	6.5	8.7	.9	6.2	1.9	1.9	1.2	.6	1.4
IN	12.8	13.1	21.0	15.8	21.6	25.2	20.8	23.4	17.2	21.0	20.4	18.0	19.3
NON	16.5	24.0	25.0	24.5	10.5	15.2	17.8	14.7	16.9	18.2	16.1	27.5	19.0
PER	4.4	2.7	4.9	3.4	7.7	5.3	4.2	5.6	1.9	3.4	2.4	2.1	2.5
PRORSUS	.36	1.7	.01	1.2	.0	.0	.0	.0	.18	.0	.0	.0	.04
SED	11.4	8.5	9.2	8.7	8.9	3.5	12.8	7.1	5.1	6.4	4.9	8.9	6.1
SI	9.1	10.4	11.8	10.9	8.0	9.9	6.6	8.6	7.9	4.6	6.7	9.9	6.7
UT	14.7	12.1	10.4	11.5	12.9	21.6	16.4	18.2	6.7	5.6	5.6	9.1	6.5
VEL	7.3	6.2	3.5	5.2	3.1	5.9	1.5	4.1	.7	1.3	1.1	1.1	1.1

a All means are weighted.

b CP, CH, CM, CS are the works of Seneca mentioned in note 6 above. My figures are based on Delatte's indexes of these works. In some cases I have hand-counted the occurrences of a word, since Delatte gives the frequency only for the dictionary entry and not for each inflection of a word. I have used his totals (5,688 for CP, 6,775 for CH, 8,384 for CM, and 5,292 for CS; a total of 26, 139), even though his counting of enclitic particles as separate words differs from my practice. This is only a small difference, probably making Delatte's totals about one percent higher than my method of counting would give.

TABLE X

Vocabulary: Distinctiveness ratio for high frequency words

	ET	IN	ENIM	NON	SI	UT	SED
(1)[a]							
EPROSE/EDIAL	1.47	1.60	.88	1.04	1.13	.86	1.07
(2)							
EDP[b]/VICTOR	1.03	.73	1.67	2.32	1.36	.89	.98
,, /FORTUN	1.17	.63	2.18	1.62	1.10	.53	2.49
,, /AMBROS	1.05	.76	.95	1.38	1.65	.70	.68
,, /VFA	1.09	.68	1.56	1.67	1.27	.63	1.22
,, /SEN	1.00	.82	1.67	1.29	1.63	1.77	1.43
(3)							
Dial/EDIAL	.95	1.06	.97	.69	.88	1.21	1.34
,, /EPROSE	.65	.64	1.10	.66	.77	1.42	1.24
,, /EDP	.82	.81	1.00	.68	.84	1.28	1.31
,, /VFA	.89	.57	1.55	1.12	1.05	.81	1.60
,, /SEN	.82	.66	2.17	.87	1.36	2.26	1.87

[a] (1), (2), (3) represent the three stages of the argument as outlined on pp.59f.
[b] $\overline{\text{EDP}}$ is the weighted mean frequency rate for EDIAL and EPROSE, reported in the fourth column of Table IX. $\overline{\text{VFA}}$ and $\overline{\text{SEN}}$ are from columns 8 and 13.

junction ET ('and'). SI ('if') and SED ('but') are weakened by the similarity to Fortunatianus on the former (D = 1.10) and to Victorinus on
the latter (D = .98). Yet on all of the words except ET Augustine is more
consistent with himself (lower D) than with the two means ($\overline{\text{VFA}}$, $\overline{\text{SEN}}$)
for the other authors. Thus the words have a general power to dis-
criminate between Augustine and other authors considered in a group.
What they fail to do is distinguish clearly between Augustine and any
other single author. Because of this failure, my study of these seven words
in De dialectica is concerned mainly with the various mean rates.

The question is whether De dialectica is more like Augustine's early
writings, writings by other fourth-century authors, or some of Seneca's
writings.[51] The answer is that there is a measurable tendency for De
dialectica to be most like Augustine's early writings and least like the
writings of Seneca. This may be seen as follows. When the distinctiveness
ratios are calculated for De dialectica in relation to the mean frequency
rates (Table X, part 3), the comparison with Augustine's early writings
yields the shortest range of variation from 1.0 (complete agreement) and

the least number of critical values of D. As a way of quantifying the variation from 1.0 I have transformed all values less than 1.0 into values above 1.0 and calculated the averages.[52] *De dialectica* has the lowest average when compared with Augustine's early writings. The figures on average, range, and critical values are:

(1) for *De dial.*/Augustine mean ($\overline{\text{EDP}}$), an average D of 1.23, a range of .68 to 1.31, with no values of D in the critical region;

(2) for *De dial.*/VFA mean, an average D of 1.36, a range of .57 to 1.60, with three critical values of D (for IN, ENIM, SED);

(3) for *De dial.*/Seneca mean, an average D of 1.65, a range of .66 to 2.26, with four critical values of D (for IN, ENIM, UT, SED).

I know of no appropriate way to evaluate the significance of the differences between the three averages. Perhaps the most important observation we can make here is to note that half of the values for the fourth century authors and for Seneca (seven of fourteen) are in the critical

TABLE XI

Vocabulary: Rank of high frequency words

	ET	IN	ENIM	NON	SI	UT	SED
EDIAL	1	4	10	2	8	7	11
EPROSE	1	4	12	3	6	7	10
EDP	1.0	4.0	11.0	2.5	7.0	7.0	10.5
VICTOR	1	3	22	7	9	4	8
FORTUN	2	3	28	7	12	4	34
AMBROS	1	2	8	4	12	5	7
VFA	1.33	2.67	19.33	6.0	11.0	4.33	16.33
De dial.	2	8	13	4	12	6	10

region, whereas none of the values for Augustine's early writings are critical. Whatever its statistical weight, the evidence is in the direction we would expect if the hypothesis that Augustine wrote *De dialectica* is true.

Since the seven words were chosen from the set of words ranking among the ten most frequent in Augustine's early writings, it is interesting to see how these words rank in the other data sets. Table XI gives the ranks and mean ranks for the seven words. The rank for *De dia-lectica* is closer to the Augustine mean rank more often (five times) than to the VFA mean (two times). The average variation of *De dialectica* ranks from the Augustine mean ranks is just over two (2.12); from the VFA means, in contrast, it is well over three (3.33). If its variation from the individual data sets is examined, it is seen that it is most like Augustine's early prose (mean variation of 2.0). It is also close to the early dialogues and Ambrose (both with a mean variation of 2.28). It is least like Victorinus (3.56), and Fortunatianus (5.46).[53] This greater degree of resemblance of *De dialectica* to Augustine's writings on rank is in harmony with the findings of the D study.

2. *Low Frequency Words*

The second group of words studied have lower frequency rates than the first group. In Augustine's early writings they occur with a frequency of from .72 per thousand to 5.8 per thousand. The first group had a range of 8.7 per thousand to 32 per thousand. Several of the low fre-quency words were located by following up on the information given by J. H. Gillis in his study of particles in Hilary, Jerome, Ambrose, and Augustine.[54] Four of the words – AUTEM, AT, ERGO, ID – are used rather consistently by Augustine. From Table XII (part 1) it can be seen that they have D values (EPROSE/EDIAL) ranging from .83 to 1.23. The fifth word – PRORSUS, an adverb or adjective meaning 'straight-way' or 'straight' – was studied because Gillis found it to be unique to Augustine.[55] It occurs frequently in the early dialogues he studied. It is much less frequent in the other works, but is found there. This difference between the dialogues and other writings is confirmed by my research, which located twenty occurrences of PRORSUS in the early dialogues and only one in the early prose. Two other words – PER and EX – though of doubtful value due to a significant discrepancy between their rate in the two Augustine strata, were studied because preliminary findings showed them to be used less frequently by Augustine than by other authors. Most of the other words studied are Augustine "plus" words.[56] It seemed desirable to test some apparently "minus" words.

Comparison of these words' rates of occurrence in Augustine's writings with the rates in other authors (Table XII, part 2) shows them to be of varying discriminating power. On the whole they are superior to the

TABLE XII

Vocabulary: Distinctiveness ratio for selected low frequency words

	AUTEM	AT	ERGO	ID	PRORSUS	PER	EX
(1)							
EPROSE/EDIAL	1.17	.83	1.23	.88	.095	1.80	.66
(2)							
EDP/VICTOR	2.08	–[a]	1.77	.59	–	.44	.41
,, /FORTUN	4.46	2.48	3.90	.44	–	.64	.49
,, /AMBROS	2.15	–	.81	4.23	–	.81	1.38
,, /VFA	2.90	4.80	1.77	.61	–	.61	.56
,, /SEN	3.62	.73	2.78	2.71	30.0	1.36	.55
(3)							
De dial./EDIAL	.94	1.87	.79	1.10	.21	1.63	2.00
,, /EPROSE	.84	2.25	.65	1.26	2.25	.90	3.00
,, /EDP	.91	1.97	.73	1.16	.31	1.29	2.27
,, /VICTOR	1.89	–	1.29	.67	–	.57	.93
,, /FORTUN	4.05	4.90	2.84	.51	–	.83	1.12
,, /AMBROS	1.96	–	.59	4.9	–	1.05	3.15
,, /VFA	2.64	9.50	1.29	.71	–	.79	1.27
,, /SEN	3.30	1.43	2.03	3.14	9.00	1.75	1.24

[a] A dash means that the word does not occur in this author. Thus there is no frequency rate by which to calculate D.

high frequency words. AUTEM, an adversative conjunction, usually translated as 'but' or 'however,' is an excellent discriminator. Augustine uses it at least twice and as much as four times as frequently as any other author. Gillis's tabulations on AUTEM show the same result.[57] AUTEM is, therefore, apparently characteristic of Augustine in comparison with a fairly large number of authors. The same may be said of PRORSUS, which I find only once in the other authors I studied (Seneca), and of ID, the neuter nominative and accusative of the demonstrative pronoun 'is' ('this'). ID does not discriminate quite as well as AUTEM because Augustine's frequency rate for it is between that of the other authors (higher than Seneca and Ambrose; lower than Victorinus and Fortunatianus) rather than consistently above or below others. The other words have less discriminating power. AT, an adversative conjunction ('but', 'moreover'), is good for distinguishing Augustine from fourth-century authors,[58] but not for distinguishing him from Seneca.

Seneca usually uses AT somewhat more frequently than Augustine but not always (*De Consolatione ad Polybium*). Moreover, AT is risky because of its extremely low rate of occurrence, less than once in a thousand in Augustine. ERGO ('therefore') is weakened as a discriminator by Augustine's similarity to Ambrose (D = .81).[59] PER ('by') and EX ('from') turn out to be weak, again because of Augustine's similarity to Ambrose, and, on PER, to Seneca.

Because these low frequency words have clearer discriminating power than the high frequency words considered above, it is worthwhile in examining their use in *De dialectica* to consider them individually as well as in a group. In addition to allowing more specific conclusions, this procedure will make it possible to distinguish among the words according to their ability to discriminate.

The best discriminators are AUTEM, ID, and PRORSUS. On the first two, *De dialectica* is very similar to Augustine's early writings (D of .91 and 1.16) and, with one exception (Seneca's *De const. sap.*, D of 1.13 for AUTEM), very different from the other authors. All of the distinctiveness ratios with other authors are in Ellegård's critical region, with two minus values (.51, .67) and plus values from 1.89 to 15.10.[60] If we consider the excellent discriminating power of AUTEM and ID, we must find these results weighty evidence in favor of Augustine's authorship of *De dialectica*. The results for PRORSUS should be treated more cautiously, since it is not used in Augustine's early writings at a consistent rate. It occurs twice in *De dialectica*. Assessment of such a rare event is difficult, but it would appear significant that a word found only once in around three quarters of a million words written by Augustine's contemporaries[61] and only once in twenty-five thousand words of Seneca, should occur twice in the less than six thousand words of *De dialectica*. This is about what we would expect if Augustine wrote the treatise.

The remaining words are of less value as discriminators and they yield mixed results for *De dialectica*. AT is used in the work at a rate most like Seneca's (D = 1.43), from whose writings Augustine's usage cannot be distinguished, and very far from the other authors' rate (D = 9.50), again like Augustine. Thus in *De dialectica* AT follows a pattern similar to Augustine's early writings. The use of ERGO does not fit a pattern at all. It occurs in *De dialectica* at a rate about equidistant between the fourth-century and Augustine means but is individually closest to one of Seneca's works, *De constantia sapientis* (D of 1.00). PER and EX, poor discriminators in the first place, yield confusing evidence. PER is used at a rate closer to the fourth-century mean (D = .79); EX at a rate closer to the Seneca mean (D = 1.24). Individually, therefore, the good discriminators support Augustinian authorship and the poorer discriminators weaken the Augustinian hypothesis.

Turning to a grouping of the data, we find a situation similar to that found for high frequency words: *De dialectica* is measurably most like Augustine's early writings. For the same three measures used above for the high frequency words, the figures are[62]:

(1) for *De dial.*/Augustine mean, an average D of 1.52, a range from .73 to 2.27, with two values of D in the critical region (for AT and EX);

(2) for *De dial.*/VFA mean, an average D of 2.90, a range from .71 to 9.50, with two values of D in the critical region (for AT and AUTEM);

(3) for *De dial.*/Seneca mean, an average D of 2.15, a range from 1.24 to 3.30, with four values of D in the critical region (for AUTEM, ERGO, ID, and PER).

The distinctiveness ratios for **PRORSUS** are not included in these figures. If they could be included somehow, the differences of *De dialectica* from the fourth-century authors and from Seneca would be increased.[63] On the high frequency words *De dialectica* was least like Seneca's writings. On the low frequency words it would appear that it is least like the three fourth-century authors, for both the average D and the range of D is largest for the comparison with them. If we eliminate the data for the poorest discriminators (PER and EX), we find *De dialectica* to be even more similar to Augustine's early writings and less similar to the fourth-century authors. The averages for D now become (in the same order as above) 1.40, 3.72, and 2.47. But whichever group of writings is least like *De dialectica*, on low frequency as on high frequency words it is most like the works written by Augustine during the years 386–391.

3. *Alternative Words*

The final kind of vocabulary study I have made is a brief investigation
of the relative frequency of two pairs of alternative words, AUT and
VEL, A and AB. The first two, usually translated as 'or,' are not strictly
alternative. Both are disjunctive particles, but AUT is generally stronger
in classical Latin, having the force of exclusive disjunction in contrast
to the inclusive sense of VEL.[64] This distinction tended to become blurred
in late Latin (after Apuleius), where AUT often means merely 'and'.[65]
The weakening of AUT appears to have increased the use of VEL. In
his research Gillis found that Augustine and Ambrose use the latter
more than the former.[66] In Table XIII I present the data from my
study in the form of the ratio of AUT to VEL. In none of the authors
does VEL exceed AUT in rate of occurrence.[67] The works of Augustine
and Ambrose and one of Seneca's come the closest to this. Because the
Ambrose and Seneca (*Cons. Helv.*) ratios are very close to Augustine's,
the AUT-VEL ratio cannot be regarded as a clear discriminator among
authors. If, however, we examine only the means, we find Augustine to
have a much lower ratio than either the fourth-century group or Seneca.
De dialectica, with a ratio of 1.60, is closest to the Augustine mean and
furthest from the mean ratio for Seneca. We can conclude, therefore,
that on the relative frequencies of AUT and VEL *De dialectica* is most
similar to Augustine's early writings. Since it has a ratio falling between
those for the dialogues and the prose, it is more likely to have been
written by Augustine than by other fourth-century authors or by any

TABLE XIII

Vocabulary: Alternative words, AUT, VEL

Data set	Ratio (AUT/VEL)	Weighted mean
EDIAL	1.11	1.28
EPROSE	1.77	
VICTOR	2.10	
FORTUN	3.10	2.80
AMBROS	1.60	
SENECA, CP	7.85	
,, , CH	1.61	3.82
,, , CM	3.44	
,, , CS	5.35	
De dialectica	1.60	

classical author. Since Fortunatianus is the only other candidate for author of the treatise, his high AUT-VEL ratio (3.10) must be considered strong evidence against that candidacy.

The second pair, A and AB ('from,' 'away from'), is a mere matter of alternative spelling. Preceding words beginning with consonants, A is used; preceding words beginning with vowels, AB is used.[68] I have found that Augustine uses A less frequently relative to AB than do other authors (Table XIV). He differs on this most from his contemporaries Victorinus, Fortunatianus, and Ambrose. Why there is this difference admits of no easy explanation. It could be that it reflects a difference in the subject matter and therefore in which nouns are used, but over relatively large samples this seems unlikely. It could also be due to some conscious or unconscious preference of Augustine for avoiding the use of A when it would be appropriate by using such synonyms as '*de*' or a noun that begins with a vowel. Whatever the explanation, the tendency to use A less relative to AB than his contemporaries is present in Augustine's early writings. This tendency is present also in *De dialectica*, and in fact is slightly more marked there. This is further evidence in favor of Augustinian authorship of the treatise.

The vocabulary study which I have reported on may be regarded as a pilot study. It does, in my opinion, support the view that Augustine wrote *De dialectica*. Its value may be challenged, however, on the grounds that it is too narrowly conceived. Only a few words are studied. They do not give us a very broad idea of the total vocabulary of the

TABLE XIV

Vocabulary: Alternative words, A, AB

Data set	Ratio (A/AB)	Weighted mean
EDIAL	1.53	1.50
EPROSE	1.40	
VICTOR	2.48	
FORTUN	2.71	2.72
AMBROS	3.00	
SENECA, CP	1.43	
„ , CH	1.65	2.00
„ , CM	3.85	
„ , CS	2.15	
De dialectica	1.33	

various authors. It might be useful to test many more words than I was able to test,[69] though there is no guarantee that other discriminator words would be discovered. I did make one study which is broader, calculating Yule's "characteristic" for all of the words in each data set. The results seem to be of no value for authorship discrimination.[70] At this point, I must be content with having discovered some words characteristic of Augustine, which are also characteristic of *De dialectica*.

D. CONCLUSION

At the beginning of this part of the Introduction I noted that a positive conclusion would be less certain than a negative conclusion and that either would be only probable and not certain. Even within these limits the evaluation of the quantitative evidence yields nothing like statistical finality. The clearest statistical outcome is in the case of mean word length, where *De dialectica* and Augustine's early writings are found to be significantly different from the other authors but not from each other. Word length distribution also yields fair statistical results, though it would be a stronger discriminator if Augustine's two strata of early writings were more similar to each other. The vocabulary study locates some Augustinian characteristics also found in *De dialectica* but it is not clear that the results of that part of the study can be translated into statistical significance.

If, however, statistical significance eludes us, an undeniable similarity of *De dialectica* to Augustine's early writings is seen in several ways. This degree of similarity should perhaps be regarded as surprising, if it is remembered that *De dialectica* is an incomplete work which may have never been revised.[71] Of course, similarity by itself proves nothing. Other authors whose writings are extant (but untested) or lost may have been like Augustine on some or all of the aspects of style I have studied. But the burden of proof should be on those who deny Augustinian authorship, for literary and historical analysis produces only this hypothesis with any force. The hypothesis that Fortunatianus wrote the treatise, a weak one to begin with, is effectively countered by the quantitative evidence. The *Ars rhetoricae* is not close to *De dialectica* on any of the matters studied. The two works are especially dissimilar on word length distribution, rank of high frequency words, frequency rate of the best discriminators among low frequency words (AUTEM, ID, PRORSUS), and the AUT-VEL ratio. The negative conclusion that Fortunatianus did not write *De dialectica* is as close to certain as statistical reasoning can take us. The same reasoning allows the positive conclusion that Augustine wrote *De dialectica*. There seems to be no sufficient reason to reject that conclusion.

NOTES

[1] *The Statistical Study of Literary Vocabulary*, 1944.
[2] *A Statistical Method for Determining Authorship: The Junius Letters, 1769–1772*, 1962.
[3] *Inference and Disputed Authorship:* The Federalist, 1964.
[4] *Paul, the Man and the Myth*, 1966, with James McLeman; "The Seventh Letter of Plato," *Mind* 77 (1968), 309–325, with M. Levison and A. D. Winspear. For a brief account of the history of such studies see Richard W. Bailey, "Statistics and Style: A Historical Survey," in Bailey and Lubomir Dolezel (eds.), *Statistics and Style*, pp. 217–236.
[5] *Augustins Geistige Entwickelung in den Ersten Jahren nach seiner "Bekehrung", 386–391.* (*Neue Studien zur Geschichte der Theologie und der Kirche*, pt. 3, Berlin, 1908), p. 10, n. 1.
[6] Hence the titles of the two most useful anthologies on the subject, Dolezel and Bailey's *Statistics and Style* and Jacob Leed's, *The Computer and Literary Style*.
[7] For a full discussion see Louis Milic, *A Quantitative Approach to the Style of Jonathan Swift*, chap. 2.
[8] Sally and Walter Sedelow, "A Preface to Computational Stylistics," in Leed, p. 1.
[9] G. Herdan, *Quantitative Linguistics*, p. 151.
[10] Morton, "Seventh Letter," p. 310; Milic, "Unconscious Ordering in the Prose of Swift," in Leed, pp. 82f.; the principle was first stated by T. C. Mendenhall in his early studies "The Characteristic Curve of Composition," *Science* 9 (1887), p. 245, and "A Mechanical Solution of a Literary Problem," *The Popular Science Monthly* 60 (1901), p. 97.
[11] Herdan, p. 11; Ellegård, p. 8; and H. H. Somers, "Statistical Methods in Literary Analysis," in Leed, p. 128.
[12] The pattern I must follow for *De dialectica* is more complicated and necessarily has a weaker conclusion than the pattern followed when there are only two candidates for authorship of a disputed work, as in the *Federalist* problem where either Hamilton or Madison is the author. In the study of a two-candidate dispute one can easily test all possible candidates whose authentic works are extant and need only choose between two candidates.
[13] Herdan, pp. 150f.; Ephim G. Fogel, "Salmons in Both, or Some Caveats for Canonical Scholars," in *Evidence for Authorship*, Fogel and David Erdman, eds. (Ithaca, 1966), p. 96.
[14] See L. R. Palmer, *The Latin Language*, pp. 190 and 202, and Christine Mohrmann, *Études sur le Latin des Chrétiens*, pp. 383ff., on the development of Augustine's Latin after his conversion.
[15] During his years in Milan Augustine was a frequent hearer of Ambrose's sermons and greatly admired their style and content. See *Conf.* V.xiii.23–xiv.24 and *De doctr. chr.* IV.xxi.48–50. One variable which I have not considered is chronological spread. Among the various data sets the spread ranges from a short time in the case of *De dial.* and, presumably, Fortunatianus to up to nineteen years in the case of Augustine's logical writings.
[16] See below, sections B.1 and C.
[17] This method is described by Phillip J. McCarthy, *Introduction to Statistical Reasoning*, 1957, pp. 280–288. Randomness is required if one is to use statistical tests.

[18] Relative size was determined by counting the columns for each work in *PL*.

[19] See Mosteller and Wallace, p. 249, who believe that even this is small for sample size.

[20] Ellegård, pp. 20f. and 77, says that 100,000 words are necessary to generalize about an author and 1,000,000 to generalize about a general population.

[21] I have tested the differences between the means by the method for multiple comparisons with one variable using the F statistic. This method is described by W. J. Dixon and F. J. Massey in *Introduction to Statistical Analysis,* 3rd edn. (New York, 1969), p. 167.

[22] Tore Janson, "Word, Syllable, and Letter in Latin," pp. 52f. Janson's samples, made up of sentences 151 through 250 of each work studied, average around 1,600 words.

[23] Stephen V. F. Waite, "Approaches to the Analysis of Latin Prose, Applied to Cato, Sallust and Livy," pp. 91–94 and Table I. Waite studied all of the Cato cited (*De agri cultura,* 15,800 words; *Orat.,* 2,700 words; other fragments, 1,400 words) and arbitrarily selected passages in Livy (16,000 words) and Sallust (11,100 words).

[24] Palmer, p. 202.

[25] Cited above note 10. Bailey, p. 217, regards Mendenhall's work as the first modern statistical study of style.

[26] "Characteristic Curve," p. 245, and "Mechanical Solution," p. 97.

[27] Mosteller and Wallace, pp. 259–262, and Claude S. Brinegar, "Mark Twain and the Quintus Curtius Snodgrass Letters: A Statistical Test of Authorship," pp.92ff.

[28] The only exception is the curve for Caesar's Commentaries given by Mendenhall, "Characteristic Curve," p. 249. It is much flatter and has three peaks – at 2, 5, and 7.

[29] "Characteristic Curve," p. 241.

[30] *Ibid.,* pp. 245f.

[31] Brinegar, p. 87. Brinegar does not say how large the sample should be; in his own study he uses samples ranging in size from 1,900 to 6,100 words.

[32] The null hypothesis holds that a difference between two sample means is due to chance and not to any difference between the populations from which the samples are drawn. Rejection of the null hypothesis means that a difference is due to a real difference between populations. Its acceptance means only that there is no evidence that the populations are different. For a description of the Chi-Square test see Paul Hoel, *Elementary Statistics,* 2nd edn. (New York, 1960), pp. 235–243. I have carried out my tests by the contingency table method described by Hoel on pp. 240–243.

[33] The critical value is determined by consulting a distribution of χ^2 table. I have used the one printed by Fisher and Yates, *Statistical Tables for Biological, Agricultural, and Medical Research,* 6th edn., 1963, Table IV. The only values not significant at the .05 level are obtained from comparing *De dial.* with EDIAL and EPROSE.

[34] Mosteller and Wallace, pp. 259–262.

[35] Moreover, the values obtained in comparing *De dial.* with the early prose and the early dialogues are not significant at the .05 level.

[36] For word lengths 1 through 14 the data was ungrouped. The data for lengths 15–18 was grouped to insure at least five occurrences in each cell, a requirement for use of the Chi-Square test.

[37] Note, however, that the value for the comparison with EDIAL is now in the critical region, whereas for the grouped data it is not. Both grouped and ungrouped data yield insignificant differences between *De dial.* and EPROSE.

[38] An investigation of sentence length was also carried out. I defined a sentence as consisting of the words between periods or question marks. Sentence length turned out not to discriminate among the authors I studied, but I will briefly report my findings. The following

mean number of words per sentence were found for each data set:

AMBROS	18.39
EDIAL	18.44
FORTUN	18.71
De dial.	19.19
VICTOR	22.55
EPROSE	23.22
LOGIC	27.27

The differences between the means were evaluated by the method used for evaluating mean word length. EDIAL and EPROSE differ significantly from each other but not from the writings of any of the other authors. Thus mean sentence length does not yield a criterion for Augustinian authorship. *De dialectica* is significantly different only from LOGIC. – Similar findings resulted from study of the sentence length distribution. Using the Chi-Square test, I obtained a higher value when comparing EDIAL and EPROSE (37.2, with 9 degrees of freedom) than when comparing these two Augustinian sets with the other authors (average with VICTOR is 23.2 (8 degrees of freedom), with FORTUN it is 16.0, and with AMBROS it is 23.5). Thus sentence length distribution does not yield a criterion for Augustinian authorship, since his writings differ from each other more than from the writings of other authors tested. The values of χ^2 when *De dial.* was compared with other data sets are: with EDIAL, 22.9, with EPROSE, 13.9, with VICTOR, 9.5, with FORTUN, 5.6, and with AMBROS, 19.4. – Other investigators have had varying success in studies of sentence length. Mosteller and Wallace, p. 6, report that mean sentence length is useless for distinguishing Hamilton and Madison from each other. Waite, pp. 96–99, finds sentence length more valuable than word length, but his definition of a sentence is different from mine. It should be noted that there are special problems in studying sentence length in ancient authors, for punctuation of ancient works is usually a matter of modern editorial decision.

[39] *A Quantitative Approach to the Style of Jonathan Swift*, pp. 139–141.

[40] *Ibid.*, p. 79.

[41] Ellegård, p. 41; Morton, *Paul*, p. 45; Mosteller and Wallace, p. 265; and Ivor Francis "An Exposition of a Statistical Approach to the *Federalist* Dispute," in Leed, pp. 69 and 76.

[42] Syntactical study requires a far more complex process of data preparation for machine analysis, since grammatical information must be included with each word. For vocabulary study only running text needs to be encoded in machine-readable form.

[43] Ellegård, pp. 13–15.

[44] The works indexed are the three *consolationes, Ad Polybium, Ad Helviam, Ad Marciam,* and the *De constantia sapientis.*

[45] A weighted mean is calculated by giving each data set influence in proportion to its size. Thus the weighted mean for EDIAL-EPROSE is closer to the mean for EDIAL, since the latter is the larger of the two data sets.

[46] The following were studied and rejected at either the first or second stage: AC, CUM, ESSE, EST, IAM, IGITUR, ITEM, LICET, NAM, QUAE, QUOD, SUNT, ULTRA, VERUMTAMEN.

[47] Due to an unexplained programming error which was detected after the data were collected the total sample size is smaller for some of the data sets here than in the word length study. EDIAL is now 11,826 words, EPROSE is 6,344, VICTOR is 3,252, and AMBROS is 3,360. VICTOR and EDIAL have the largest losses in total, 13.0 and 8.5 percent. I was able to determine which passages were omitted. From EDIAL about two samples from *De musica* were not indexed; since there are six other samples from *De musica*

this does not seem a major loss. VICTOR is more seriously affected, for about one sample from the *Explan. in Cic. rhet.* is omitted. AMBROS loses about one third of a sample from *De virg.* EPROSE loses one third of one of the three samples from *De Gen. c. Man.*

[48] Ellegård, pp. 15f., prefers low frequency words; but Mosteller and Wallace, p. 265, found strong discriminators among high frequency function words.

[49] Ellegård, p. 15.

[50] They are, in order of mean rank: ET, EST, NON, IN, QUOD, ESSE, SI, UT, CUM, SED, ENIM, QUAE.

[51] Although Seneca wrote at a time much earlier than *De dialectica* is likely to have been written, data from his writings is useful for the purposes of assessing the significance of differences. Without Seneca there would be only two means to be compared with *De dialectica*.

[52] Such a transformation is necessary if one is to treat plus words (above 1.0) and minus words (below 1.0) together (Ellegård treats them separately). Otherwise the average of 1.5 and .5 would be the same as the average of 1.25 and .75, namely, 1.0, whereas the first pair of D values would represent a much larger variation from agreement than the second pair. If the "minus" values are transformed, the averages are 1.75 for the first pair and 1.29 for the second. Such averages give a way to express average variation from complete agreement (1.0). The first of the hypothetical averages above, 1.75, reflects, for example, an average variation of three quarters (.75) more or less of one author from the other author or group of authors with whom he is being compared.

[53] I did not include Seneca in this part of the study, largely because of the difficulty of getting comparable figures from the Delatte indexes. See the note to Table IX.

[54] *The Coordinating Particles in Saints Hilary, Jerome, Ambrose, and Augustine.* His data are not strictly comparable to mine because his samples were not randomly taken and he does not give the total sample size for each author from which the rate of occurrence could be computed. Also, he considered a different set of authors. Nevertheless, several of the tendencies Gillis observes are borne out by my research. For Augustine, Gillis studied the three Cassiciacum dialogues (*C. Acad.*, *De beata vita*, and *De ordine*), *Confessions*, *De civitate Dei*, *Epistles* 1–43, and *Sermons* 1–12.

[55] Gillis, p. 76. He does find one occurrence in Jerome.

[56] Gillis, p. 213, notes that Augustine's works surpass the other authors he studied in number and uses of particles. It may be, therefore, that there are few "minus" function words in Augustine.

[57] *Ibid.*, pp. 42–46. His totals are: Hilary, 392; Jerome, 375; Ambrose, 360; Augustine, 789, with the *dialogi* contributing over a quarter of this total though they are only a fifth of the total sample.

[58] Gillis also found this to be true. *Ibid.*, pp. 40f.

[59] Gillis's findings agree. *Ibid.*, pp. 75–82.

[60] The D of 15.10 is for *De dial.*/Seneca – CM on AUTEM. It is not given in Table XII but may be calculated from information given in Table IX. The D for *De dial.*/VFA (.71) on ID is not critical; this is due to the VFA mean being based on one low and two high frequency rates.

[61] I find no occurrences in Victorinus, Fortunatianus, or Ambrose; Gillis finds one in Jerome. I estimate his total sample for each author to be around 250,000 words (he did counts for 500 columns of Migne's *Patrology*; an average of 500 words per col. gives my figure).

[62] Again I have transposed D values below 1.0 into values above 1.0. Thus the average of D measures the degree of variation from 1.0 but not the direction of variation.

[63] This is a weakness of Ellegård's D as a measure of distinctiveness: in a case where one author is truly unique in using a word not used at all by the other, there is no way to express this quantitatively. In this case, Augustine makes considerable use of PRORSUS, a word not found at all in the samples taken in Victorinus, Fortunatianus, and Ambrose.

[64] Lewis and Short, *A Latin Dictionary* (Oxford, 1879), p. 210.

[65] Gillis, p. 30.

[66] *Ibid.*, pp. 33–37. Gillis says that only Augustine does this (pp. 37, 215), but his figures show that he found 301 occurrences of VEL and 274 of AUT in Ambrose.

[67] For Augustine's dialogues Gillis has a similar result: AUT, 158; VEL, 117; ratio of 1.35. I did find one instance of VEL exceeding AUT, namely, in Augustine's logical writings where the numbers are: AUT, 18; VEL, 28; ratio, .64.

[68] Lewis and Short, p. 2.

[69] One may be excused for envying the facilities and large number of personnel available to such researchers as Mosteller and Wallace (p. ix).

[70] Yule's characteristic or K is a measure of the repeat rate or variety of an author's vocabulary. A high value indicates a rich vocabulary. Calculating K for all words (where a word is any unique alphabetic character string), I get the following results ordered from highest to lowest:

EPROSE	59.3
FORTUN	58.4
De dial.	51.2
VICTOR	40.0
EDIAL	38.6
AMBROS	36.2

Because EPROSE and EDIAL are quite different, it is not possible to draw any authorship conclusions from these results. There are several possible reasons why K is of no value to my study. (1) Yule studied only nouns; I do all words, a procedure which Yule questions (p. 28). (2) According to Yule (pp. 120, 133, 231) K varies depending on whether samples are drawn from one or several works. My data sets include both kinds. (3) Yule uses spread sampling not random sampling (pp. 47, 57–68).

[71] It seems unlikely that an incomplete work would have been revised. It would be interesting to know how Augustine composed his early works. His later works were dictated. (See *Epistle* 174, *De trin.* III, proem. 1 *in.*, and Brown, *Augustine*, p. 272.) If *De dialectica* were dictated and not revised or corrected, then it might have some non-Augustinian elements attributable to the stenographer.

INTRODUCTION TO THE TEXT

by JAN PINBORG

This edition was originally planned as a complete critical edition. But while I was preparing the work I learned that a similar project was planned and almost finished by H. Braakhuis, Nijmegen. So I decided to use only a selection of the thirty-seven manuscripts known to me for this hand edition.[1] I believe, however, that the reduced apparatus gives all of the relevant readings for the constitution of the text, though of course not everything of interest for the history of the text.

Roughly speaking, the witnesses of the tradition can be divided into three strata. I doubt that it is possible to determine exactly all stemmatic relations of the manuscripts; there are too many instances of contamination for that. But a rough division into three strata, which represent as it were cross sections of one tradition in distinct stages of corruption, can be established from the evidence with sufficient certainty.[2]

Group I. The first and oldest stratum is represented by the following eleven manuscripts:

> B = Bern, Bürgerbibliothek 363, s.IX.
> D = Köln, Dombibl. 166 (= Darmstadt 2191), s.VIII.
> d = Vaticana, Pal. lat. 1588, s.IX.
> P = Paris, BNat. lat. 7730, s.IX/X.
>   Firenze, BLaur. S.Marco 264, s.XV.
>   Firenze, BLaur. Aed.flor.eccl. 168, s.XV.
>   Firenze, BRicc. 709, s.XV.
>   Oxford, Bodl.Libr. 587 (2359), s.XV.
>   Vaticana, Urb.lat. 1180, s.XV.
>   Vaticana, Vat.lat. 1485, s.XV.
>   Vaticana, Chigi H VI 186, s.XV.

To this group belong also the oldest editions. With the exception of B, where Augustine is named as author, the text is anonymous or ascribed to Fortunatianus. d is an old copy from D. P is corrected by another hand, on the basis of a group II manuscript; together with B it makes it possible to discard some faulty readings peculiar to D. According to Billanovich all of the fifteenth-century manuscripts in this group depend on the copy of D which Giovanni Aurispa had made in 1433. Several conjectures and contaminations have, however, crept into these later manuscripts.

The manuscripts of this group give us a text that is on the whole sound. Their text is generally in a better condition than it is in all of the remaining manuscripts. For some errors unique to this group see e.g. notes 28, 56, 64, 66, 139 etc.

I have newly collated B and D, two of the manuscripts used by Crecelius. I have used d for the pages where D is mutilated. Also I have newly collated P which was partly used by Funaioli.[3] Of the later manuscripts, I have collated Urb.lat. 1180, but I have not included it in the apparatus.

Group II. This group consists of eight manuscripts, most of them from the tenth century:

> Berlin (Ost), Pr.Staatsbibl., Phillips 1780 (Rose 176), s.X.
> Bern, Bürgerbibl. 548, s.XI.[4]
> Einsiedeln, B. Abbat. 324, s.X.
> Leningrad, B Publ. F V class.lat. N 7, s.IX.[5]
> Leiden, Bibl.univ. Voss. lat. 8° 88, s.X.
> O = Orléans, Bibl.mun. 263 (219), s.X. Mutilated, the rest of the original manuscript, however, is found in:
> O = Paris, BNat. lat. 6638.
> Q = Paris, BNat. lat. 7581, s.X.
> Vercelli, Bibl.cap. CXXXVIII (143), s.X.

On the average the text of this group is good. In several cases the manuscripts of group II avoid errors that are found in group I. Other errors, however, are common to both groups, and several new ones are added in II. Within this group one can see a continual deterioration of the text. O is easily the best manuscript. Q, which has narrow connections with the Berlin manuscript, belongs to a middle stage. I have sample collated the remaining manuscripts of this group, but I have not included them in the apparatus.

Group III. This group consists of eighteen mostly later manuscripts. The text is altered by errors and arbitrary additions. What has been called the *textus receptus* is located within this group. A great majority of the manuscripts, like most of the manuscripts of group II, also include Pseudo-Augustine's treatise on the Categories. L. Minio-Paluello has thoroughly analysed the stemmatic relations of the manuscripts for this treatise.[6] He found that the manuscripts of group III are all contaminated and dependent on the manuscripts of group II. My sample collating led to similar results for the Augustine text. The oldest manuscripts of the group are the Cambridge manuscript and G. The Cambridge text is very bad, while G is still in a transitional stage from group II to group III. I have included G in the apparatus, first, in order to show the oldest source of several errors of the *textus receptus* and, second, because G sometimes offers interesting readings, going back to old conjectures or perhaps even to another Ms. of the group I-type. G is the manuscript of a Carolingian scholar (cp. above p. 20f.). Examples of the progressive deterioration of the text through group II to group III with conjectures appearing in G are found in notes 6, 77, 78, 111, 127 etc.

I have not seen all of the manuscripts of this group or sample collated them, but only those indicated by +. The manuscripts investigated by Minio-Paluello are designated by §.

       + Bern, Bürgerbibl. A 92 n.35 (Fragment), s.X.
       § Bruxelles, BRoyale 49–62 (1117), s.XIV.
    +§ Cambridge, Corp.Christi 206, s.IX.
          Charleville, BMun. 187, s.XII.
       § Eton, BColl. 120, s.XIV.
       + Firenze, BLaur. S.Marco 113, s.XII.
       § Paris, BArs. 350, s.XIV.
       § Paris, BArs. 351, s.XII.
       § Paris, BMaz. 632, s.XIII.
       § Paris, BNat. lat. 2083, s.XIII.
G = +§ Paris, BNat. lat. 12949 (Olim Germanensis), s.IX.
       § Paris, BNat.lat. 16598, s.XIII.
          Philadelphia, Univ.Libr. lat. 63, s.XII.[7]
       § Troyes, BMun. 40, s.XII.
          Troyes, BMun. 70, s.XIII.

+§ Vaticana, Reg.lat. 233, s.XI.
+ Vaticana, Urb.lat. 393, s.XII.
+ Venezia, BMarc. lat. VI 68 (3633), s.XIII.

Selected instances of the distribution of variant readings among the groups I–III[8]

Textual note no.	Reading	Gr. I	Gr. II	Gr. III
6	expectant aliquid	DBP	OCFQLVE	
	alia quae non			
	comprehendunt,			G dett.
	sed expectant aliquid			
7	ambulat		OCFQLVE	G dett.
	om.	DBP		
46–50	cum...quibus de	DBP	OCFQLV	
	tunc...de quibus		E	G dett.
80, 82	origo dum esse	DB(P)		
	origo quaerendum esse		OCFQVE	
	originem quaerendam esse		L	G dett.
132	Cotta	DBP	O(Cottam)	
	quoddam		QVC	393, Marc.
	quiddam		FLE	G Cam. 233, 113
150	ferret	DBP^{ac}	OCFQLV	
	offenderet	P^{pc}	E	G dett.
197	ambigua se	DBP	OCFQLVE	G
	ambiguose			dett.
200	facete	P^{pc}	O	G(supra lin.)
	facie	DBP^{ac}		
	facile		CFQLVE	G dett.
255	At		OV^{pc}	
	ut	DBP	CFQL	
	ex diversa origine ut		E	G dett.
272	tu	DBP	O	
	istud		CFQELV	G dett.

The Edition and Variant Readings

With some hesitation I have adopted a 'normalized' orthography. Anyone interested in the orthography of the oldest manuscripts may be referred to Crecelius.

The apparatus is selective. Only readings of the Mss. B, D/d, G, O, P and Q are mentioned. Minor isolated errors in one manuscript have not been included. Exceptions have been made for some variant readings of G, since such errors of G are often reflected in the *textus receptus*.

Stemma of the Mss. employed:

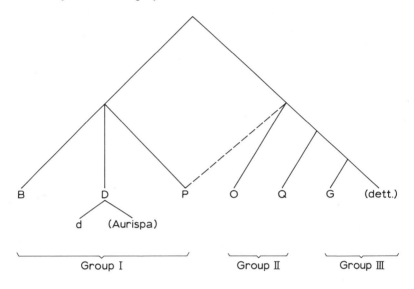

The apparatus is negative, which means that when a Ms. is not mentioned in the critical note it can be assumed that it has the reading offered in the text.

The page numbering and every fifth line of the Crecelius edition is printed in the margin and indicated in the text by a slash mark (/). A vertical stroke ($^{|}$) indicates the endings of the remaining lines of the Crecelius edition.

NOTES

[1] I have to thank l'Institut de recherche et d'histoire des textes (Paris) which has generously helped me in locating and describing the Mss. and also put at my disposal microfilms of some of the Mss. I should also like to thank Professor Jackson who has translated this introduction from an earlier German version and through his thorough reading of the text has saved me from several errors. Finally, I wish to thank Mr. Sten Ebbesen, Copenhagen, who made a sample collation of some Mss. and with whom I have discussed many problems of the text.

[2] For some examples of this division see p. 79. For further information on the Mass. I refer to Professor Jackson's introduction, above pp. 7–22.

[3] In: *Grammaticae Romanae fragmenta.* Leipzig (Teubner) 1907, pp. 278–86.

[4] This Ms. was partially employed by Crecelius. Hagen (1872) gives a complete collation.

[5] I have only been able to see this Ms. after the manuscript of this introduction was completed. So it is not included in the examples given on p. 79. The readings of this Ms. are pretty close to Q.

[6] *Aristoteles latinus* I (1961) p. LXXX ff.
[7] For the text of this Ms. cp. above p. 40, note 113.
[8] Abbreviations used in this paradigm: C=Bern 548. E=Einsiedeln 324. F=Berlin 1780. L=Leiden 88. V=Vercelli 143. *dett.*=consensus of the Mss.: Cam=Cambridge 206, Marc=Venezia VI 68, 393=Urb. lat. 393, 233=Reg. lat. 233 and 113=Firenze Laur. 113.

ABBREVIATIONS
CRITICAL APPARATUS

Manuscripts:
B =Bern, Bürgerb. 363.
D=Köln, Bibl. capit. 166.
d =Vat. Pal. lat. 1588.
G=Paris BN lat. 12949.
O =Orléans, B. Mun. 263 (219)+Paris BN lat. 6638.
P =Paris BN lat. 7730.
Q =Paris BN lat. 7581.

Sigla:
X^{ac}: ante correctionem
X^{pc}: post correctionem
+ : addidit (addiderunt)
om.: omisit (omiserunt)
secl.: seclusit
conj.: conjecit (conjecerunt)
codd.: consensus codicum BDGOPQ
suppl.: supplevit.

Editions Quoted:
Ed. *Erasmus*, Basel 1528.
Ed. per theologos Lovanienses (*Lovan.*). Antwerpen 1577.
Ed. "opera et studio monachorum ordinis S. Benedicti" (*Ben.*), 1797.
These three editions are quoted from *Crecelius*: Augustini de dialectica liber. Recensuit et adnotavit W. Crecelius. Jahresbericht über das Gymnasium zu Elberfeld. 1857.

Emendations:
Funaioli: cp. note 3. The emendations of Buecheler and Usener are taken over from Funaioli.
Hagen: H. Hagen, Zur Kritik und Erläuterung der Dialectik des Augustinus. *Neue Jahrbücher für Philologie und Pädagogik* 42. Jhg., 105 Bd. (=*J. für classische Philologie*, 18. Jhg.). Leipzig 1872, 757–780.
Keil: ibid. 29. Jhg., 79. Bd. (*J. für classische Philologie*, 5. Jhg.) 1859, 154–157.

ON DIALECTIC

CHAPTER I. SIMPLE WORDS[1]

[5] Dialectic is the science of disputing well.[2] We always dispute with words. Now words are simple or combined.[3] Words which signify some one thing are simple, as when we say '*homo,*' '*equus,*' '*disputat,*' '*currit*' (man, horse, disputes, runs). Do not be surprised that '*disputat*' is classified as simple although it is composed of two elements.[4] This is made clear by our definition; for that is said to be simple which signifies some one thing. And so '*disputat*' is included in this definition. On the other hand, the word[5] '*loquor*' (I speak) is not included. For even though the latter is one word, it does not have a simple signification, since it also signifies the person who speaks. Now for this reason it is subject to truth or falsity, for it can be denied and affirmed. So every first and second person verb, although it is expressed singly, nevertheless is classified as a combined word, because it does not have a simple signification. For whoever says '*ambulo*' (I am walking) causes both the walking and he himself, who is walking, to be understood. And whoever says '*ambulas*' (you are walking) in a similar manner signifies both the thing which is done and the person who does it. On the other hand, whoever says '*ambulat*' (walks) signifies only walking. For this reason a third person verb is always classified as simple and it cannot be affirmed or denied except in the case of verbs which have the signification of the person necessarily attached to them in ordinary usage. For example, the verbs '*pluit*' (it is raining) or '*ninguit*' (it is snowing) cannot be classified as simple words because, even though it is not added "who" rains or snows, it is understood.[6]

CHAPTER II. COMBINED WORDS

Combined words are those which, when connected to one another, signify many things, for example, when we say 'the man is walking' or 'the man

S. AURELII AUGUSTINI DE DIALECTICA LIBER

I

[5] Dialectica est bene disputandi scientia. Disputamus autem utique verbis.
Verba igitur aut simplicia| sunt aut coniuncta. Simplicia sunt quae unum
quiddam significant ut cum dicimus 'homo, equus, disputat,| currit'. Nec
mireris, quod 'disputat' quamvis ex duobus compositum sit tamen inter
5   simplicia numeratum est. / Nam res definitione illustratur. Dictum est
enim id esse simplex quod unum quiddam significet. Itaque hoc| inclu-
ditur[1] hac definitione qua non includitur[2] cum dicimus 'loquor'. Quam-
vis enim unum verbum sit, non| habet tamen simplicem significationem,
siquidem significat etiam personam quae loquitur. Ideo iam obnoxium|
est veritati aut falsitati, nam et negari et affirmari potest. Omnis itaque
prima et secunda persona verbi quam|vis singillatim enuntietur tamen
inter coniuncta verba numerabitur, quia simplicem non habet significa-
10 tionem. / Siquidem quisquis dicit 'ambulo' et ambulationem facit intel-
legi et se ipsum qui ambulat, et quisquis dicit[3]| 'ambulas' similiter et rem
quae fit et eum qui facit significat. At vero qui dicit 'ambulat' nihil aliud
quam| ipsam significat ambulationem. Quamobrem tertia persona verbi
semper inter simplicia numeratur[4] et nondum| aut affirmari aut negari
potest, nisi cum talia verba sunt, quibus necessario cohaeret personae
significatio con|suetudine loquendi, ut cum dicimus 'pluit' vel 'ninguit'[5],
15 etiamsi non addatur quis pluat aut ninguat, tamen / quia intellegitur
non potest inter simplicia numerari.

II

Coniuncta verba sunt quae sibi conexa res plures significant, ut cum
dicimus 'homo ambulat' aut| 'homo festinans in montem ambulat' et
siquid tale. Sed coniunctorum verborum alia sunt quae sen|tentiam com-

---

1 & 2 includimur G.   3 dicat QG.   4 numerabitur OG.   5 ninguet D ningit B.

[6] prehendunt, ut ea quae dicta sunt: 〈alia quae〉 expectant aliquid 〈ad completionem sententiae〉[6] ut eadem / ipsa quae nunc diximus, si subtrahas verbum quod positum est 'ambulat'[7]. Quamvis enim verba coniuncta sint[|] 'homo festinans in montem', tamen adhuc pendet oratio. Separatis igitur his coniunctis verbis quae non[|] implent sententiam restant ea verba coniuncta quae sententiam comprehendunt. Horum item duae species sunt.[|] Aut enim sic sententia comprehenditur, ut vero aut falso

5　teneatur obnoxia, ut est 'omnis homo ambulat' / aut 'omnis homo non ambulat' et si quid huiusmodi est. Aut ita[9] impletur sententia, ut licet perficiat pro[|]positum animi, affirmari tamen[10] negarive non possit, ut cum imperamus, cum optamus, cum execramur[11] et[12|] similia. Nam quisquis dicit[13] 'perge ad villam' vel 'utinam pergat ad villam' vel[14] 'dii illum perduint[15'],[|] non potest argui quod mentiatur aut credi quod verum dicat[16]. Nihil enim affirmavit[17] aut[18] negavit[19]. Ergo nec[|] tales sententiae in quaestionem veniunt, ut disputatorem requirant.

III

10　Sed illae quae requirunt aut simplices / sunt aut coniunctae. Simplices sunt, quae sine ulla copulatione sententiae alterius enuntiantur, ut est illud[|] quod dicimus 'omnis homo ambulat'. Coniunctae sunt, de quarum copulatione iudicatur, ut est 'si am[|]bulat, movetur'. Sed cum de coniunctione sententiarum iudicium fit, tamdiu est, donec perveniatur ad[|] summam. Summa est autem quae conficitur ex concessis. Quod dico tale est. Qui dicit 'si ambulat, mo[|]vetur', probare vult aliquid, ut cum hoc[20]

15　concessero[21] verum esse, restet illi docere quod ambulet et[22] summa / consequatur, quae iam negari non potest, id est quod moveatur[23] – aut restet illi docere quod non moveatur[23],[|] ut consequatur summa, quae item non potest non[24] concedi, id est quod non ambulet. Rursus si hoc modo velit[|] dicere 'homo iste ambulat', simplex sententia est: quam si concessero et[25] adiunxerit aliam 'quisquis autem[|] ambulat movetur' et

---

6 alia – sententiae *conj. Crecelius, cf. etiam n. 25:* expectant aliquid DBPOQ alia quae non comprehendunt sed expectant aliquid G.   7 *om.* DBP.   9 itaque DPQ sic G.   10 tunc O *om.* G.   11 execramus DBP.   12 et: +his OG.   13 quisquis dicit: si quis dicat (dicit O) OQG.   14 aut OG.   15 perdant B^{ac}QG perdunt B^{pc} P.   16 dicit DBPQ.   17 affirmabit OQG.   18 vel OG.   19 negabit OQG.   20 hoc: +non DBP.   21 concesso G.   22 ut *conj. Hagen.*   23 *conj. Crecelius:* movetur *codd.*   24 *om.* OQG.   25 et: *om.* QG +alia (aliam et aliam QG) quae aliquid expectant ad completionem sententiae sententiam comprehendunt (comprehendit G) *codd. Cf. etiam n.* 6.

is walking quickly toward the mountain' and others of this kind. But among combined words there are some which make a statement, for example, those just cited, and there are others which require something [6] further to complete the statement,[1] as in the case of the second example if we omit 'is walking.' For even though the words 'the man quickly toward the mountain' are combined, still the utterance is left hanging. If we leave aside these combined words which do not make a statement, there remain those combined words which do make a statement. But again there are two species of these. For either a statement is made in such a way that it is held to be subject to truth or falsity, such as 'every man is walking' or 'every man is not walking' and others of this kind. Or a statement is made in such a way that, although it fully expresses what one has in mind, it cannot be affirmed or denied, as when we command, wish, curse, and the like.[2] For whoever says 'go into the house' or 'oh that he would go into the house' or 'may the gods destroy that man' cannot be thought to lie or to tell the truth, since he did not affirm or deny anything. Such statements do not, therefore, come into question so as to require anyone to dispute them.[3]

CHAPTER III. SIMPLE AND COMBINED STATEMENTS

But those statements which require disputation are either simple or combined. Those are simple which are spoken without any connection with another statement, for example, 'every man is walking.' Those are combined in which a judgment is made in respect of their connection,[1] for example, 'if he is walking, he is moving.' Now when a judgment is made in respect of the connection of statements, a conclusion can be reached.[2] The conclusion is what is established on the basis of what is conceded. Here is what I mean. Whoever says 'if he is walking, he is moving' wishes to prove something, so that when I concede that this combined statement is true he only needs to assert that he is walking and the conclusion that he is moving follows and cannot now be denied, or he need only assert that he is not moving and the conclusion that he is not walking must be agreed to. Or, to put it another way, one can say 'that man is walking.' This is a simple statement. But if I concede its truth, then he can add a further statement: 'whoever is walking is moving.'

hanc etiam[26] concessero, ex hac coniunctione sententiarum quamvis
singillatim enun'tiatarum et concessarum illa summa sequitur, quae iam
20   necessario concedatur, id est 'homo iste igitur / movetur'.'

IV

His[27] breviter constitutis singulas partes consideremus. Nam sunt primae[28] duae: una de his quae simpli'citer dicuntur, ubi est quasi materia
dialecticae, altera de his quae coniuncta dicuntur, ubi iam quasi opus'
apparet. Quae de simplicibus est vocatur de loquendo. Illa vero quae de
[7]   coniunctis est in tres partes dividitur. / Separata enim coniunctione verborum quae non implet sententiam, illa, quae sic implet sententiam, ut
nondum' faciat quaestionem vel disputatorem requirat, vocatur de elo-
quendo; illa, quae sic implet sententiam, ut de sen'tentiis simplicibus
iudicetur, vocatur de proloquendo; illa, quae sic comprehendit sententiam, ut de ipsa etiam' copulatione iudicetur donec perveniatur ad sum-
5   mam, vocatur de proloquiorum summa. Has ergo singulas / partes dili-
gentius explicemus.'

V

Verbum est uniuscuiusque rei[29] signum, quod ab audiente possit intellegi,
a loquente prolatum. Res est' quidquid vel sentitur vel intellegitur vel
latet. Signum est quod et se ipsum sensui et praeter se aliquid' animo
ostendit. Loqui est articulata voce signum dare. Articulatam autem dico
quae[30] comprehendi litteris' potest. Haec[31] omnia quae definita sunt,
10   utrum recte definita sint et utrum hactenus verba definitionis aliis / definitionibus persequenda fuerint, ille indicabit locus, quo[32] definiendi
disciplina tractatur. Nunc quod instat' accipe intentus. Omne verbum

---

26 etiam: +si OQG.   27 His: +igitur OQG.   28 primae: +et DB +rasura P.   29 om.
DBP.   30 quod G.   31 Haec: +autem OG.   32 quo: in quo P^{pc}OQG.

And if I agree to this, even though the two statements now conceded were stated singly, there follows from the connection of them a conclusion, which must be agreed to, namely, 'therefore, that man is moving.'[3]

CHAPTER IV. THE PARTS OF DIALECTIC[1]

Having given this brief exposition, let us now consider the parts [of dialectic] one by one. The first division is twofold: one concerning those things which are spoken simply, and this is, as it were, the raw material of dialectic; the other concerning those things which are spoken in combination, and in this we see, as it were, the finished product of dialectic. The part of dialectic which is about simple words is called 'on naming.'

[7] That which concerns combined words is divided into three parts. Leaving aside that combining of words which does not make a complete statement, there is, first, that which makes a complete statement but in such a way as not to require questioning or disputing. The part of dialectic concerning such statements is called 'on expressing.' There is, second, that combining of words which makes a complete statement in such a way that a judgment is made in respect of simple statements. The part of dialectic concerning such statements is called 'on asserting.' Finally, there are words which make a statement in such a way that a judgment is made in respect of the connection of statements in it so as to arrive at a conclusion. The part of dialectic dealing with such statements is called 'on concluding from assertions.' Therefore we shall carefully set forth these parts, one by one.[2]

CHAPTER V. SIGNIFICATION[1]

A word is a sign of any sort of thing. It is spoken by a speaker and can be understood by a hearer. A thing is whatever is sensed or is understood or is hidden.[2] A sign is something which is itself sensed and which indicates to the mind something beyond the sign itself.[3] To speak is to give a sign by means of an articulate utterance. By an articulate utterance I mean one which can be expressed in letters.[4] Whether all these things that have been defined have been correctly defined and whether the words used in definition so far will have to be followed by other definitions, will be shown in the passage in which the discipline of defining is discussed.[5] For the present, pay strict attention to the material at hand.

sonat. Cum enim est in scripto, non verbum sed verbi signum est; quippe|
inspectis a legente litteris occurrit animo, quid[33] voce prorumpat. Quid
enim aliud litterae scriptae[34] quam se| ipsas oculis,[35|] praeter se
voces animo ostendunt. Et[36] paulo ante diximus signum esse quod se
ipsum sensui et| praeter se aliquid animo ostendit. Quae legimus igitur

15 non verba sunt sed signa verborum. Sed ut, ipsa lit/tera cum sit pars
minima vocis articulatae, abutimur tamen hoc vocabulo, ut[37] appellemus
litteram etiam cum| scriptam[38] videmus, quamvis omnino tacita sit neque
ulla pars vocis sed signum partis vocis appareat, ita etiam| verbum ap-
pellatur cum scriptum est, quamvis verbi signum id est signum signifi-
cantis vocis non[39] ⟨verbum⟩[40] eluceat. Ergo| ut coeperam dicere omne
verbum sonat. Sed quod sonat nihil ad dialecticam. De sono enim verbi
agitur,| cum quaeritur vel animadvertitur, qualiter[41] vocalium vel dis-

20 positione[42] leniatur vel concursione dehiscat, item con/sonantium vel
interpositione nodetur vel congestione asperetur, et quot vel qualibus
syllabis constet, ubi poe|ticus rhythmus accentusque, ⟨quae⟩[43] a gram-
maticis solarum aurium tractantur[44] negotia.[45] Et tamen cum de his dis-
putatur,| praeter dialecticam non est. Haec enim scientia disputandi est.

[8] Sed cum[46] verba sint[47] ⟨signa⟩[48] rerum, quando de ipsis[49] / obtinent,
verborum autem illa, quibus de[50] his disputatur – nam cum de verbis
loqui nisi verbis nequeamus et| cum loquimur nonnisi de aliquibus rebus
loquimur – occurrit animo ita esse verba signa rerum, ut res esse| non
desinant. Cum ergo verbum ore procedit, si propter se procedit id est ut
de ipso verbo aliquid quaeratur| aut disputetur, res est utique disputationi

5 quaestionique subiecta, sed ipsa res verbum vocatur. Quidquid autem /
ex verbo non aures sed animus sentit et ipso animo tenetur inclusum,
dicibile vocatur. Cum vero verbum| procedit non propter se sed propter
aliud aliquid significandum, dictio vocatur. Res autem ipsa, quae iam|
verbum non est neque verbi in mente conceptio, sive habeat verbum
quo[51] significari possit, sive non habeat,| nihil aliud quam res vocatur
proprio iam nomine. Haec ergo quattuor distincta teneantur; verbum,

---

33 quod OQ.   34 inscriptae OQG.   35 oculis: + et G *Crecelius*.   36 ut *conj. Crecelius*.   37
ut: et ut DBPOQ.   38 scriptum DBPOQ.   39 *erasit* G *secl. Crecelius*.   40 *supplevi duce*
Hagen.   41 qualiter *conj. Usener*: quanta *codd*.   42   disputatione DBP^ac.   43 *supplevi*.
44 tractatur QG.   45 negotio P^pcG.   46 tunc G.   47 sunt G.   48   *suppl. Hagen*.   49
ipsis: +disputatur haec rerum vim *suppl. Hagen* scilicet intellectum *glossavit* G obtinent=
=τυγχάνουσιν(?).   50 quibus de: de quibus G.   51 quod DQ.

Every word is a sound, for when it is written it is not a word but the sign of a word. When we read, the letters we see suggest to the mind the sounds of the utterance.[6] For written letters indicate to the eyes something other than themselves and indicate to the mind utterances beyond themselves. Now we have just said that a sign is something which is itself sensed and which indicates to the mind something beyond the sign itself. Therefore, what we read are not words but signs of words. For we misuse the term 'letter' when we call what we see written down a letter, for it is completely silent and is no part of an utterance but appears as the sign of a part of an utterance; whereas a letter as such is the smallest part of an articulate utterance. In the same way [we misuse the term 'word'] when we call what we see written down a word, for it appears as the sign of a word, that is, not as a word but as the sign of a significant utterance. Therefore, as I said above, every word is a sound.

But sounds are not the concern of dialectic. We concern ourselves with the sound of words when we ask about or attend to the use of vowels to make speech lighter, or to the combination of vowels in a word, or again to the arrangement of consonants for articulation, or their concentration for asperity of speech, to the number and quality of syllables, or the matter of poetic rhythm and accent. All such matters having to do with hearing alone are treated by the grammarian. Nevertheless, when there is dispute about these subjects, it is a concern of dialectic, for dialectic is the science of disputing. Words are signs of things whenever they refer to them, even though those [words] by which we dispute about [words] are [signs] of words. For since we are unable to speak of words except by words and since we do not speak unless we speak of some things, the mind recognizes that words are signs of things, without ceasing to be things. When, therefore, a word is uttered for its own sake, that is, so that something is being asked or argued about the word itself, clearly it is the thing which is the subject of disputation and inquiry; but the thing in this case is called a *verbum*.[7] Now that which the mind not the ears perceives from the word and which is held within the mind itself is called a *dicibile*. When a word is spoken not for its own sake but for the sake of signifying something else, it is called a *dictio*. The thing itself which is neither a word nor the conception of a word in the mind, whether or not it has a word by which it can be signified, is called nothing but a *res* in the proper sense of the name. Therefore, these four are to be kept

dicibile,| dictio, res. Quod dixi verbum, et verbum est et verbum significat.

10   Quod dixi dicibile, verbum est, nec / tamen verbum, sed quod[52] in verbo intellegitur et animo continetur, significat. Quod dixi dictionem, verbum| est, sed quod iam illa duo simul id est et ipsum verbum et quod fit in animo per verbum significat. Quod| dixi rem, verbum est, quod praeter illa tria quae dicta sunt quidquid restat significat. Sed exemplis haec| illustranda esse perspicio. Fac igitur a quoquam[53] grammatico[54] – puerum interrogatum hoc modo: 'arma quae| pars orationis est?' quod dictum est 'arma', propter se dictum est id est verbum propter ipsum

15   verbum. / Cetera vero, quod ait 'quae pars orationis', non propter se, sed propter verbum, quod 'arma' dictum est,| vel animo sensa vel voce prolata sunt. Sed cum animo sensa sunt, ante vocem dicibilia erunt[55]; cum autem| propter id quod dixi proruperunt in vocem, dictiones factae sunt. Ipsum vero 'arma' quod hic verbum est,| cum a Vergilio pronuntiatum est, dictio fuit: non enim propter se prolatum est, sed[56] ut eo significarentur vel| bella quae gessit Aeneas vel scutum vel[57] cetera[58] quae

20   Vulcanus heroi[59] fabricatus est. Ipsa vero bella vel / arma, quae gesta aut ingestata[60] sunt ab Aenea – ipsa inquam quae, cum gererentur atque essent, videbantur,| quaeque si nunc adessent vel digito monstrare possemus aut tangere, quae etiamsi non cogitentur non eo| tamen fit ut non fuerint – ipsa ergo per se nec verba sunt nec dicibilia nec dictiones, sed res quae iam pro|prio nomine res vocantur. Tractandum est igitur nobis in hac parte dialecticae de verbis, de dicibilibus, de| dictionibus, de rebus. In quibus omnibus cum partim verba significentur partim non verba,

25   nihil est tamen[61], / de quo non verbis disputare necesse sit. Itaque de his primo disputetur per quae de ceteris disputare conceditur.|

VI

Igitur verbum quodlibet excepto sono – de quo bene disputare ad facultatem dialectici pertinet, non| ad dialecticam disciplinam, ut defensiones Ciceronis sunt quidem rhetoricae facultatis sed non his docetur ipsa| rhetorica – ergo omne verbum praeter id quod sonat quattuor quaedam

---

52 quod: tale quo G.   53 quodam G.   54 grammaticum OQ.   55 sunt OQ.   56 *om.* DBP[ac].   57 et DBP.   58 cetera: +arma G.   59 aerea G.   60 bella – ingestata: bella quae gesta vel arma quae gestata *emendavit Keil approbante Hagen.* ingestata: igestata D ingesta BPOQG.   61 enim G.

distinct: the *verbum,* the *dicibile,* the *dictio,* and the *res.* '*Verbum*' both is a word and signifies a word. '*Dicibile*' is a word; however, it does not signify a word but what is understood in the word and contained in the mind. '*Dictio*' is also a word, but it signifies both the first two, that is, the word itself and what is brought about in the mind by means of the word. '*Res*' is a word which signifies whatever remains beyond the three that have been mentioned. But I recognize that these must be illustrated by examples.

Let us take as an example a grammarian questioning a boy in this manner: "What part of speech is '*arma*'?"[8] '*Arma*' is said for its own sake, the word for the sake of the word itself. The other words that he speaks, 'what part of speech,' whether they are understood by the mind or uttered by the voice, are not an end in themselves but concern the word '*arma*.' Now when we consider words as perceived in the mind, prior to utterance they are *dicibilia,* but when they are uttered, as I have said, they become *dictiones.* As for '*arma*,' in the context we supposed, it is a *verbum,* but when it was uttered by Vergil it was a *dictio,* for it was not said for its own sake but in order to signify either the wars which Aeneas waged, or his shield, or the other arms which Vulcan made for the hero. These wars or weapons, which were waged or worn by Aeneas, which were seen when they were waged or when they were, which, if they were now present, we could touch or point to, which, even if they were not thought of, would not be prevented from having existed – these things are neither *verba* nor *dicibilia* nor *dictiones;* they are things which are called '*res*' in the proper sense of the name. In this part of dialectic we must treat of *verba, dicibilia, dictiones,* and *res.*[9] Among all these it is sometimes words that are signified, sometimes not; but there is nothing about which it is not necessary to dispute with words. Therefore we will first dispute about words, by means of which, as all agree, other disputes are carried out.

CHAPTER VI. THE ORIGIN OF WORDS[1]

Any word whatsoever though not its sound – since its sound belongs to the exercise of dialectic to dispute well about but does not belong to the science of dialectic, just as the speeches of Cicero belong to the exercise of rhetoric but rhetoric itself is not taught by means of those speeches – every word, I say, apart from its sound, necessarily raises questions about

necessario[62] vocat in quaestionem:| originem suam, vim, declinationem, ordinationem.|

[9] / De origine verbi quaeritur, cum quaeritur unde ita dicatur, res mea sententia nimis curiosa et minus[63]| necessaria. Neque hoc eo mihi placuit dicere, quod Ciceroni[A] quoque idem videtur.| Quis enim egeat auctoritate in re tam perspicua? Quod si omnino multum iuvaret explicare[64] originem verbi,| ineptum esset aggredi quod persequi profecto infinitum est.

5   Quis enim[65] reperire possit, quidquid dictum / fuerit unde ita dictum sit? Huc accedit quod ut somniorum interpretatio ita verborum origo pro cuiusque| ingenio iudicatur. Ecce enim 'verba' ipsa quispiam ex eo putat dicta quod aurem quasi verberent. Immo| inquit alius quod aërem. Sed quid nostra[66]? Non magna lis est, nam uterque a verberando huius vocabuli| originem trahit. Sed de transverso tertius vide quam rixam inferat. Quod enim verum nos ait[67] loqui oportet| odiosumque[68] sit[69] natura ipsa iudicante mendacium, 'verbum' a vero cognominatum est.

10   Nec ingenium quartum / defuit. Nam sunt qui verbum a vero quidem dictum putant, sed prima syllaba satis animadversa secundam| neglegi non oportere. 'Verbum' enim cum dicimus, inquiunt, prima eius syllaba verum significat, secunda| sonum. Hoc enim[70] volunt esse 'bum', unde Ennius sonum pedum 'bombum[71] pedum' dixit et βοῆσαι[72] Graeci| clamare et Vergilius[B] 'reboant silvae'. Ergo verbum dictum est quasi a[73] verum[74] boando| hoc est verum[75] sonando. Quod si ita est, praescribit

15   quidem hoc nomen, ne cum verbum facimus mentiamur; / sed vereor, ne ipsi qui dicunt ista mentiantur. Ergo ad te iam pertinet iudicare, utrum 'verbum' a verbe|rando an a vero solo an a[76] verum boando dictum putemus, an potius unde sit dictum non curemus, cum| quid significet intellegamus. Breviter tamen hunc locum notatum, hoc est de origine verborum, volo paulisper| accipias, ne ullam partem suscepti operis praetermississe videamur. Stoici autumant, quos Cicero in hac re| ut Cicero inridet, nullum esse verbum, cuius non certa explicari origo[77]

[A] Cicero, De natura deorum III, 24, 63.   [B] Vergil, Georgica III, 223.

62 necessaria G.   63 nimis P^{ac}Q non nimis OGP^{pc}.   64 explicaret DBP.   65 quis enim: quamvis quis G.   66 nostram DBP^{ac}.   67 nos ait: ait nos POQG.   68 otiosumquae D odiosum que G.   69 est *conj. Crecelius* fit *conj. Usener.*   70 autem OQG.   71 bumbum O bonbum D.   72 boesae D boesei B boese P^{ac}Q boece O boose G.   73 *om.* OG.   74 vere OQG.   75 vere OG.   76 *om. G.*   77 explicari origo: explicari Q ratio explicari G.

[9] four things: its origin, force, declension, and arrangement.[2] We ask about the origin of a word when we ask why it is called such and such; but in my opinion this is more a matter of curiosity than necessity. And I do not feel that I am bound to say this because it is the opinion of Cicero.[3] For who needs authority in such a clear matter? Even though it is a great help to explicate the origin of a word, it is useless to start on a task whose prosecution would go on indefinitely. For who is able to discover why anything is called what it is called? Discerning the origin of words is like the interpretation of dreams; it is a matter of each man's ingenuity. Let us take as an example 'verbum.'[4] One man thinks that verba are so called because, as it were, they verberent (strike or reverberate on) the ear; another man says they reverberate in the air. But what difference does this make to us? Their dispute is not great, for in either case the word is derived from 'verberans.' But a third man introduces a dispute. He says that we ought to speak what is true and that a lie is judged hateful by its own nature; therefore a verbum is named from 'verum' (true). And there is a fourth piece of cleverness, for there are those who agree that a verbum is named from 'verum,' but think that attention should not be directed to the first syllable to the neglect of the second. For when we say 'verbum,' they surmise, the first syllable signifies what is true, the second sound. And this latter they decide is 'bum.' Thus Ennius calls the sound of hooves "bombum pedum"[5]; and in Greek 'to shout' is βοῆσαι. And Vergil says, "reboant silvae" (the woods resound).[6] Therefore 'verbum' is derived, as it were, from 'verum boans,' that is, from a sounding of what is true. If this be so, this word 'verbum' certainly forbids us to lie when we produce a word. But I am afraid that those who say this are lying. Consequently it is up to you to judge whether you think 'verbum' comes from 'verberans' or from 'verum' alone or from 'verum boans' or whether its origin is a matter of indifference so long as we understand what it signifies.

Nevertheless I do wish for you to consider for a little while this topic which we have indicated briefly, namely, the origin of words, so that we might not seem to neglect any part of the work we have begun. The Stoics, whom Cicero ridicules in this matter, as only Cicero can, think that there is no word whose definite origin cannot be explained.[7] Because it would

20 possit. Et quia hoc modo eos urguere[78] / facile fuit, si diceres hoc infinitum esse, quibus verbis alicuius verbi originem interpretaris[79], eorum
[10] rursus / a te origo[80] ⟨quaeratur, aiunt hoc⟩[81] quaerendum[82] esse, donec
perveniatur eo, ut res cum sono verbi aliqua similitudine^l concinat, ut
cum dicimus aeris tinnitum, equorum hinnitum, ovium balatum, tuba-
rum clangorem, stridorem^l catenarum. Perspicis enim haec verba ita[83]
sonare ut ipsae res quae his verbis significantur. Sed quia sunt res^l quae
non sonant, in his similitudinem tactus valere, ut, si leniter vel aspere
5 sensum tangunt, lenitas vel / asperitas litterarum ut tangit auditum[84] sic
eis nomina pepererit: ut ipsum 'lene' cum dicimus leniter sonat.^l Quis
item 'asperitatem' non et ipso nomine asperam iudicet? Lene est auribus
cum dicimus 'voluptas',^l asperum cum dicimus 'crux'. Ita res ipsae af-
ficiunt[85], ut verba sentiuntur.[86] Mel, quam suaviter gustum res ipsa,^l
tam leniter nomine tangit auditum. 'Acre' in utroque asperum est. 'Lana'
et 'vepres', ut audiuntur verba, sic^l illa tanguntur. Haec quasi cunabula
10 verborum esse crediderunt, ubi sensus rerum cum sonorum sensu con-/
cordarent. Hinc ad ipsarum inter se rerum similitudinem processisse
licentiam nominandi; ut cum verbi causa^l 'crux' propterea dicta sit, quod
ipsius verbi asperitas cum doloris quem crux efficit asperitate concordat[87], 'crura'^l tamen non propter asperitatem doloris sed, quod longitu-
dine atque duritie[88] inter membra cetera sint ligno^l ⟨crucis⟩[89] similiora,
sic appellata sint. Inde ad abusionem ventum, ut usurpetur nomen[90] non
rei similis sed quasi^l vicinae. Quid enim simile habet significatio 'parvi'
10 et 'minuti', cum possit par⟨v⟩um[91] esse quod non modo nihil / minutum sit, sed aliquid etiam creverit? Dicimus tamen propter quandam
vicinitatem 'minutum' pro 'parvo'.^l Sed haec abusio vocabuli in potestate
loquentis est; habet enim 'parvum' ut 'minutum' non dicat[92]. Illud magis^l
pertinet ad id quod nunc volumus ostendere, quod, cum 'piscina' dicitur

78 eos urguere: eos arguere P eos urgere O eos surgere Q suggerere G.   79 interpretareris
G*Crecelius*.   80 originem G.   81 *suppl. Hagen*.   82 dum DB quaerendam G dicenda est
P faciendum *conj. Crecelius*.   83 ista BOQ.   84 auditam D audita P.   85 efficiunt B^{ac}P.
86 sentiantur D^{pc}BOP.   87 concordaret B concordet D.   88 duritiae BQ duritia G +et
codd. (secl. Crecelius).   89 crucis: *om.* DBPOQ.   90 *conj. Lovan. ex codice Carthusiano
nondum reperto*: tamen *codd*.   91 parum DBPOQ.   92 dicatur POQG.

be easy to refute them by saying that this would be an infinite process, for by whichever words you interpret the origin of any one word, the origin of these words would in turn have to be sought, they assert that you must search until you arrive at some similarity of the sound of the [10] word to the thing,[8] as when we say 'the clang of bronze,' 'the whinnying of horses,' 'the bleating of sheep,' 'the blare of trumpets,' 'the rattle of chains.' For you clearly see that these words sound like the things themselves which are signified by these words. But since there are things which do not make sounds, in these touch is the basis for similarity. If the things touch the sense smoothly or roughly, the smoothness or roughness of letters in like manner touches the hearing and thus has produced the names for them. For example, '*lene*' (smoothly) itself has a smooth sound. Likewise, who does not by the name itself judge '*asperitas*' (roughness) to be rough? It is gentle to the ears when we say '*voluptas*' (pleasure); it is harsh when we say '*crux*' (cross). Thus the words are perceived in the way the things themselves affect us. Just as honey itself affects the taste pleasantly, so its name, '*mel*,' affects the hearing smoothly. '*Acre*' (bitter) is harsh in both ways. Just as the words '*lana*' (wool) and '*vepres*' (brambles) are heard, so the things themselves are felt.[9] The Stoics believed that these cases where the impression made on the senses by the things is in harmony with the impression made on the senses by the sounds are, as it were, the cradle of words. From this point they believed that the license for naming had proceeded to the similarity of things themselves to each other. For example, take the words '*crux*' (cross) and '*crura*' (legs).[10] A *crux* is so called because the harshness of the word itself agrees with the harshness of the pain which the cross produces. On the other hand, *crura* are so called not on account of the harshness of pain but because their length and hardness as compared with the other members is more similar to the wood of the cross. Next we come to the transferred use of words, when a name is derived not from a similar thing but, as it were, from a nearby thing. For what is there similar between the signification of '*parvum*' (small) and the signification of '*minutum*' (diminutive), since something can be small which is in no way diminished but has even grown? Nevertheless we say '*minutum*' for '*parvum*' according to a certain proximity of signification. But this transferred use of a name is within the discretion of the speaker, for he has the word '*parvum*' and need not use '*minutum*.' This bears more on what I now wish to show, namely, that when '*piscina*' (fish-pond) is applied to

in balneis, in qua piscium nihil sit[|] nihilque simile piscibus habeat, videtur tamen a piscibus dicta[93] propter aquam, ubi piscibus vita est. Ita vocabulum non translatum similitudine sed quadam vicinitate usurpatum est[94]. Quod si[|] quis dicat homines piscibus similes natando fieri et inde

20 piscinae nomen esse natum, stultum est repugnare[95], / cum ab re neutrum abhorreat et utrumque lateat. Illud tamen bene accidit, quod hoc[96] uno exemplo diiudicare[|] iam possumus, quid distet[97] origo verbi quae de vicinitate adripitur ab ea quae de similitudine ducitur. Hinc[|] facta progressio usque ad contrarium. Nam 'lucus' eo dictus putatur quod minime luceat et 'bellum' quod[|] res bella non sit et 'foederis' nomen quod res foeda

[11] non sit. Quod si a foeditate porci dictum est, ut non/nulli volunt, redit origo[98] ad illam vicinitatem, cum id quod fit ab eo per quod fit nominatur. Nam ista[|] omnino vicinitas late patet et per multas partes secatur: aut per efficientiam, ut hoc ipsum a foeditate porci,[|] per quem 'foedus' efficiatur – aut per effecta[99], ut 'puteus', quod eius effectum[100] potatio est, creditur dictus –[|] aut per id quo[101] continetur[101a], ut 'urbem' ab orbe

5 appellatam volunt, quod auspicato locus[102] aratro circumduci[103] / solet, cuius rei et Vergilius^C meminit, ubi "Aeneas urbem designat aratro" – aut[|] per id quod continet[104], ut si quis 'horreum' mutata[105] littera affirmet ab hordeo nominatum – aut per[|] abusionem, ut cum 'horreum' dicimus et ibi[106] triticum conditur – vel a parte totum, ut 'mucronis' nomine,[|] quae summa pars gladii est, gladium vocamus[107] – vel a toto pars, ut 'capillus' quasi capitis pilus. Quid[|] ultra provehar? Quidquid aliud adnumerari potest, aut similitudine rerum et sonorum aut similitudine / rerum ipsarum aut vicinitate aut contrario contineri videbis

10 originem verbi. Quam persequi non quidem[|] ultra soni similitudinem possumus, sed hoc non semper utique possumus. Innumerabilia sunt enim verba,[|] quorum origo[108], de qua[109] ratio reddi[110] possit, aut non est, ut ego arbitror, aut latet, ut Stoici contendunt.[|] Vide tamen paulu-

---

^C Vergil, Aeneis V, 755.

93 dictam DBP. 94 Ita – est: *om. Crecelius errore.* 95 reputare Q refutare G. 96 *om.* QG. 97 quid distet: qui distet DBG^{ac} quid ista P. 98 ergo G. 99 effectum P^{pc}G. 100 effectus G. 101 quod OQG. 101a continet G. 102 loco G. 103 aratro circumduci: circumduci aratro OQG. 104 continetur G. 105 mutata: +d P^{pc}G. 106 ubi D. 107 vocant QG dicimus B. 108 *om.* QG. 109 de qua: *om.* G. atque *conj. Crecelius.* 110 reddi: +non *suppl. edd.*

baths, in which there are no fish and nothing like fish, the baths are, nevertheless, named from *pisces* (fish) because they contain water, in which fish live.[11] Thus the term is not applied by any similarity but is borrowed because of a certain proximity. But if someone should think that men are like fish because they swim and that the term '*piscina*' comes from this, it is foolish to oppose his theory, since neither explanation is incongruous with the thing and each is obscure. It is fortunate that we can see by means of one example the difference between the origin of a word which is drawn from proximity and the origin of a word which is derived from similarity. We can thus move on to contrariety. It is thought that a *lucus* (sacred grove) is so called because *minime luceat* (it has little light);[12] and *bellum* (war) because it is not *bella* (pretty); and that has the name '*foedus*' (alliance) which is not *foeda* (dishonorable). But if, as

[11]   many think, *foedus* is named from *foeditas porci* (the filthiness of the pig), then its origin is based on the proximity we were talking about, since that which is made is named from that by which it is made.[13] Proximity is a broad notion which can be divided into many aspects: (1) from influence, as in the present instance in which an alliance is caused by the filthiness of the pig; (2) from effects, as *puteus* (a well) is named, it is believed, from its effect, *potatio* (drinking); (3) from that which contains, as *urbs* (city) is named from the *orbis* (circle) which was by ancient custom plowed around the area after taking auspices at the place (Vergil mentions where "Aeneas laid out the city by plowing");[14] (4) from that which is contained, as it is affirmed that by changing a letter *horreum* (granary) is named after *hordeum* (barley); (5) or by transference, as when we say '*horreum*' and yet it is *triticum* (wheat) that is preserved there; (6) or the whole from a part, as when we call a *gladium* (sword) by the name '*mucro*' (point), which is the terminating part of the sword; (7) or the part from the whole, as when a *capillus* (hair) is named from *capitis pilus* (hair of the head). How do I go beyond that? Whatever else is added you will see that the origin of a word is contained either in the similarity of things and sounds, in the similarity of things themselves, in proximity, or in contrariety.

We cannot pursue the origin of a word beyond a similarity of sound, and at times we are unable to do even this. For an explanation can be sought for innumerable words for which there either is no origin, as I believe, or for which it is hidden, as the Stoics maintain.[15] But now con-

lum, quomodo perveniri putant ad illa verborum cunabula vel stirpem potius atque adeo[|] sementum, ultra quod quaeri originem vetant nec si

15 quisquam velit potest quicquam invenire. Nemo abnuit / syllabas, in quibus v littera locum obtinet consonantis, ut sunt in his verbis primae 'vafer, velum, vinum,[|] vomis, vulnus' crassum[111] et quasi validum sonum edere. Quod approbat etiam loquendi consuetudo, cum de[|] quibusdam verbis eas subtrahimus, ne onerent aurem. Nam unde[112] est, quod 'amasti' dicimus libentius quam[|] 'amavisti',[113] et 'abiit' non 'abivit' et in hunc modum innumerabilia. Ergo cum dicimus[|] 'vim', sonus verbi ut dictum est quasi validus[114] congruit rei quam significat. Iam ex illa vici-

20 nitate per id quod / efficiunt, hoc est quia[115] violenta sunt, dicta 'vincula'
[12] possunt videri et 'vimen' quo aliquid vinciatur. Inde[116] / 'vites', quod adminicula quibus innituntur[117] nexibus prendunt[118]. Hinc iam propter similitudinem incurvum senem[|] 'vietum' Terentius[D] appellavit. Hinc terra, quae pedibus itinerantium flexuosa et trita est,[|] 'via' dicitur. Si autem 'via', quod vi pedum trita est, magis[119] creditur dicta, redit origo ad illam vicinitatem.[|] Sed faciamus a similitudine vitis vel viminis hoc

5 est a flexu esse dictam. Quaerit ergo[120] me quispiam: quare / 'via' dicta est? respondeo: a flexu, quod flexum velut incurvum 'vietum' veteres dixerunt, unde 'vietos' [|]etiam[121] quae[122] cantho[123] ambiantur rotarum ligna vocant. Persequitur quaerere, unde 'vietum' flexum dicatur: et[|] hic respondeo a similitudine vitis. Instat atque exigit, unde ita[124] sit 'vitis' nomen; dico, quod vinciat ea quae[|] comprehenderit. Scrutatur, ipsum 'vincire' unde dictum sit; dicemus a vi. 'Vis' quare sic appellatur, requi-ret;[|] reddetur ratio, quod robusto et quasi valido sono verbum rei quam

10 significat congruit. Ultra quod requirat / non habet. Quot modis autem origo verborum corruptione vocum varietur, ineptum est persequi. Nam et[|] longum et minus quam illa quae dicta sunt necessarium.[|]

[D] Terentius, Eunuchus IV, 4, 21.

111 grassum DQ grossum G.   112 inde PG^{s.l.}.   113 amavisti: +et nosti quam novisti D.
114 validius DBPOQ.   115 qui Q quod O.   116 unde O nd G.   117 innitantur QG^{ac}.
118 *om.* Q prendent G pendent *edd.*   119 *om.* QG.   120 ergo: +a *edd.*   121 *om.* QG.
122 quod OQG.   123 *conj. Crecelius*: canthu O cantu DBPQG.   124 ista Q istud G.

sider for a moment the way in which the Stoics think they arrive at that cradle or root of words, or more precisely the seed of words, beyond which they deny that the origin can be sought or that anything can be found even if someone wishes to search. No one denies that syllables in which the letter 'v' functions as a consonant produce a dense and powerful kind of sound, for example, in the first syllable of the words '*vafer*,' '*velum*,' '*vinum*,' '*vomis*,' '*vulnus*.'[16] Thus ordinary usage approves our removing this sound from certain words lest they oppress the ear. For this reason we say '*amasti*' more readily than '*amavisti*' and '*abiit*' not '*abivit*.' There are innumerable examples of this. Therefore when we say '*vis*' (force), the sound of the word is, as I said, in a way powerful, congruous with the thing signified. We can see that chains are called '*vincula*' from a proximity with that which they do, that is, because they are *violenta* (forcible) and that a *vimen* (withe) is so called because by it something is

[12] *vinciatur* (bound). In the same way, *vites* (vines) are so named because they seize the stakes which they press upon by entwining.[17] On account of this Terence called a bent old man '*vietum*' (withered) by similarity.[18] And the ground which is winding and worn by the feet of travelers is called '*via*' (road). If it is thought to be called '*via*' more because it is worn by the *vis* (force) of feet, then the origin of the word returns to the realm of proximity. But let us derive it from a likeness to a vine or a withe, that is, from its winding; then if someone were to ask me why it is called '*via*,' I would answer, from winding, because the ancients called what is wound or bent '*vietus*' (withered). For this reason they called the woods of wheels which are encircled by iron '*vieti*.' Then another question arises. Why is something bent called '*vietus*'? And to this[19] I answer, from the similarity to *vites* (vines). This raises the question why a *vitis* has this name and I say that it is because it *vincit* (binds) that which it lays hold of. If it is asked why '*vincire*' itself is thus spoken, we say, from '*vis*.' If it is asked again why it is called '*vis*,' the reason can be given that the word, with its robust and powerful sound, is congruent with the thing that is signified. No further explanation is required. But it is useless to inquire about the number of ways in which the origin of words is varied by the alteration of utterances, for such an inquiry is long and it is not as crucial as these matters of which we have spoken.

VII

Nunc vim verborum, quantum res patet, breviter consideremus. Vis verbi
est, qua cognoscitur quan¦tum valeat. Valet autem tantum quantum movere audientem[125] potest. Porro movet audientem aut secundum se¦ aut
secundum id quod significat aut ex utroque communiter. Sed cum secun-
15   dum se movet, aut ad solum / sensum pertinet aut ad artem aut ad utrumque. Sensus aut natura movetur aut consuetudine. Natura movetur[126]
¦cum[127] offenditur, si quis nominet Artaxerxen regem, vel mulcetur,
cum audit Euryalum. Quis¦ enim etiamsi nihil umquam de his[128]
hominibus audierit, quorum ista sint[129] nomina, non tamen et[130] in illo
asperi¦tatem maximam et in hoc iudicet esse lenitatem? Consuetudine
movetur sensus, cum offenditur, si[131] quis verbi¦ causa vocetur 'Motta',
et non offenditur[131], cum audit 'Cottam'[132]. Nam hic ad soni suavitatem
20   vel insuavitatem / nihil interest, sed tantum valent aurium penetralia[133],
utrum per se transeuntes sonos quasi hospites notos an¦ ignotos recipiant.
Arte autem movetur auditor, cum enuntiato sibi verbo attendit, quae sit
[13]   pars orationis, vel / si quid aliud in his disciplinis quae de verbis tradun-
tur accepit. At vero ex utroque id est et sensu et arte¦ de verbo iudicatur,
cum id, quod aures metiuntur, ratio notat et nomen ita ponit[134], ut,
cum[135] dicitur[136] 'optimus',¦ mox, ut aurem longa una syllaba et duae
breves huiusce nominis percusserint, animus ex arte statim pedem¦ dac-
tylum agnoscit[137]. Iam[138] vero non secundum se, sed secundum id quod
5   significat verbum movet, quando per / verbum[139] accepto signo animus
nihil aliud quam rem ipsam intuetur, cuius illud signum est quod accepit:
ut¦ cum Augustino nominato nihil aliud quam ego ipse cogitor ab eo cui
notus sum, aut quilibet[140] hominum menti¦ occurrit[141], si forte hoc nomen
vel qui me ignorat audierit, vel qui alium novit qui Augustinus vocetur.
Cum¦ autem simul et secundum se verbum movet audientem et secundum id quod significat, tunc et ipsa enuntiatio¦ et id quod ab ea[142] nun-

---

125 movere audientem: audientem movere OQG.   126 movetur *conj. Hagen*: vitiavit
DBP vitiabit Q vitiatur G *om.* O iudicabit *conj. Crecelius.*   127 quod Q in eo quod G.
128 iis D.   129 sunt BG sicut Q.   130 *om.* QG.   131 si – offenditur: *om.* BPOQG.   132
Cotta DBP quoddam Q quiddam G.   133 sed tantum (tamen G) valet, aurium
penetralia utrum *maluit Hagen.*   134 ponitur P^{pc}OG.   135 *om.* QG.   136 dicimur G.
137 agnoscat *conj. Crecelius.*   138 Iam *conj. Crecelius*: scientiam DBPQ scientia OG sensum
conj. edd.   139 urbem DBP aurem *conj. Crecelius.*   140 quilibet *conj. Ben.*: cuilibet *codd.*
141 menti occurrit: mentio currit DB.   142 eo G.

CHAPTER VII. THE FORCE OF WORDS

Now we shall consider, as briefly as the matter allows, the force of words. The force of a word is that whereby the extent of its efficacy is learned. It has efficacy to the extent to which it is able to affect a hearer. Now a word affects a hearer either on its own account or on account of what it signifies or on account of both together.[1]

When a word affects a hearer on its own account, it does so either by sense alone or by art or by both. Sense is affected either by nature or by custom.[2] Sense is affected by nature when, for example, it is offended if someone names King Artaxerxes or is soothed when it hears 'Euryalus.' For who, even though he has heard nothing about the men who are named, will not suppose that there is great harshness in the former and mildness in the latter?[3] Sense is affected by custom when, for example, it is offended if someone is named 'Motta' and not offended when it hears 'Cotta.'[4] This has nothing to do with the smoothness or roughness of sound, but rather with the extent to which the passing sounds themselves are received by the inner chambers of the ears as familiar guests or as strangers. The hearer is affected by art when he [13] considers the part of speech of a word spoken to him or undertakes some other investigation belonging to those disciplines that are devoted to words. And the hearer is affected by both, that is the word is judged by sense and art, whenever reason takes note of what the ears take the measure of and a name is thus supplied. For example, if someone says 'optimus,' as soon as the one long and the two short syllables of this word strike the ear, the mind by art immediately recognizes a dactylic foot.

A word affects sense on account of what it signifies rather than on its own account when the mind receives a sign by a word and considers nothing other than the thing itself whose sign has been received. Suppose, for example, that Augustine has been named and a man to whom I am known thinks of nothing except I myself, or another man comes to mind if this name happens to be heard by someone who does not know me but knows another man called 'Augustine.'[5]

When, however, a word moves a hearer both on its own account and on account of what it signifies, then both the statement itself and that

tiatur[143] simul advertitur. Unde enim[144], quod non offenditur aurium

10 castitas, cum[145] audit[E] / manu ventre pene[146] bona patria laceraverat?
Offenderetur autem, si obscena pars| corporis sordido ac vulgari nomine
appellaretur, cum res eadem sit cuius utrumque vocabulum est, nisi quod|
in[147] illo turpitudo rei quae significata est decore verbi significantis[148]
operitur[149], in hoc autem sensum animumque| utriusque deformitas
fer⟨i⟩ret[150]: veluti non alia[151] meretrix, sed aliter tamen videtur eo
cultu, quo ante iudicem stare| adsolet, aliter eo quo in luxuriosi cubiculo

15 iacere[151a]. Cum igitur tantam vim tamque multiplicem appareat esse /
verborum, quam breviter pro tempore summatimque attigimus, duplex
hinc[152] ex consideratione[153] sensus nascitur: partim| propter explican-
dam veritatem, partim propter conservandum decorem; quorum primum
ad dialecticum, secundum| ad oratorem maxime pertinet. Quamvis enim
nec disputationem deceat ineptam[154] nec eloquentiam oporteat[155] esse
men|dacem, tamen et in illa saepe, atque adeo paene semper, audiendi
delicias discendi cupido contemnit et in hac imperitior| multitudo quod
ornate dicitur etiam vere dici arbitratur. Ergo cum appareat, quid sit

20 uniuscuiusque proprium, mani/festum est et disputatorem, si qua ei
[14] delectandi cura est, rhetorico colore aspergendum, et oratorem, si veri- /
tatem persuadere vult, dialecticis quasi nervis atque ossibus esse robo-
randum, quae ipsa natura in[156] corporibus| nostris nec firmitati[157]
virium subtrahere potuit nec oculorum offensioni[158] patere permisit.|

VIII

Itaque nunc propter veritatem diiudicandam, quod dialectica profitetur,
ex hac verborum vi, cuius| quaedam semina sparsimus, quae impedimen-

5 ta nascantur, videamus. Impedit enim auditorem ad veritatem[159] / vi-
dendam in verbis aut obscuritas aut ambiguitas. Inter ambiguum et ob-
scurum[160] hoc interest, quod in| ambiguo plura se ostendunt, quorum

---

[E] Sallust, Catilina 14, 2.

143 enuntiatur G.   144 enim: *om.* B +fit G +est P[pc] *Crecelius*.   145 quod OQ.   146
pone DB paene Q pede P[pc]G[pc].   147 *om.* BPOQ.   148 significanti DBP[ac]Q.   149 operire-
tur G oritur Q.   150 feriret *conj. Crecelius*: ferret DBOQ offenderet GP(*super rasuram*).
151 aria DBPO.   151a *conj. Hagen*: iaceret *codd.*   152 hic QG.   153 ex consideratione:
consideratio *conj. Crecelius*.   154 incomptam *conj. Hagen*.   155 oportet DBP[ac].   156 *om.*
G.   157 firmitate G.   158 offensionem DBOQ offensioni P[pc]G offensione *conj. Crecelius*.
159 varietatem DBP[ac]G[pc].   160 ambiguum et obscurum: obscurum et ambiguum OG.

which is stated by means of it are attended to together. Why is the chastity of the ears not offended when one hears "He had squandered his patrimony by hand, by belly, and by penis"?[6] It would be offended if the private part of the body were called by a low or vulgar name, though the thing with a different name is the same. If the shamefulness of the thing signified were not covered over by the propriety of the signifying word, then the base character of both would affect both sense and mind. Similarly, although a harlot *is* no different, she nevertheless looks different because of the clothes she wears when she stands before a judge than she looks when she lies in her dissolute bedchamber.

Thus since the force of words appears to be as complicated as our treatment of it has been brief and cursory, our reflections give rise to two ways of looking at the subject: partly through presenting truth, partly through observing propriety. The first of these is the concern of the dialectician, the second mainly of the orator. For although disputation need not be inelegant and eloquence need not be deceptive, still in the former the passion of learning often – indeed, nearly always – scorns the pleasures of hearing, while in the latter the more ignorant multitude think that what is said elegantly is said truly. Therefore, when it becomes apparent what is proper to each, it is clear that a disputer who has any concern to make his points appealing will sprinkle them with rhetorical color, and an
[14] orator who wishes to convince people of the truth will be strengthened by the sinews and bones, as it were, of dialectic, which are indispensable to the strength of the body but are not allowed to become visible to the eye.[7]

CHAPTER VIII. OBSCURITY AND AMBIGUITY[1]

Because the business of dialectic is to discern the truth, let us look now at the hindrances which may arise because of the force of words – a matter about which we have just now made some scattered remarks. Either obscurity or ambiguity hinders the hearer from discerning the truth in words. The difference between what is ambiguous and what is obscure is this: in what is ambiguous more than one thing is presented,

quid potius accipiendum sit ignoratur, in obscuro autem nihil aut parum[|]
quod attendatur apparet. Sed ubi parum est quod apparet, obscurum est
ambiguo simile: veluti si quis[|] ingrediens iter excipiatur aliquo bivio vel
trivio vel etiam ut ita dicam multivio loco, ibique[161] densitate nebulae[|]
nihil viarum quod est eluceat. Ergo a pergendo prius obscuritate terre-

10   tur[162]; at ubi aliquantum[163] rarescere nebulae / coeperint, videtur aliquid, quod utrum via sit an terrae proprius et [163a] nitidior color incertum
est. Hoc est obscurum ambiguo simile[164]. Dilucescente[|] autem[165] caelo
quantum oculis satis sit iam omnium viarum deductio clara est, sed qua
sit pergendum non[|] obscuritate sed ambiguitate dubitatur. Item sunt
obscurorum genera tria. Unum est quod sensui patet,[|] animo clausum
est: tamquam si quis malum punicum pictum videat, qui neque viderit
aliquando nec[|] omnino quale esset audierit, non oculorum est, sed animi,

15   quod cuius rei pictura sit nescit. Alterum / genus est, ubi res animo
pateret, nisi sensui clauderetur: sicuti est homo pictus[166] in tenebris.
Nam ubi oculis[|] apparuerit, nihil animus hominem pictum[167] esse du-
bitabit[168]. Tertium genus est, in quo etiam sensui absconditur,[|] quod
tamen si nudaretur nihilo magis animo emineret, quod genus est om-
nium obscurissimum: ut si imperitus[|] malum illud punicum pictum etiam
in tenebris cogeretur agnoscere.[|]

Refer[169] nunc animum ad verba, quorum sunt istae[170] similitudines.
20   Constitue[171] animo[172] quempiam grammaticum / convocatis discipulis
factoque silentio suppressa voce dixisse 'temetum', quod ab eo dictum
qui prope adsi[|]debant satis audierunt, qui remotius parum, qui autem
remotissime nulla omnino voce perstricti sunt. Horum[173][|] autem illi
⟨qui prope adsidebant, quid esset 'temetum' ignorabant, illi autem⟩[174]
qui remotiores erant nescio quo casu partim sciebant, quid esset teme-
tum, partim ignorabant; illos[|] vero, qui magistri vocem nec[175] accepe-
rant, quid esset temetum prorsus latebat; omnes obscuritate impedie-
bantur.[|] Et hic iam perspicis omnia illa[176] genera obscuritatum. Nam
25   qui de[177] auditu nihil dubitabant, primum illud / genus patiebantur, cui
simile est malum punicum ignorantibus sed in luce pictum. Qui noverant

---

161 ubique Q ubi POG.   162 tenetur QG.   163 aliquantulum P aliquanto OG aliquando Q.
163a sed *conj. Hagen.*   164 Hoc – simile: *om. Crecelius errore.*   165 *om.* QG.   166 vinctus
QG.   167 vinctum QG.   168 dubitavit DQ.   169 refert DB.   170 sunt istae: istae sunt
OG.   171 constitutae QG.   172 pone QG.   173 *hic deest unum folium in D (usque ad n.*
201). Ubi D deficit d *adhibemus.*   174 *suppl. Hagen.*   175 ne dBOP bene *conj. Crecelius.*
176 Illa: +tria QG.   177 *om. G.*

but one does not know which of them is to be understood; in what is obscure, on the other hand, nothing or very little appears to be considered. When a little appears, obscurity is similar to ambiguity, as when someone who is walking on a road comes upon a junction with two, three, or even more forks of the road, but can see none of them on account of the thickness of a fog. Thus at first he is kept from proceeding by obscurity. When the fog begins to lift a bit, something can be seen, but it is uncertain whether there is any road or any of the bright colors typical of the earth. This is obscurity similar to ambiguity. When the sky clears enough for good visibility, the direction of all the roads is apparent, but which is to be taken is still in doubt, not because of any obscurity but solely because of ambiguity.[2]

There are three kinds of obscurity. The first is when something is manifest to the senses but is closed to the mind, as, for example, if someone sees a picture of a red apple, who has never seen an apple or heard what it is; his failure to know what it is a picture of is due not to his eyes but to his mind. There is another kind of obscurity when the thing would be manifest to the mind if it were not closed to the senses, as in the case of a picture of a man which is in the dark; for as soon as it is visible to the eyes the mind will in no way doubt that a man is pictured. There is a third kind of obscurity, the most obscure of all three, when something is hidden to the senses and even if it were to be revealed nothing more would be clear to the mind, as when a man with no knowledge of apples tries to recognize a picture of an apple in the dark.

Now turn your attention to words, of which these are likenesses. Imagine a teacher of grammar who, when he had called his class together and gotten silence, said in a low voice, 'temetum' (wine).[3] Those who were seated nearby heard what he said quite distinctly; those who were some distance from him caught something of it; and those who were farthest from him heard no sound at all. Of these three groups, those who sat near him did not know what temetum is;[4] those who were further from him in some cases knew and in other cases, for some reason, did not know what temetum is; and those who did not hear his voice at all were utterly ignorant of what temetum is. All three groups were hindered by obscurity. And here you see all three kinds of obscurity. For those who had no doubt about what they heard experienced that first kind of obscurity which is similar to the case of those who saw the picture in the light and

verbum sed[l] auribus aut parum aut omnino non acceperant vocem, se-
cundo illo genere laborabant, cui similis est hominis[l] imago sed in non[178]
perspicuo aut omnino tenebricoso[179] loco. Qui autem non solum vocis
sed et significationis[l] verbi expertes erant, tertii generis, quod omnium
[15]   taeterrimum[180] est, caecitate involvebantur. Quod[181] autem dictum /
est[182] quiddam obscurum ambiguo simile, in his perspici potest, quibus
verbum erat quidem[183] notum sed vocem[l] nec penitus nullam nec omnino certam perceperant. Omnia igitur obscure loquendi genera vitabit[184], qui et[l] voce quantum satis est clara nec ore impedita[184a] et verbis
notissimis utetur. Vide nunc in eodem grammatici[l] exemplo, quam longe
aliter[185] impediat ambiguitas quam obscuritas verbi. Fac enim eos qui
5   aderant et satis / sensu accepisse vocem magistri et illum id[186] verbum
enuntiasse quod esset omnibus notum, ut puta fac eum[l] dixisse 'magnus'
et deinde siluisse. Attende, quae incerta[187] hoc audito nomine patiantur.
Quid si enim[188] dicturus est[l] 'quae pars orationis'? quid si de metris
quaesiturus 'qui[189] sit pes'? quid si de[190] historia[191] rogaturus[192] ut
puta 'magnus[l] Pompeius quot bella gesserit'? quid si commendandorum
carminum gratia[193] dicturus est 'magnus et[l] paene solus poeta Vergilius'?
10   quid si obiurgaturus neglegentiam discipulorum in haec deinde verba /
prorumpet[194] 'magnus vos erga studia[195] torpor invasit'? videsne re-
mota nebula obscuritatis illud quod[l] supra dictum est quasi eminuisse
multivium? nam hoc unum quod dictum est 'magnus' et nomen est et
pes[l] chorius est et Pompeius est et Vergilius et neglegentiae torpor et si
qua alia vel[196] innumerabilia non com[l]memorata sunt, quae tamen per
hanc enuntiationem verbi possunt intellegi.[l]

IX

Itaque rectissime a dialecticis dictum est ambiguum esse omne verbum.
15   Nec moveat quod apud Cice/ronem calumniatur Hortensius hoc modo
"ambigua se[197] aiunt audere[198] explicare dilucide. Idem[199] omne[l] ver-

---

178 in non: non in OG non Q.   179 tenebroso OQG.   180 deterrimum G.   181 quid
dBP[ac] cum Q.   182 esse dB.   183 quidem: +non *suppl. Hagen.*   184 vitavit dBP.   184a
impedito dBPO.   185 aliud QG.   186 illum id: illud id Q illud G.   187 quae incerta: qui
incerta Q quid incerti G.   188 eum Q *om.* G.   189 quid dP.   190 *om.* QG.   191 historiam
G.   192 interrogaturus G.   193 grama Q grammaticus G.   194 prorumpat QG.   195
studium G.   196 qua alia vel: qua alia P qualia dB.   197 ambigua se: ambiguose G.   198
audere *conj. Erasmus, Crecelius*: audire acute *codd.*   199 id est P[pc]O *om.* G.

had no knowledge of a red apple. Those who knew the word but heard a little of the utterance or none at all labored under the second kind of obscurity, as in the example of the man's portrait hung in a shadowy or completely dark place. But those who not only failed to hear the utterance but were ignorant of the signification of the word are enveloped in the blindness of the third kind, which is the worst of all three. What we [15] have called obscurity similar to ambiguity can be clearly seen in those to whom the word was indeed known but who did not apprehend the utterance entirely, or at least with any certainty. Therefore one who speaks in a loud enough voice, with good articulation, and using the best known words, will avoid all the varieties of speaking obscurely.

Notice now in the same example of the teacher of grammar how the ambiguity of a word hinders in a way very different from obscurity. Suppose that those who were with him heard the teacher's voice clearly and that he spoke a word known to everyone. For example, suppose he said 'magnus' (great) and then was silent. Notice the uncertainties that result from hearing the name. For what if he were going to say, 'What part of speech is it?' What if he were going to ask about its meter, 'What sort of foot is it?' What if he were going to raise a historical question, for example, 'Great Pompey, how many wars did he wage?'[5] What if he were going to say for the sake of commending some poems, 'Great and almost unique is the poet Vergil?' What if he were going to scold the negligence of the students, blurting out, 'Great laziness toward studies has come upon you!' Do you see that when the fog of obscurity is removed, the word which was spoken above is like a crossroads with many paths? For the one thing that is said – 'magnus' – is a name and a chorius and Pompey and Vergil and the laziness of negligence. And innumerable other things, even though not mentioned here, can also be understood as a result of this utterance of the word.

CHAPTER IX. AMBIGUITY[1]

Therefore it is said quite correctly by the dialecticians that every word is ambiguous.[2] It is beside the point when Hortensius in Cicero misrepresents them in this way: "They say that they listen for ambiguous words in order to explain them clearly; and yet they say that every word is

bum ambiguum esse dicunt. Quomodo igitur ambigua ambiguis explicabunt? Nam^l hoc est in tenebras extinctum lumen inferre.'^F Facete[200] quidem atque callide dictum, sed hoc est quod^l apud eundem Ciceronem Scaevola dicit Antonio^G "denique ut sapientibus diserte,^l stultis etiam vere videaris dicere." Quid enim aliud illo loco fecit Hortensius nisi

20 acumine ingenii et / lepore sermonis quasi meraco[201] et suavi poculo

[16] imperitis caliginem obfudit? Quod enim dictum est omne verbum / esse ambiguum de verbis singulis dictum est. Explicantur autem ambigua disputando et nemo utique verbis^l singulis disputat. Nemo igitur ambigua verba verbis ambiguis explicabit. Et tamen cum omne verbum ambiguum^l sit, nemo verborum[202] ambiguitatem[203] nisi verbis sed iam[204] coniunctis quae ambigua non erunt explicabit. Ut enim,^l si dicerem[205] 'omnis miles bipes est', non ex eo sequeretur, ut cohors ex militibus utique[206] bipedi-

5 bus ita[207] / constaret[208], ita, cum dico ambiguum esse omne verbum, non dico sententiam, non disputationem, quamvis^l verbis ista texantur. Omne igitur ambiguum verbum non ambigua disputatione explicabitur.^l

Nunc ambiguitatum genera videamus; quae prima duo sunt, unum in his etiam quae dicuntur, alterum^l quod in his solis quae scribuntur dubitationem facit. Nam et[209] si quis audierit 'acies' et si quis legerit, potest^l incertum habere, nisi per sententiam clarescat, utrum acies militum an

10 ferri an oculorum dicta vel scripta sit. / At vero si quis inveniat scriptum verbi causa 'leporem' nec appareat qua sententia positum sit, profecto dubi^ltabit, utrum paenultima huius verbi syllaba producenda sit ab eo quod est 'lepos' an ab eo quod est 'lepus'^l corripienda – quam scilicet non pateretur ambagionem[210], si accusativum huius nominis casum voce loquentis^l acciperet. Quod si quis dicat etiam loquentem male pronuntiare potuisse, iam non ambiguitate sed obscuritate^l impediretur auditor ex illo tamen genere quod ambiguo simile est, quia male latine pronun-

15 tiatum verbum / non in diversas notiones[211] trahit cogitantem sed ad id quod apparet impellit. Cum igitur duo ista genera inter^l se plurimum distent, primum genus rursus in duo dividitur. Nam quidquid dicitur et

---

^F Cicero, Hortensius frg.   ^G Cicero, De oratore I, 10, 44.

200 facete: facile QG (*s.l.add.* vel facete G) facie dBP^{ac} (facete P^{pc}).   201 *Hic iterum incipit* D.   202 verbum G.   203 ambiguum G.   204 etiam OG.   205 diceret G.   206 *om.* G. 207 ista DBPO tota *conj. Lovan.*   208 constarent DP.   209 *om.* G.   210 ambaginem D ambagem G.   211 nationes B rationes POQG.

ambiguous. How will they explain ambiguities by ambiguities? This is like bringing an unlighted lamp into the darkness."[3] Indeed, this is wittily and skillfully said, but this is what Scaevola says to Antony, also in Cicero: "Lastly, you should seem to speak clearly to the wise and truly to the ignorant as well."[4] For in that other passage what does Hortensius do except pour obscurity into a pure and sweet cup for the uninstructed by means of the sharpness of his genius and the charm of his speech? For when it is said that every word is ambiguous, it is said of isolated

[16] words. But ambiguities are explained through discussion and certainly no one carries on a discussion by means of isolated words. Thus no one explains ambiguous words by ambiguous words; and although every word is ambiguous, no one will explain the ambiguity of words except by means of words, but words already combined which will not be ambiguous. For if I were to say, 'Every soldier is two-footed,' it would not follow from this that a platoon made up of two-footed soldiers would itself be two-footed. So when I say that every word is ambiguous, I do not say that every statement or every discussion [is ambiguous], although these are built of words. Every ambiguous word will, therefore, be explained by non-ambiguous discussion.

Now let us look at the kinds of ambiguity. First, these two: one produces doubt even in spoken expressions, the other only in those that are written. For whether one hears 'point' or reads it, he might be uncertain whether the point of a military formation or of a sword or of vision is spoken or written about unless it is made clear by a statement in which it occurs.[5] And if someone comes upon the written word 'leporem,' for example, and it is not apparent in which sentence[6] it was located, he will be uncertain whether the penultimate syllable of the word is to be drawn out as a form of 'lepos' (wit) or whether it is to be shortened as a form of 'lepus' (hare). There would not be this degree of ambiguity if he had heard the accusative case of this name in the voice of a speaker. But if someone says that even a speaker can pronounce badly what he says, then the hearer is hindered not by ambiguity but by obscurity. Yet it is the kind of obscurity which is similar to ambiguity, because the word pronounced badly in Latin does not lead a thinker to different ideas but forces him to that which he thinks he heard.

Since these two kinds of ambiguity differ very greatly from each other, the first kind [that is, about what is said,] is again divided into two. For

per plura intellegi potest,¦ eadem scilicet plura aut non[212] solum vocabulo uno sed una etiam definitione contineri queunt aut tantum com¦-
muni tenentur vocabulo[212] sed diversis expeditionibus explicantur. Ea
quae una definitio potest includere[213] 'univoca'¦ nominantur, illis autem
quae sub uno nomine necesse est diverse definiri[214] 'aequivocis'[215] no-

20   men est. Prius ergo / consideremus univoca, ut, quoniam genus hoc iam
definitione patefactum est, illustrentur[215a] exemplis. Hominem¦ cum dicimus, tam puerum dicimus quam iuvenem, quam senem, tam stultum quam
sapientem, tam magnum¦ quam parvum, tam civem quam peregrinum,
tam urbanum quam agrestem, tam qui iam fuit quam qui nunc¦ est, tam
sedentem quam stantem, tam divitem quam pauperem, tam agentem
aliquid quam cessantem, tam¦ gaudentem quam maerentem vel neutrum.

25   Sed in his omnibus dictionibus nihil est, quod non ut hominis / nomen
accepit ita etiam hominis definitione claudatur. Nam definitio hominis

[17] est 'animal rationale / mortale'. Num[216] ergo quisquam potest dicere
animal rationale mortale iuvenem tantum, non etiam puerum¦ aut senem
esse[217], aut sapientem tantum, non etiam stultum? immo et ista et cetera
quae numerata sunt sicut¦ hominis nomine ita etiam definitione continentur. Nam sive puer sive stultus sive pauper sive etiam dormiens,¦ si
animal rationale mortale non est, nec homo est; est autem homo; illa

5   igitur etiam[218] definitione contineatur / necesse est. Et de ceteris quidem
nihil ambigetur. De puero autem parvo aut stulto seu prorsus fatuo aut
de¦ dormiente vel ebrio vel furente dubitari[219] potest, quomodo possint[220] esse animalia rationalia[221]. Potest omnino de¦fendi, sed ad alia
properantibus longum est. Ad id quod agitur illud satis: non esse istam[222]
definitionem hominis¦ rectam et ratam, nisi et omnis homo eadem contineatur et praeter hominem nihil. Haec sunt igitur univoca,¦ quae non
solum nomine uno sed una etiam eiusdem nominis definitione claudan-

10   tur[223], quamvis et inter se pro/priis nominibus et definitionibus dis-
tingui possint[224]. Diversa enim nomina puer, adulescens, dives, et pauper,
liber,¦ et servus, et si quid aliud differentiarum est; ideo diversas[225] inter

---

212 non-vocabulo: non solum vocabulo uno Q (*per homoioteleuton*) uno vocabulo et una
interpretatione aut tantum uno v. G.   213 potest includere: est includere DB includit P.
214 diverse definiri: definiri diverse OG.   215 aequivoci G.   215a illustretur BO.   216 non
G.   217 puerum – esse: senem aut puerum et cetera G.   218 *om.* G.   219 dubitare QG^(ac).
220 sint P possunt G.   221 rationabilia OG.   222 ista DB.   223 clauduntur G.   224 possunt G.   225 diversas: et G.

whenever something is said and can be understood in more than one
way, these ways can either be included in a single name and a single
definition or they are held together only by a name but are separated
out by means of definitions. Those which one definition can include are
called 'univocal,' but the name for those which must be variously defined
under a single name is 'equivocal.'[7] First, we shall consider univocals,
and since this kind is already clear from the definition, they will be illustrated by examples. When we speak of a man we speak equally of a boy
and of a young man and of an old man, equally of a fool and of a wise
man, equally of someone large and of someone small, of a citizen and a
foreigner, of a city-dweller and a country-dweller, of one who was and
of one who now is, of someone sitting and of someone standing, of a
plutocrat and a pauper, of one doing something and of one doing nothing,
of one who rejoices and of one who mourns and of one who does neither.
Among all these expressions[8] there is not one which does not accept the
name 'man' in such a way as to be included by the definition of man.
[17]   For the definition of 'man' is 'a rational, mortal animal.'[9] Can anyone
say that only a youth is a rational, mortal animal and not also a boy
or an old man, or that only a wise man is and not also a fool? On the
contrary, all these and the others which were listed above are contained
in the name of man in such a way as to be contained in the definition as
well. For whether it is a boy or a fool or a pauper or even someone sleeping, if it is not a rational, mortal animal, it is not a man; but it is a man.
Therefore it is necessarily contained in that definition. And about the
others mentioned there should be no doubt. One may wonder how a boy
who is small and stupid, or at least silly, or a man who is sleeping or
drunk or in a rage, can be rational animals. This can certainly be defended,
but it would take too long to do this because we must hasten on to other
subjects. For the matter at hand it is enough to say that the definition
of 'man' is correct and certain only if it includes every man and nothing
beyond men. Therefore univocals are those which are included not only
in one name but also in a single definition of that name, even though
they can be distinguished among themselves by their own special names
and definitions. For these names are different, 'boy,' 'youth,' 'plutocrat'[10]
and 'pauper,' 'slave' and 'freeman,' and, if there are such, [the names for]
other differences. Thus they have special definitions different from one

se proprias definitiones habent[226]. Sed ut illis¹ unum commune nomen
est homo, sic et[227] animal rationale mortale definitio una communis est.¹

X

Nunc aequivoca videamus, in quibus[228] ambiguitatum perplexio prope
infinita silvescit. Conabor tamen¹ eas in genera certa distinguere. Utrum
15   autem conatum meum facultas sequatur, tu iudicabis. Ambiguitatum /
igitur quae ab aequivocis veniunt prima genera tria sunt: unum ab arte,
alterum ab usu, tertium ab utroque.¹ Artem nunc dico propter nomina,
quae in verborum disciplinis verbis imponuntur. Aliter enim definitur
apud¹ grammaticos, quid sit⟨nomen, aliter quid sit pes dactylus, aliter
quid sit⟩[229] aequivocum[230]. Et tamen unum hoc[231] quod dico 'Tullius'
et nomen¹ est et pes dactylus et aequivocum. Itaque si quis ex me efflagitet
ut definiam quid sit 'Tullius', cuiuslibet¹ notionis explicatione respondeo?
Possum enim recte dicere: Tullius est nomen, quo[232] significatur homo,
20   summus / quidam orator, qui Catilinae coniurationem consul oppressit.
Subtiliter attende me nomen ipsum definisse.¹ Nam si mihi Tullius ipse
ille, qui si viveret digito demonstrari posset, definiendus foret, non dicerem: Tullius¹ est nomen, quo[233] significatur homo; sed dicerem: Tullius
est homo et ita cetera adiungerem. Item respondere¹ possem hoc modo:
Tullius est pes dactylus his litteris constans – quid enim nunc opus est
eas litteras¹ enumerare[234]? Licet etiam illud dicere: Tullius est verbum,
25   per quod aequivoca inter se sunt[235] omnia[236] cum hoc ipso / quae supra
dicta sunt et si quid aliud inveniri potest. Cum igitur hoc unum quod
dixi 'Tullius' secundum¹ artium vocabula tam varie mihi definire licue-
rit[237], quid dubitamus esse ambiguorum genus ex aequivocis¹ venientium,
quod merito dici possit ex arte contingere? Diximus enim aequivoca esse,
quae non ut uno¹ nomine ita etiam una definitione possunt teneri. Vide
nunc alterum genus[238], quod ex loquendi usu venire¹ memoravimus.
Usum nunc appello illud ipsum propter quod verba cognoscimus. Quis
30   enim verba propter / verba conquirat et colligat? Itaque iam constitue

226 habebunt G.   227 *om.* G.   228 in quibus: *om.* DBP.   229 *supplevi.*   230 aequivocum: +aliter apud dialecticum *suppl. Lovan. codicem Carthusianum nondum repertum
secuti.*   231 unum hoc: hoc unum G.   232 quod DQ.   233 quod DQ.   234 opus –
enumerare: eas litteras opus est numerare OG.   235 aequivoca – sunt: aequivocantur inter
se G.   236 nomina P.   237 licuit G.   238 genus: +est G.

another. But just as the one name 'man' is common to them, so the definition 'rational, mortal animal' is common to them.

CHAPTER X. EQUIVOCATION[1]

Now let us look at equivocals, in which the tangle of ambiguities runs
wild, almost without limits. Nevertheless I shall attempt to sort them
into definite kinds and you may judge whether my attempt succeeds.[2]

There are three main kinds of ambiguity that are based on equivocals.
One is from art, another from use, and a third from both of these together.
I say art because of the names which are imposed upon words by the
disciplines dealing with words.[3] For grammarians define a word in one
way when they say that it is a name, in another way when they say it is
a dactylic foot, and in another way when they say that it is an equivocal.
This one word which I speak, 'Tullius,' is both a name and a dactylic
foot and an equivocal. Hence if someone asks me to define 'Tullius,' I
may reply with an explication of one or another of these notions. I can
correctly say that 'Tullius' is a name by which a man is signified, the
greatest orator, who as consul overcame the conspiracy of Catiline.[4]
Observe carefully that I have defined the name itself. For if one had
demanded of me that I define Tullius himself, to whom I would be able
to point with my finger if he were living, I would not say that Tullius is
a name by which a man is signified, but I would say that Tullius is a
man, and then I would add other things in that fashion. I could also say
that 'Tullius' is a dactylic foot consisting in these sounds – is it necessary
to enumerate them? It is also possible to say that 'Tullius' is a word by
which all the things said above are equivocal among themselves with this
very expression.[5] Since, therefore, this one word which I spoke, namely,
'Tullius,' can be so variously defined by me according to the terms of art,
can we doubt that there is a type of ambiguity that is derived from
equivocals and which may be rightly said to come from art? For we have
said that equivocals are those which cannot be contained by one definition as they can by one name.

Look now at another kind of equivocals which we said comes from
the use of the speaker.[6] Now I call 'use' that for the sake of which we
learn words. For who seeks and collects words for their own sake? And
so now let us suppose someone who hears what is spoken, but in such

[18]   aliquem sic audire, ut ei notum sit nihil de partibus orationis / aut de
metris quaeri aut de verborum aliqua disciplina. Tamen adhuc potest,
cum dicitur 'Tullius', aequi^lvocorum ambiguitate impediri. Hoc enim
nomine et ipse qui fuit summus orator et eius picta imago vel^l statua et
codex quo eius litterae continentur et si quid est in sepulchro eius ca-
daveris significari potest.^l Diversis enim notionibus[239] dicimus: 'Tullius
5   ab interitu patriam liberavit' et 'Tullius inauratus in Capitolio stat' et /
'Tullius totus tibi legendus est' et 'Tullius hoc loco sepultus est'. Unum
enim nomen, sed diversis haec omnia^l definitionibus explicanda sunt.
Hoc igitur genus aequivocorum est, in quo iam nulla de disciplina ver-
borum^l oritur ambiguitas sed de ipsis rebus quae significantur. At si
utrumque confundat audientem vel legentem,^l sive quod ex arte sive
quod ex loquendi usu dicitur, nonne tertium genus recte adnumerabitur?
cuius^l exemplum in sententia quidem apertius apparet, ut si quis dicat:
10   'multi dactylico metro scripserunt ut est / Tullius'. Nam hic incertum,
utrum 'Tullius' pro exemplo dactyli pedis an dactylici[240] poetae positum
sit, quorum^l illud ex arte hoc ex usu loquendi accipitur. Sed in simplicibus
etiam verbis contingit, tamquam si hoc ver^lbum grammaticus audienti-
bus discipulis enuntiet, ut[241] supra ostendimus.^l
   Cum igitur haec tria genera manifestis inter se rationibus differant,
rursum primum genus in duo^l dividitur. Quidquid enim ex arte verborum
15   facit ambiguitatem, partim sibi pro exemplo esse potest, partim / non
potest. Cum enim definiero, quid significet[242] 'nomen', possum hoc ipsum
exempli gratia supponere. Etenim^l hoc quod dico 'nomen' utique nomen
est; hac enim lege per casus flectitur[243] cum dicimus "nomen, nominis,^l
nomini et cetera". Item cum definio[244] quid significet 'dactylus pes'[245],
hoc ipsum potest esse pro exemplo. Etenim^l cum dicimus 'dactylus', unam
longam syllabam et duas deinde breves enuntiamus. At vero cum defini-
tur^l 'adverbium' quid significet, non potes[246] hoc ipsum in exemplum
20   dicere[247]. Etenim cum 'adverbium' dicimus, / haec ipsa enuntiatio nomen[248] est. Ita secundum aliam notionem adverbium utique adverbium
est et non[249] est^l nomen, secundum aliam vero adverbium non est adverbium quia nomen est. Item 'pes creticus' quando quid^l significet defi-

---

239 rationibus QG.   240 dactylici *conj. Erasmus, Lovan.*: dactyli et *codd.*   241 et DB.
242 significat G.   243 plectitur DB.   244 definiero *conj. Crecelius.*   245 pes *conj. Keil*:
per DBPOQ *om.* G *secl. Crecelius.*   246 potest DBPOQ.   247 dici *conj. Crecelius.*   248
non O.   249 *conj. Ben.* nomen *codd.*

[18] a way that he pays no attention to parts of speech or meter or anything else having to do with the study of words. It is still possible for him to be hindered by the ambiguity of equivocals when someone says 'Tullius,' for by this name can be signified the man who was the greatest orator and his picture or statue and a book which contains his writings and his corpse in the grave, if there is anything of it left. It is with different things in mind that we say, 'Tullius freed the fatherland from ruin' and 'Tullius stands gilded on the Capitol,' and 'You must read all of Tullius,' and 'Tullius is buried in this place.'[7] For there is one name, but all of these things must be explained by different definitions. This, therefore, is the kind of equivocals in which ambiguity arises not from the study of words but from the very things that are signified.

But if a combination of both confuses a hearer or a reader, whether it is called 'from art' or 'from the use of the speaker,' should not a third kind be recognized? This will become clearer if we illustrate with the statement, 'Many wrote in dactylic meter, for example, Tullius.' It is uncertain in this statement whether 'Tullius' is given as an example of a dactylic foot or as a dactylic poet. Of these, the former arises from art, the latter from ordinary use. This can also occur in simple words, as when a teacher of grammar utters this word to his listening students, as we pointed out above.

Since these three kinds differ among themselves for clear reasons, the first kind is again divided into two. For whatever causes ambiguity from the art of words can in some cases be examples of themselves and in other cases cannot. When I define what 'name' signifies, I am able to give this itself as an example, for 'name' is certainly a name, since it is declined regularly by case, as we say *nomen, nominis, nomini,* and so on.[8] Likewise when I define what 'dactylic foot' signifies, the word itself can be an example. For when we say 'dactylus,' we pronounce one long syllable and then two short ones. But when we define what 'adverb' signifies, we cannot use the word as an example of itself, since this expression itself is a name. Thus in one sense an adverb is certainly an adverb and not a name, but in another sense 'adverb' is not an adverb because it is a name. Likewise when we define what 'creticus' signifies, we cannot use it as an example

nitur, non potest hoc ipsum exemplo esse. Haec enim enuntiatio quan-
do[250] dicimus 'creticus' prima| longa syllaba deinde duabus brevibus
constat, quod autem significat longa syllaba et brevis et longa est. Ita|
et hic secundum aliam notionem creticus nihil est aliud quam creticus

25   et dactylus non est, secundum aliam / vero creticus non est creticus quia
dactylus est.|

Secundum item[251] genus, quod iam praeter disciplinas verborum ad
loquendi usum dictum est pertinere,| duas habet formas. Nam aequivoca
inde[252] sunt aut ex eadem origine[253] aut ex diversa. Ex eadem origine
appello|, quae quamvis uno nomine ac non sub una definitione teneantur,

[19]   uno tamen quasi fonte demanant; ut est / illud quod 'Tullius' et homo
et statua et codex et cadaver intellegi potest. Non possunt quidem ista
una| definitione concludi, sed tamen unum habent fontem, ipsum scilicet
verum hominem, cuius et illa statua et| illi libri[254] et illud cadaver est.
At[255] cum dicimus 'nepos', longe ex diversa origine filium filii et luxurio-
sum| significat[256]. Haec ergo distincta teneamus, et vide illud genus,

5   quod ex eadem origine appello, in quae iterum[257] / dividatur. Nam dividitur in duo, quorum unum translatione alterum declinatione contin-
git[258]. Translationem| voco cum vel similitudine unum nomen fit multis
rebus, ut 'Tullius' et ille in quo magna eloquentia fuit et| statua eius dici-
tur – vel ex toto cum pars cognominatur ut cum cadaver eius[259] Tullius
dici potest – vel ex| parte totum ut cum 'tecta' dicimus totas domos – aut
a genere species: 'verba' enim principaliter omnia dicuntur[260]| quibus
loquimur, sed tamen verba proprie nominata sunt quae per modos et per

10   tempora declinamus – aut / a specie genus: nam cum 'scholastici' non
solum proprie sed et primitus dicantur hi, qui adhuc in scholis| sunt, in
omnes tamen qui in litteris vivunt nomen hoc usurpatum est – aut ab
efficiente effectum ut 'Cicero' est| liber Ciceronis – aut ab effecto efficiens
ut 'terror' qui terrorem facit – aut a continente quod continetur,| ut
'domus' etiam qui in domo sunt dicuntur – aut conversa vice ut 'castanea'
etiam[261] arbor dicitur[262] – vel| si quid aliud inveniri[263] potest, quod ex

15   eadem origine quasi transferendo cognominetur. Vides ut arbitror, /

250 quod DBPO.   251 igitur G.   252 dicta G.   253 origine: +venientia G.   254 illi
libri: ille liber G.   255 ut DBPQ ex diversa origine ut G.   256 significet G.   257 item QG.
258 contigit DB.   259 illius OG.   260 omnia dicuntur: dicuntur omnia O dicunt Romani
G.   261 *om.* G.   262 dicitur: +quae non est OQG +et fructus B.   263 invenerit D in-
venire P.

of itself. For when we utter this expression 'creticus,' there is first a long syllable and then two short ones, but what it signifies is a long syllable, then a short and a long. Thus here, too, in one sense a creticus is none other than a creticus and is not a dactyl; in another sense 'creticus' is certainly not a creticus because it is a dactyl.

Now the second kind, which has been said to pertain to the use of the speaker apart from the disciplines dealing with words, also has two forms. For equivocals are either from a single source or from different sources. I say that equivocals have a single source when they are included by a single name and, though they are not included by a single definition, still [19] they flow as from a single spring, for example, in the case above where 'Tullius' can be understood as a man and a statue and a book and a corpse. Although these are not included under one definition, they have one source, namely, the man himself whose statue and books and corpse they are. On the other hand, '*nepos*' signifies both a son's son and a spendthrift from very different sources.[9]

Let us, therefore, keep these distinct and look further at the first kind, which I say comes from the same source. It is once again to be divided into two classes, of which one happens through transference, the other through declension. I call it transference (1) when by similarity one name is used of many things, as both the man, renowned for his great eloquence, and his statue can be called 'Tullius.' Or (2) when the part is named from the whole, as when his corpse can be said to be Tullius; or (3) the whole from the part, as when we call whole houses 'roofs.' Or (4) the species from the genus, for '*verba*' is used chiefly of all the words by which we speak, although the words which we decline by mood and tense are named '*verba*' in a special sense. Or (5) the genus from the species, as 'scholars' were originally and properly those who were still in school, though now all who pursue a literary career use this name. Or (6) the effect from the cause, as 'Cicero' is a book of Cicero's. Or (7) the cause from the effect, as something is a terror which causes terror. Or (8) what is contained from the container, as those who are in a house are called a household. Or (9) vice versa, as a tree is called 'chestnut.'[10] Or if any other manner is discovered in which something is named by a transfer, as it were, from the same source. You see, I believe, what makes for am-

quam faciat in verbis ambiguitatem. Quae autem ad eandem originem
pertinentia condicione declinationis¹ ambigua esse diximus, talia sunt.
Fac verbi causa quemquam dixisse 'pluit', ⟨∗∗∗⟩²⁶⁴ et haec diverse utique
definienda¹ sunt. Item 'scribere' qui dicit, incertum est utrum infinitivo²⁶⁵
activi an imperativo passivi pronuntiaverit. 'Homo'¹ quamvis unum
nomen sit et una enuntiatio, tamen fit aliud ex nominativo aliud ex
vocativo ²⁶⁵ᵃ quomodo ²⁶⁶¹ 'doctus' et 'docte' ubi enuntiatio quoque di-

20 versa est. ['Doctius' aliud est cum dicimus 'doctius mancipium', / aliud
cum dicimus 'doctius illo iste disputavit'.]²⁶⁷ Declinatione igitur ambiguitas orta est. Nam declina¹tionem nunc appello, quidquid sive per
voces sive per significationes flectendo verba contingit. 'Hic doctus'¹
enim²⁶⁸ et 'o docte' etiam²⁶⁹ per voces flexum est, 'hic homo' autem et
'o homo' per solas significationes. Sed¹ hoc genus ambiguitatum minuta-
tim concidere ac persequi paene infinitum est. Itaque locum ipsum hac-
tenus¹ notasse suffecerit, ingenio praesertim tuo. Vide nunc ea quae²⁷⁰

25 diversa origine veniunt. Nam et²⁷¹ ipsa divi/duntur adhuc in duas
primas formas, quarum una est, quae contingit diversitate linguarum: ut,
cum dicimus¹ 'tu'²⁷², haec una vox aliud apud Graecos aliud apud nos

[20] significat. Quod genus notandum omnino²⁷³ fuit; non / enim praescrip-
tum est unicuique, quot²⁷⁴ linguas nosset aut quot²⁷⁵ linguis disputaret.
Altera forma est, quae in²⁷⁶¹ una quidem lingua facit ambiguitatem, diversa tamen eorum origine, quae in uno vocabulo significantur²⁷⁷, quale¹
est illud quod de nepote supra posuimus. Quod rursus in duo scinditur.
Aut enim sub eodem genere partis¹ orationis fit – tam²⁷⁸ nomen est enim
nepos cum filium filii, quam cum luxuriosum significat – aut sub²⁷⁹ di-

5 verso: / nam non solum aliud est cum dicimus 'qui'²⁷⁹ ⟨∗∗∗ aliud⟩²⁸⁰

---

264 *puto supplendum esse e.g.*: incertum est utrum praesenti tempori an praeterito pronuntiaverit.   265 infinito DP.   265a *Hic desinit* D; *pro reliqua parte tractatus adhibemus* d.
266 quomodo *conj. Hagen*: quam *codd.* quam ambiguitatem vitabit qui vocabulum aliquod
addet ut *conj. Crecelius.*   267 *Haec verba secludenda aut alio loco inserenda puto quippe quae
argumentationem interrumpunt.*   268 *om.* G.   269 tantum G.   270 quae: +ex G.   271 *om.*
G.   272 istuc QG.   273 notandum omnino: non tantum omnino Q non tamen omnis
novis *conj. Lovan. corruptelam, fortasse lacunam suspicor.*   274 quod dᵃᶜBQG.   275 quod
dᵃᶜOQG.   276 *om.* G.   277 significatur dBPO.   278 *om.* G.   279 sub – qui: *om.* Q etiam
sub alio genere fit partis orationis G.   280 *lacunam indicavit Crecelius.*

biguity in words. But those which we have said are ambiguous relative to a single source because of declension are such as the following. Take, for example, someone saying '*pluit*.' This can certainly be taken in different ways.[11] Again, if he were to say '*scribere*,' it is uncertain whether he has uttered the active infinitive or the passive imperative. '*Homo*' (man), although it is a single name and a single utterance, does one thing in the nominative case and another in the vocative, as do '*doctus*' and '*docte*' where the utterance is different. '*Doctius*' is one thing when we say '*doctius mancipium*' (the more learned slave), another when we say '*doctius illo iste disputavit*' (this man disputed more learnedly than that one).[12] Therefore ambiguity has its origin in declension, understanding by declension whatever happens as a consequence of changing words either in utterance or in signification. For '*hic doctus*' and '*o docte*' are changed in utterance as well; '*hic homo*' and '*o homo*' in signification alone. But to pursue and defeat, one by one, this kind of ambiguities is an endless task. And so it should be enough to take note of the topic and leave the rest to your ingenuity.

Now let us look at ambiguities which come from different sources. These are again divided into two primary forms. One depends on the diversity of languages. Thus when we say '*tu*,' this one utterance signifies one thing to the Greeks and another thing to us.[13] This kind ought merely to be noted; for it is not necessary for anyone [to study it, unless] he knows or disputes in several languages.[14] The other form is that which produces ambiguity in one language; nevertheless the things that are signified by a single word have different sources, just as we showed above in the case of '*nepos*.'[15] This is divided again into two. It occurs either under the same kind of part of speech, as '*nepos*' is just as much a name when it signifies a son's son as when it signifies a spendthrift. Or it occurs under different parts of speech, for '*qui*' can be not only a pronoun but,

[20]

ut dictum est[281] 'qui scis᷑ ergo istuc nisi periculum feceris',[H] sed etiam illud pronomen, hoc adverbium.|

Iam ex utroque id est et ex arte et ex usu verborum, quod in aequivocis tertium genus posueramus,| tot ambiguitatum formae possunt existere quot[282] in duobus superioribus enumeravimus[283]|.

Restat illud genus ambiguum, quod in scriptis solis reperitur, cuius
10   tres sunt species. Aut enim spatio / syllabarum fit tale ambiguum aut acumine aut utroque: spatio[284], ut cum scribitur 'venit' de tempore incertum| est propter occultum primae syllabae spatium; acumine autem, ut cum scribitur 'pone' utrum ab eo quod est| 'pono' an ut dictum est[J] 'pone sequens namque hanc dederat Proserpina| ⟨legem'⟩[285] incertum est propter latentem acuminis locum; at vero ex utroque fit, ut est quod superius de lepore| diximus. Nam non solum producenda sed acuenda etiam est paenultima syllaba huius verbi, si ab eo quod est 'lepos', non
15   ab eo quod / est 'lepus' deflexum est.

[H] Terentius, Andria III, 3, 33.   [J] Vergil, Georgica IV, 487.

281 est: +a Terentio G.   282 quod dO.   283 enumerabimus dBO posueramus QG.   284 spatio: +autem G.   285 *suppl.* G *ex loco Vergilii: om.* dBPOQ.

as in the line "*Qui scias ergo istuc nisi periculum feceris?*" (How do you know unless you make a try?),[16] it can be an adverb.

Now in the third kind of equivocals, which arises from art and from the use of words together, as many forms of ambiguity can exist as we have set down in the two classes above.

There still remains that kind of ambiguity which is found only in writings. There are three species in this kind of ambiguity, for it is caused either by the length of syllables or by accent or by both. By length as when '*venit*' is written. The tense is uncertain because the length of the first syllable is not disclosed.[17] By accent as when '*pone*' is written and it is doubtful whether it is from the verb '*pono*,' as in the line "*Pone sequens, namque hanc dederat Proserpina legem*" (Following behind, for Proserpina had ordained this condition),[18] because the accent is not disclosed. And it is from both length and accent, as we have said above in the case of '*lepore*.'[19] For the penultimate is to be not only lengthened but accented if the word is a form of '*lepos*' but not if it is a form of '*lepus*.'

NOTES

CHAPTER I

[1] On the chapter divisions and titles see the Introduction, p. 25. When I do not follow the title given in *PL* 32 I will note my divergence.

[2] Augustine uses the Stoic name for logic, 'dialectic,' as had Cicero (*Top.* XII.53, *Or.* XXXII.113) and Varro (Pfligersdorffer, p. 137) before him. His definition of dialectic is also Stoic. It appears to be a mixture of the definitions given by Diogenes, VII.42: (1) rhetoric is the science of speaking well(ἐπιστήμην... εὖ λέγειν);(2) dialectic is the science of carrying on a discussion correctly (ὀρθῶς διαλέγεσθαι). Augustine was not the first to give this definition. Barwick, p. 8, cites J. von Arnim, *Stoicorum Veterum Fragmenta*, vol. III, frag. 267:διαλεκτικὴ δὲ ἐπιστήμη τοῦ εὖ διαλέγεσθαι.This fragment is from the Περὶ παθῶν falsely attributed to Andronicus of Rhodes (ed. by F. W. A. Mullach, *Fragmenta Philosophorum Graecorum*, III, Paris, 1881, pp. 570–578; the fragment is on p. 575). This little eclectic work is assigned to the second century A. D. See Pauly-Wissowa, I, col. 2167, and

Der Kleine Pauly, I, col. 349 (in the latter it is incorrectly titled Περὶ ἀρχῶν). I do not know
of Augustine's definition occurring in earlier Latin authors, but similar definitions are found
in Cicero, who calls dialectic *"ars bene disserendi"* (*De or.* II.xxxviii.157), and in Quintilian,
who calls rhetoric *"bene dicendi scientia"* (*Inst. or.* II.xv.34). When I wrote "The Theory of
Signs," p. 37, I did not know of the Περὶ παθῶν definition.
³ Augustine here begins a classification which extends through Ch. III and which gives the
basis for the division of dialectic into four parts (Ch. IV). The classification, with the
corresponding parts, is as follows:

           1. Simple words   *(de loquendo)*
           2. Compound words
              a. Do not make a statement
              b. Make a statement
                  i. Neither true nor false   *(de eloquendo)*
                  ii. True or false
                      α. Simple   *(de proloquendo)*
                      β. Compound *(de proloquiorum summa)*

Pinborg, p. 158, Duchrow, p. 43, and Barwick, pp. 8ff., have noted the similarity of Augustine's classification to the Stoic classification of λεκτά given by Diogenes (VII.63–75) and
Sextus Empiricus (*Adversus mathematicos* VIII.69–74 and 93). Benson Mates, *Stoic Logic*,
p. 16, gives a summary diagram of this Stoic classification. But Augustine is discussing
words, the Stoic φωναί. In this respect he is closer to Aristotle's *De interpretatione* 1–5
(summarized by I. M. Bocheński, *Ancient Formal Logic*, p. 28). In any case the *simplex-
coniuncta* distinction is common in the logical writings of antiquity. We know that Augustine would have encountered it when he read Aristotle's *Categories*. In Ch. 2 Aristotle says,
"Of things that are said, some involve combination (συμπλοκήν) while others are said
without combination. Examples of those involving combination are 'man runs', 'man
wins'; and of those without combination 'man', 'ox', 'runs', 'wins'." (Trans. by J. L. Ackrill,
Clarendon Aristotle Series, p. 3.) In his translation of the *Categories* Boethius translated
συμπλοκή as *'complexio'* (*Ar. Lat.* I, p. 5, ed. L. Minio-Paluello), but the earlier Pseudo-
Augustinian *Categoriae decem* may be closer to the language Augustine would have found
in the Latin translation which he read. In it we find, *"Scire etiam debemus verba aut simplicia
esse aut certe coniuncta: coniuncta sunt 'equus currit'; simplicia, cum haec separantur et
dicuntur singula, ut 'equus', 'currit'."* (*Ar. Lat.* I, p. 139; *PL* 32, 1422). The most important
parallel to the first two chapters is Capella's *De dialectica* 388–392 (Book IV of his *De
Nuptiis*), which Crecelius, p. 5, and others have cited. Capella makes the basic distinction
between simple and compound words using *'separata'* instead of *'simplicia'* for the former;
but he discusses first, second, and third person verbs in the same way as Augustine does in
Ch. I and makes points about *sententia* similar to those Augustine makes in Ch. II (see note 1
on Ch. II). This parallelism has led scholars to infer that Augustine and Capella have a
common source. Fischer, esp. pp. 52f. and 62f., has argued rather convincingly that this
common source is Varro's *De dialectica*, the second book of his lost *Disciplinarum libri*.
Fischer argues against the view of R. Reitzenstein (*Varro und Johannes Mauropus*, pp. 69–80)
that *De lingua Latina* I, also not extant, is the main source. Several of the editors of Varro
have viewed Augustine's *De dialectica* I–IV as a fragment of Varro. August Wilmanns gives
these chapters (omitting a few sentences) as a fragment of *De ling. Lat.* XIV–XVI (fr. 32,
pp. 161–166). Later editors of Varro are uncertain which of Varro's works *De dial.* draws
upon (Funaioli, fr. 265, pp. 278–280, and Goetz and Schoell, fr. 130, pp. 234–236).
⁴ Augustine is apparently referring to the fact that *'disputare'* is composed of the inseparable

prefix *'dis'* and the verb *'putare'*. He thus makes it clear that the basis for the distinction between simple and compound words is the signification of words and not their phonetic makeup.

⁵ I have here translated *'cum dicimus 'loquor''* as 'the word *'loquor''*.' The phrase *'cum dicimus'* occurs so frequently throughout the work that it would be tiresome to continually translate it as 'when we say.' Moreover, it may be that Augustine is using the phrase in a way similar to the way later medieval writers used *'hoc quod dico'*, namely, to indicate mention rather than use of a word. On the other hand, I have occasionally retained 'when we say' as a reminder that Augustine is almost always thinking of spoken words. See Ch. V, 7, 11–18, where spoken words are said to be words in the proper sense of the term.

⁶ First and second person verbs in Latin signify the person speaking or the person spoken to, whereas third person verbs are by themselves indeterminate as to a subject, except in the case of impersonal verbs. Martianus Capella, IV.389, also uses the verb *'pluit'* to make the same point as Augustine makes here.

CHAPTER II

¹ *'Sententia'* has several meanings and in this context could be translated in several ways. I have chosen 'statement' because it has the connotation in English of something spoken which is more complete than an utterance (the latter term I will often use to translate *'vox'*). I have decided against translating *'sententia'* by 'sentence' because the latter refers properly to a set of written words and, as a technical term, is more appropriate to grammar than to logic. The phrase *'quae sententiam comprehendunt'* could be translated as 'which express a meaning' or 'thought' or 'judgment', but the second seems too psychological and all three would require circumlocutions if they were consistently used for *'sententia.'* One disadvantage of 'statement' is that it has the connotation of a declarative or truth-claiming utterance. It should be clear from the context, however, that Augustine means for *'sententia'* to apply to any set of combined words which express any sort of complete meaning. The same usage is found in Capella, IV.390–392. Varro used *'sententia'* in his definition of the Stoic ἀξίωμα as a *"sententia in qua nihil desideratur"* (Wilmanns fr. 36, Aulus Gellius, *Noctes Atticae* XVI.viii.6).

² For a longer list of kinds of non-truth-claiming statements see Apuleius (?), *Peri hermeneias* I, p. 176 (ed. of P. Thomas, 1921). Interest in such statements as a part of logic goes back to Stoic sources. See Diogenes Laertius, VII.67–68, and Sextus Empiricus, VIII.71–72. Aristotle, on the other hand, relegates them to rhetoric and poetics (*De int*. 4).

³ By this last sentence Augustine does not intend to place such statements outside of the domain of the dialectician, which is clear from Ch. IV; rather he is saying that they do not come under discussion with respect to truth-values. Capella, IV.391, also uses *'quaestio'* to speak of the appropriateness of discussing the truth or falsity of a statement.

CHAPTER III

¹ I translate *'de'* by 'in respect of' to make it clear that the connection itself is not judged but rather the statements in relation to the connection which relates them.

² Barwick, p. 9, notes that Cicero in *De oratore* II.xxxviii.158 uses *'summa'* as the name for the conclusion of an argument. It would not seem to have been the name commonly used by Latin authors; *'conclusio'* and *'complexio'* are the more usual names for a conclusion (Cicero, *De inv*. I.xlvii.87; Quintilian, V.xiv.1–2 and 5; Apuleius, VII, p. 183; Capella, IV.407). Quintilian (V.xiv.11) and Gellius (II.viii.8–9) do use *'summa'* and *'finis'* when they discuss the position of a conclusion in an argument. *'Summa'* may be an attempt to translate

the Stoic technical term for a conclusion, συμπέρασμα (see Mates, p. 135, for this term). Literally it means that which is finished by joining together and it could be literally translated into Latin by *'consumma'* or *'consummatio'*. See p. 40, n. 118, above for Erasmus's scholium on *'summa'*. – In the same *De oratore* passage where he uses *'summa'* Cicero, describing the Stoics' science of dialectic, also distinguishes between statements expressed simply (*simpliciter*) and those expressed in conjunction with other statements (*coniuncte*), a distinction Augustine has just made at the beginning of this chapter.

[3] Augustine's examples of deductive arguments are Stoic in form, the first and second undemonstrated arguments of the Stoic system – known since the Middle Ages as *modus ponens* and *modus tollens*. The presence of the second is obscured in the Augustine editions by the omission of the ten words *"aut restet illi docere quod non moveatur, ut consequatur summa"* (p. 6, 15f.). Crecelius restored them on the basis of his three MSS. I find that his reading is supported by Paris 7730 (P), Orleans 263 (O), Paris 12949 (G), and Einsiedeln 324, as well as by the Venice edition. The words are omitted by Troyes 40 and Philadelphia 63. For full accounts of Stoic deduction theory see Mates, pp. 67ff., and Kneale and Kneale, pp. 158ff. As noted in the Introduction, p. 5, the theory of deduction in Augustine's other works is also Stoic.

CHAPTER IV

[1] I have supplied the title. The one printed by the Maurists – *Conjunctas sententias subdividit* – is innaccurate.

[2] Capella, IV.338–343, uses these same rubrics for the parts of dialectic and organizes his book by them. Barwick, p. 10, points to Diogenes VII.63 for the Stoic background of the fourfold division given in this chapter. Fischer, pp. 28f., believes that the source for the rubrics used by Augustine and Capella is Varro; Pfligersdorffer, pp. 140–147, argues for a later origin. Whatever their common source(s), Augustine and Capella differ from each other in a number of ways. In the first place, Capella lists fifth and sixth parts – *de iudicando* and *quae dicenda rhetoribus commodata est* – which belong more appropriately to grammar and rhetoric. In the second place, the specific contents of the parts differ. Capella is much more Aristotelian than Augustine. A detailed comparison can be made for the first part only, since that is as far as Augustine gets. In Chs. V and VI he says that under *'de loquendo'* he will discuss *verba*, *dicibilia*, *dictiones*, and *res*, and concerning *verba* he will discuss the origin, force, declension, and arrangement of words. Under *'de loquendo'* Capella, on the other hand, dicusses the predicables (*genus, forma, differentia, accidens, proprium*), definition and partition, equivocation, the ten categories of Aristotle, and the theory of opposition (IV.344–387). The only shared topic is equivocation, which Augustine takes up in the last chapters. Judging from the examples he gives in Ch. III, we would expect Augustine to have given the Stoic theory of deduction had he gotten to the fourth part. Capella gives both the Stoic and the Aristotelian theories (IV.404–422).

In my translation of the rubrics for the parts of dialectic I have tried to convey the progression from simple to compound words, and for the latter, from general to more specific kinds of compound words. 'On naming' connotes singularity. 'On expressing' implies that single words have been put together to say something. 'On asserting' refers to a certain kind of expression, namely, an affirming or a denying of something. 'On concluding from assertions' indicates a specific kind of interest with respect to assertions. Augustine does not use the nominal *'eloquium'* and uses *'proloquium'* only this one time. On these terms see Capella, IV.389–391. The latter term was apparently one of the translations of the Stoic ἀξίωμα. See Gellius, XVI.viii.1–8. In my translation of the rubrics I have been helped by the translations given by C. S. Baldwin, *Medieval Rhetoric and Poetic* (New York, 1928), p. 94, for Capella (on naming, defining, affirming, and concluding), and by Duchrow, p. 43 (vom Sprechen, vom Ausrufen, von der vollständige Aussage, vom Schluss).

[1] I have supplied this title in place of the more elaborate one given by the editions – *Quomodo de rebus, verbis, dicibilibus, dictionibus tractetur in logica*. A large portion of this chap. is regarded as a fragment of Varro by Wilmanns (fr. 1, pp. 142–144), Funaioli (fr. 265, pp. 280f.), and Goetz and Schoell (fr. 130, pp. 236f.). They omit from the fragment the explanation of the relation of spoken and written signs (7, 12–16) and the illustration at the end of the chapter (8, 12ff.).

[2] At this point the Augustine editions include the following sentences: Sciuntur enim corporalia, intelliguntur spiritalia, latet vero ipse deus et informis materia. Deus est quod neque corpus est neque animal est neque sensus est neque intellectus est neque aliquid quod excogitari potest. Informis materia est mutabilitas mutabilium rerum, capax omnium formarum. ("For corporeal things are sensed and spiritual things are understood; but God himself and formless matter are truly hidden. God is neither body, nor animal, nor sense, nor understanding, nor anything which can be thought. Formless matter is the changeableness of changeable things, the capacity for all forms.") This apparent interpolation is absent from all of the MSS which I have examined and is not in the Venice edition. Its source is probably a gloss which was copied as part of the text in some MS. Glosses in Paris B. N. lat. 7730 and 12949 are close in content to the *'corporalia,' 'spiritalia,'* and *'deus et informis materia'* of the interpolated passage. The former (fol. 16v) glosses Augustine's *"sentitur vel intellegitur vel latet"* with *"ut terrena," "celestia,"* and *"divina."* The latter (fol. 13r) glosses the three verbs more elaborately: *"Sicut sol et cetera quae in mundo sunt"; "Sicut natura angelorum";* and *"Sicut deus et eius invisibilitas vel maiestas et natura investigabilis."*

[3] Compare the definitions of 'thing' and 'sign' with Augustine's *De doctrina christiana* I.ii.2 and II.i.1, particularly with the definition of a sign in the latter passage as "... a thing which causes us to think of something beyond the impression the thing itself makes upon the senses." (Trans. by D. W. Robertson, 1958, p. 34).

[4] Augustine's definitions of *'loqui'* and *'articulata'* should be compared with the Stoic definitions given by Diogenes (VII.55–57). Augustine's *'vox'* corresponds to the Stoics' φωνή and his *'loqui'* corresponds to the Stoics' λέγειν or, as a substantive, λόγος. Augustine seems to have no equivalent to the Stoics' λέξις, an articulate but non-significant sound. See Kneale and Kneale, p. 139, for a brief discussion of these notions. I have translated *'litteris'* as 'letters,' even though Augustine makes it clear a few lines later that a *littera* is a spoken and not a written entity. Both the English and the Latin term ordinarily refer to a written entity. Augustine's use apparently goes back to Stoic sources, for according to Diogenes (VII.56) the Stoics said that 'letter' (τὸ γράμμα) signifies the sound, as well as the written symbol and the name of the sound or symbol. Definitions similar to Augustine's are found in a passage in the fourth-century Latin grammarian Diomedes which is regarded as a fragment of Varro's *De grammatica* by Goetz and Schoell (fr. 111, p. 228; the Diomedes is in Keil, *Grammatici Latini* I, p. 420). Diomedes says that an *articulata vox* is one uttered by a rational, verbal man and that it is also called *'litteralis vel scriptilis'* because *'litteris comprehendi potest.'* Augustine's *'comprehendi litteris potest'* clearly echoes this Varronian passage.

[5] Augustine did not get to this and he does not say where it would be discussed. Capella includes a paragraph on defining under *de loquendo* (IV.349). It is clear from *De ordine*

II.xiii.38 and *De doctrina christiana* II.xxxv.53 that Augustine regards definition as an appropriate topic for dialectic.

[6] See Aristotle, *De interp.* 1, 16a 5, for the view that written marks are symbols of spoken sounds.

[7] Augustine here begins the account of four elements in signification upon which the chief fame of the work in the history of logic rests. See Kneale and Kneale, p. 188, and Kretzmann, "History of Semantics," p. 366. I have not translated the four terms Augustine uses for two reasons. First, they are technical terms and by leaving them untranslated I call attention to this and force the reader to attend to the definitions given. This consideration is particularly compelling in the case of *'verbum,'* which in the opening statement of the chapter is defined as a *rei signum* but here is said to be an utterance given not in order to signify something. Second, it is difficult to translate *'dicibile'* and *'dictio'* without interpreting them more than I wish to in the text itself. There is a precedent for leaving *'dicibile'* untranslated. In his exposition of Stoic logic, Thomas Stanley used the Anglicized 'dicible' for the Stoic *lekton* (*The History of Philosophy*, The Eighth Part, London, 1656, p. 40). His source for this term is almost certainly *De dialectica*, for he knows our work (see note 8 on Ch. VI and note 1 on Ch. IX) and translates V, 8, 9f. (without credit) in his chapter on dicibles: "Dicible therefore is a word, and yet signifies not a word, but that which is understood in the word, and is contained in the minde." (p. 40) His immediate source may, however, be the *Dialectica Ciceronis* by Adam Bursius (Samoscius, 1604), a work Stanley refers to in a marginal note on the paragraph from which the sentence just quoted is taken. I have not seen the work by Bursius. If I were to translate *'dicibile'* and *'dictio'*, I would use something like 'the sayable' or 'the expressible' for the former and 'saying' or 'significant utterance' for the latter.

[8] Augustine doubtless has in mind the first word of Vergil's *Aeneis* and portrays here what seems to have been the standard classroom practice of considering even literary texts one word at a time. See, for example, Servius' commentary on the *Aeneis* (ed. by G. Thilo and H. Hagen, Leipzig, 1881, vol. 2, pp. 5f.) and Marrou, *A History of Education in Antiquity* (New York: Mentor, 1956), p. 376.

[9] Thus Augustine's account of signification gives him the topics to be considered under *'de loquendo.'* In Ch. VI he begins detailed discussion of *verba*, but he never got to further discussion of the *dicibile, dictio,* and *res*. Similar notions appear in his later works, especially in *De doctrina christiana* and *De trinitate* (see my article, "The Theory of Signs"), not, however, dressed in the same technical terminology as is found in Ch. V. This chapter has been dealt with by almost everyone who has written on *De dialectica*. Certain things about it are fairly clear, in part thanks to Augustine's own illustration. The *verbum* is described in contrast to the *dictio*; the former is uttered for its own sake, the latter in order to signify something else. This distinction seems to be the same as our distinction between the mention and ordinary use of a word. The grammarian in Augustine's example does not use *'arma'* to signify anything; he merely mentions it for the purpose of analyzing its grammatical properties. Had he been using the word, his attention would have been directed not to the word itself but rather to other things, to *res* in the proper sense of the term. These three elements – *verbum, dictio, res* – are relatively easy to understand. The difficulty comes when we turn to the *dicibile*. Among interpreters of the chapter there is agreement that Augustine's notion is very close to the Stoics' notion of the *lekton*. Due, however, to the obscurity of the latter as it is known to us, this does not help a great deal in understanding the *dicibile*. I do not know of the term being used in a technical sense before Augustine and as far as I know he did not use it again in this sense. Moreover, it is rarely used by later writers on logic. Norman Kretzmann, "Medieval Logicians on the Meaning of the *Propositio*," *The Journal of Philosophy* **67** (1970), p. 773, n. 7, cites one instance of its use by William of Moerbeke to translate *'lekton'* and I have found that it is used by William of Sherwood to define a

predicable as what can be said (*Introductiones in logicam* II.1). The word itself is formed by adding the suffix *'-ibile'* to the root of *'dico,'* to say or speak. Thus literally it is the sayable. Augustine believes that prior to and independent of speaking there is something in the mind which may be expressed by speech and which in turn is understood when one hears intelligible speech. This would not seem to be merely a thought or an idea in the psychological sense of those terms, but Augustine does not tell us how it is related to thought. Here we are in a subject which cannot be dealt with adequately in a note. I refer the reader to my article (mentioned above) and to the excellent discussions of Stoic theories of meaning in Mates, pp. 11–33, and Kneale, pp. 138–149. It would, of course, be interesting to know how Augustine would have discussed the *dictio, dicibile,* and *res* had he gotten that far in *De dial.* How the notion of the *res* would have been discussed in a book on logic is a puzzle. Barwick, p. 13, believes that Augustine would have dealt with the Stoic doctrine of categories.

CHAPTER VI

[1] Crecelius's change in the punctuation of 8, 26–30 (the earlier editions made this into two sentences) requires a change in the placement of the chapter beginning. It is moved to the beginning of Crecelius's paragraph.

[2] These four topics and the four introduced in Ch. V give the following outline of topics to be covered under *de loquendo*:

1. *De verbis*
   a. Origin (Ch. VI)
      i. Has no explanation
      ii. Has an explanation
         α. Similarity of things and sounds
         β. Similarity of things to each other
         γ. Proximity
         δ. Contrariety
   b. Force (Chs. VII–X; see below for outline)
   c. Declension
   d. Arrangement
2. *De dicibilibus*
3. *De dictionibus*
4. *De rebus*

Augustine gets through only the topic of the force of words. He does not say here what he means by *'declinatio'* and *'ordinatio.'* In X, 19, 20f. he uses the former to refer to changes in both the inflection and the function of words. Barwick, pp. 23 and 26f., notes that three of Augustine's topics – *origo, declinatio,* and *ordinatio* – are the topics by which Varro organizes the twenty-four books of his *De lingua Latina* (VII.110 and VIII.1). By *'declinatio'* Varro means not only grammatical inflection but also other forms of alteration of words. See esp. *De ling. Lat.* VIII.5–24 and X.3ff., and Barwick, pp. 34–57 (on the Stoic theory of declension, κλίσις). By *'ordinatio'* (Varro uses *'coniunctio'* in the passages cited by Barwick) Varro means syntax, according to Barwick, p. 21. The part of *De ling. Lat.* covering this is lost.

[3] Crecelius cites Cicero's *De natura deorum* III.xxiv.61–63, a passage in which the Stoic practice of explaining the names of the gods by etymologies is criticized and ridiculed. Duchrow, pp. 56–59, notes that Augustine's attitude toward etymology is also Varronian. See, for example, *De lingua Latina* VIII.xii.27. The greater part of Ch. VI has been regarded as a fragment of Varro (Wilmanns, fr. 1 and 2, pp. 144–150; Funaioli, fr. 265, pp. 281–284;

Goetz and Schoell, fr. 130, pp. 237–241). Though Augustine apparently owes nothing to it directly, no study of etymology in antiquity can be made without reference to Plato's *Cratylus*.

[4] Since in most cases translating the words which Augustine gives as examples would obscure the etymology, I have left all of the examples untranslated for the sake of consistency. I have put a translation in parentheses following the first use of each word. Many of the examples given by Augustine can be found in other writers. I will refer to some of these which have been located by Crecelius and others. On the derivations for *'verbum'* the most interesting parallels are in a statement attributed to Varro that *verba a veritate dicta esse* (Goetz and Schoell, p. 238) and in Augustine's own *De magistro* V.12 where *verba* are said to be named *a verberando*.

[5] J. Vahlen, *Ennianae Poesis Reliquae* (Leipzig, 1903), p. 238, lists this among the fragments of Ennius (no. L). Vahlen is uncertain about which work it is from. In an earlier edition (1854) he attributed this fragment to Fortunatianus; in this edition he gives the source as Augustine. According to Hagendahl, pp. 170–172 and 377, Augustine's knowledge of Ennius was indirect. Hagendahl does not include this or other quotations from *De dial.* in his list of Testimonia, since he does not regard *De dial.* as authentic.

[6] *Georgica* III.223. For Augustine's quotations from the *Georgica*, see Hagendahl, pp. 369–375; on his knowledge of Vergil, see pp. 384–463.

[7] Augustine is here an important source for information about the Stoic theory of the origin of words. Since, however, he disagrees with the Stoics, his account of their theory cannot be regarded as unbiased. See W. S. Allen, "Linguistic Problems and Their Treatment in Antiquity," unpublished Cambridge University dissertation, pp. 440–442.

[8] This is a puzzling sentence to this point. The tradition is clearly confused here. – Stanley translates Ch. VI from here to the next to the last sentence of the chapter as part of his account of Stoic teachings on Voice, Speech, and Words (pp. 30–32). He gives credit by the marginal note *"S. August. de Dialect. cap. 6."*

[9] See the fragment of Varro's *De Grammatica* (Goetz and Schoell, fr. 113, p. 229) where, in a discussion of the various qualities of *syllabae*, *'crux'* is given as an example of a rough *(aspera)* sound and *'lana'* as an example of a light *(levis)* sound.

[10] The similarity of these two words is more obvious if the latter is taken in the singular – *crus* – instead of in the plural.

[11] On this derivation of *'piscina'* see Donatus, *Ars grammatica* III.6.2, and *De doctrina christiana* III.xxix.40, where the same account is given.

[12] This etymology is also given in *De doctr. chr.* III.xxix.41 and by Quintilian, I.vi.34, and Capella, IV.360.

[13] This explanation of the origin of *'foedus'* is obscure. Crecelius refers to Isidore, *Etym.*, X.100 (actually 101), but Isidore derives it from *'haedo'* (goat) by the change of a letter. A note in Barreau's French translation of *De dialectica* (p. 58) says that the head of a pig placed on a pike was sometimes a military insignia. Thus the etymology would apparently be based on the army's function in forming alliances. A similar explanation could be made on the basis of the use of *'caput porci'* to describe a certain battle formation (see Ammianus Marcellinus, *Rerum Gestarum* XVII.13.9). Stanley, p. 31, mistranslates the sentence as: "But, if we derive *porcus*, as some do, *a foeditate*, ..."

[14] *Aeneis* V.755. Hagendahl, pp. 321–364, assembles Augustine's many quotations from Vergil's epic. Varro, V.143, gives the same explanation of *'urbs.'*

[15] This sentence is awkward as it stands in the best MSS. Crecelius reads 'origo *adque* ratio reddi *non* possit' for which the translation would be: "For there are innumerable words whose origin and cause cannot be discovered. Either there is none, as I believe, or it is

hidden, as the Stoics maintain." Only Paris 12949 (G) includes the *'non'* which the context seems to require.

[16] The phrase "'v' functions as a consonant" sounds odd to English speakers, since 'v' is always a consonant in modern English. In classical Latin, however, the same written form (usually 'u') was used to represent both the English 'u' sound and the English 'w' sound. Since the Renaissance, 'v' has often been used to represent the latter.

[17] Augustine does not seem to have given a complete explanation of the origin of *'vites.'* He apparently means that the seizing and pressing of vines involves force *(vis)* in the same way as chains and withes do. See Isidore, *Etym.* XVII.v.2.

[18] Terence does this in *Eunuchus* IV.iv.21, line 688: *"hic est vietus vetus veternosus senex."* According to Hagendahl, p. 378, Augustine quotes Terence more than he quotes any other poet except Vergil. See pp. 259–262 for quotations from the *Eunuchus*.

CHAPTER VII

[1] In this chapter Augustine develops a notion broader than signification, describing a variety of ways in which words affect hearers. See Kretzmann, "History of Semantics," p. 366. Augustine's classification gives the following outline of topics for the chapter:

1. Words affect a hearer on their own account.
    a. By sense
        i. By nature
        ii. By custom
    b. By art
    c. By sense and art together
2. Words affect a hearer on account of what they signify.
3. Words affect a hearer both on their own account and on account of what they signify.

[2] The nature-custom distinction was commonly used in antiquity in discussions of word origins. The distinction is implicit in this sense in Ch. VI. See my article, "Signs," pp. 14f. In this chapter, however, Augustine is using the notions to distinguish between the sensible qualities of words which seem to him intrinsic and those which are relative to a hearer's experience.

[3] 'Artaxerxes' was the name of several Persian kings. For 'Euryalus' Augustine may be thinking of the boy described in *Aeneis* 5.294f. as "famed for beauty and flower of youth."

[4] On the authority of the Cologne MS Crecelius restored this sentence. In the earlier editions it had hardly made sense. As restored the sentence is obviously parallel to the sentence in 12, 15f. about 'Artaxerxes' and 'Euryalus'. The interpretation of the passage is not difficult. Whereas 'Motta' is an uncommon name, 'Cotta' is a common Roman cognomen, borne, for example, by Gaius Aurelius Cotta, consul in 75 B.C., who appears in Cicero's *De natura deorum*. Even though the names sound almost alike (and if anything, 'Cotta' is a bit harsher than 'Motta'), one is unfamiliar and therefore somehow "offends" the ears.

[5] I take *'vel... vel...'* in 13, 6f. as equivalent to *'et... et...'*. If Augustine's statement were taken as disjunctive, then it would describe two cases, in one of which there could be no possibility of being affected by what the name signifies (the one who does not know the Augustine who is writing this). The MSS I have examined all read *'Augustino'* and *'Augustinus'* for this passage.

[6] Sallust, *Bellum Catilinae* 14.2. Augustine quotes Sallust with great frequency. See Hagen-

dahl, pp. 226–239, for quotations from the work on Catiline, and pp. 630–649.

[7] In Ch. V Augustine distinguished dialectic from grammar by saying that the latter is concerned with sounds, with hearing of words alone. Now he distinguishes dialectic from rhetoric by saying that the latter is concerned with the pleasures of hearing, a more specific interest in sound than the grammarian has. Dialectic, on the other hand, is concerned with truth. Yet Augustine believes that both the dialectician and the orator should make use of the other's art. To find this idea expressed about the orator we need look to no less obvious a predecessor than Cicero, who says the orator should have the *acumen dialecticorum* (*De or.* I.xxviii.128) and who spells out in detail the dialectic which orators should master (*Orator* xxxii.113–xxxiii.117). Cicero may also be a source for Augustine's view of the style of most dialecticians (*De or.* II.xxxviii.159). For Stoic views on rhetoric and dialectic see the references given by Barwick, pp. 15f.

CHAPTER VIII

[1] The title printed by the Maurists is *'Obscurum et ambiguum,'* literally, 'The obscure and the ambiguous.' The outline for the remaining three chapters, which cover the ways hearers are kept from learning the truth in words, is:

    1. Obscurity (Ch. VIII)
        a. Manifest to the senses, closed to the mind
        b. Closed to the senses, open to the mind
        c. Closed to both mind and senses
    2. Ambiguity (Chs. IX–X)
        a. Doubt about what is said
          i. in univocals
          ii. in equivocals (see Ch. X)
        b. Doubt about what is written
          i. Length of syllables
          ii. Accent
          iii. Both length and accent

Notice that even though the topic is hindrances to the hearer Augustine also discusses ambiguity in *written* words, albeit briefly. For Augustine's views on obscurity and ambiguity in the written words of Scripture see the second and third books of *De doctrina christiana*. The chapter division for Ch. VIII has been moved to the beginning of Crecelius's paragraph, one sentence earlier than in the Maurist edition.

[2] In the Introduction (p. 31, note 13) I have noted Fischer's interpretation of Augustine's *Epistle* 26 and the accompanying poem of Licentius. On Fischer's view the books on the liberal arts were in the main a presentation of Varro's doctrines with elaborations and illustrations by Augustine for the benefit of his students. Ch. VIII fits this view well. In it Augustine explains the technical notions of obscurity and ambiguity by the use of two extended metaphors (the one just given and one soon to follow). He also uses again (as he had in Ch. V) the example of a teacher uttering a single word to a class. These metaphors and examples are probably the sort of thing that Licentius had come to expect from Augustine at Cassiciacum and hoped to find more of in the completed books on the liberal arts.

[3] *'Temetum'* refers to any intoxicating drink. The term is ante-classical and poetic and hence likely to be unknown to some students.

[4] Since the example is about a word, it would have been more accurate for Augustine to say that the students were ignorant of *quid significaret temetum* rather than *quid esset temetum*.

At 14, 27f. the use of *'significationis verbi'* makes it clear that it is the signification of the word that the students do not know. I have left *'temetum'* untranslated in order to convey Augustine's meaning.

⁵ In these sentences I have departed from normal English word order in order to place 'great' at the beginning of the sentences, as it must be if they are to illustrate the point.

CHAPTER IX

¹ I have shortened the title from the one given by the Maurists – *Ambiguitatum genera duo*. Stanley, pp. 32f., translated the first part of this chapter (to 16, 6) as part of his chapter on the Stoic doctrine of Voice, Speech, and Words. He gives his source in a marginal note as *"D. August. de dialect."*, without indication of chapter.

² Crecelius, p. 15, and others cite Aulus Gellius, XI.xii.1 as evidence that this is the view of Chrysippus, the greatest of the Stoic logicians. Diogenes Laertius, VII.193, lists several works of Chrysippus on ambiguity (ἀμφιβολία). According to Diogenes (VII.62) ambiguity was discussed by the Stoics under the part of dialectic which they called περὶ φωνῆς. This part corresponds to Augustine's *de loquendo*. Ambiguity was also a common topic in works on rhetoric. See, for example, Quintilian, VII.ix.1–9.

³ The following editors list this quotation as a fragment of Cicero's lost *Hortensius*: C. F. W. Mueller, *M. Tulli Ciceronis Scripta quae Manserunt Omnia*, pt. IV, vol. III (Leipzig, 1890), fr. 99, p. 326; Michel Ruch, *L'Hortensius de Cicéron, Histoire et Reconstitution* (Paris, 1958), fr. 28, pp. 92f.; and Albertus Grilli, ed., *M. Tulli Ciceronis, Hortensius* (Milan, 1962), fr. 24, p. 25. Crecelius, p. 15, conjectures that the fragment is to be placed in the first part of the dialogue. Ruch and Grilli, who try to reconstruct the work, agree with Crecelius. From the time he read it in Carthage as a young man (*Conf.* III.iv.7), Augustine was greatly influenced by the *Hortensius*. He quotes it often, including many times in the Cassiciacum dialogues, which were written just before he undertook to write the books on the liberal arts. On Augustine and the *Hortensius*, see Hagendahl, pp. 81–94 and 486–497, and Maurice Testard, *Saint Augustin et Cicéron*, vol. I (Paris, 1958), pp. 19ff.

⁴ Cicero, *De oratore* I.x.44. Crecelius, p. 15, notes that Augustine has changed Cicero's *'prudentibus'* to *'sapientibus'* and infers from this that he is quoting from memory. Further evidence of this is that Augustine says that Scaevola is speaking to Antony but in fact he is talking specifically to Crassus. Augustine quotes Scaevola in order to accuse Hortensius of using eloquence to mislead the ignorant, whereas Scaevola says that one should speak truly to the ignorant. Augustine knew Cicero's works well and quoted him often throughout his literary career. See Hagendahl, pp. 159–161, for other quotations of *De oratore* in Augustine, and pp. 477–588, for Cicero's influence on Augustine. Testard's two volume work, *Saint Augustin et Cicéron*, is a major study of this topic.

⁵ *'Acies'* was commonly used of both a military formation and the point of a sword, as well as of sharpness or acuteness of vision.

⁶ I have translated *'sententia'* as 'sentence' because Augustine is clearly referring to written words here. By this example Augustine seems to have in mind coming upon a single written word. It is possible, however, that he is thinking of coming upon a sentence in which *'leporem'* occurs and is still ambiguous (for example, *'Leporem eius admiror'*). If so, the translation of *'qua sententia positum sit'* would more properly be 'with what thought it is put forth.' See Ch. II, note 1, above on *'sententia.'*

⁷ The ultimate source of these definitions of 'univocal' and 'equivocal' is the first chapter of Aristotle's *Categories* (read by Augustine according to *Conf.* IV), where Aristotle speaks of things which are συνώνυμα (synonymous) and ὁμώνυμα (homonymous). The standard Latin translation for *'synonyma'* and *'homonyma'* was apparently *'univoca'* and *'aequivoca,'*

if we may judge from Boethius' translation of the *Categories* (*Ar. Lat.* I, p. 5). Capella also used the same terms (IV.355f.). (Augustine, Capella, and Boethius use different terms for Aristotle's ὄνομα and λόγος. For the former Augustine uses *'vocabulum'* and Capella and Boethius use *'nomen'*; for the latter Augustine and Capella use *'definitio'* and Boethius uses *'ratio.'*) I have used the standard English translation of these terms – 'univocal' and 'equivocal' – though they may be misunderstood. For in normal English usage these terms are applied to words. We ordinarily say that a *word* is used equivocally in two places, and so on. We do not say that *things* are equivocals or univocals, though we might sometimes say that two things are equivocally named. But it is of things that Aristotle is talking, not of words. On this see Kneale, pp. 25–29, and Ackrill's note on his trans. of the *Categories*, pp. 70f. The problem, at least in the definitions we are considering, is that Aristotle uses no technical term for 'thing.' He uses instead only a relative pronoun (ὧν, *quorum* in Boethius). Augustine's manner of speaking here and throughout the last two chapters seems similar to Aristotle's. Instead of using the technical term *'res'* he uses many pronouns and substantival adjectives or simply speaks of univocals and equivocals. In my translation I have been literal, refraining form supplying 'thing' in most cases.

[8] Since Augustine is talking about things in the preceding sentence, it is odd that he should use *'dictionibus'* here rather than something like *'dictis,'* which could be translated as 'things mentioned.' His choice of words may indicate an ambivalence on whether he is talking about univocal words or univocal things. See note 7, above.

[9] This definition is commonplace. It is found, for example, in Porphyry, *Isagoge* 1b 2–3, *Categoriae decem* XIX (*Ar. Lat.* I, p. 172, 20), Capella, IV.399, and Augustine, *De magistro* viii.24.

[10] Although 'plutocrat' may have a more special connotation than Augustine intends by *'divis,'* I have used it in order to have a one word translation which avoids the use of a qualifying adjective, as 'rich man' would.

CHAPTER X

[1] I have shortened the title from the one given by the Maurists – *'Ambiguitas ex aequivocis varia.'*

[2] Augustine's classification of equivocals is:

1. From art
   a. Can be examples of themselves
   b. Cannot be examples of themselves
2. From use
   a. From the same source
      i. Transference
         α. From whole to part
         β. From part to whole
         γ. Etc.
      ii. Declension
         α. By voice
         β. By signification
   b. From different sources
      i. Diversity of languages
      ii. In one laguage
         α. Same part of speech
         β. Different parts of speech

³ See Ch. VII where *ars* also has to do with the disciplines which deal with words. There it is contrasted with *sensus*, here with *usus*.

⁴ 'Tullius' is, of course, Cicero's *nomen*. Augustine uses it only in this chapter. I have not used the English form 'Tully,' since some of Augustine's comments are about the metric quality of the name.

⁵ This is a somewhat puzzling sentence. *'Aequivoca'* is clearly applied to things, which in this case are the name of a man and a dactylic foot. A less literal translation would be: 'Tullius' is a word by which all the things said above are together equally signified (for *aequivoca*) by this expression. See note 7, Ch. IX.

⁶ Notice that Augustine has added *'loquendi'* to the name for this kind of equivocation. When it was first introduced (17, 15), he called it merely *'usus.'* Probably he does not mean to add anything to the notion; the phrase *'usus loquendi'* is fairly common in earlier writers, for example, Varro (IX.6 and X.74). In any case it is clear that Augustine is now going to describe the types of ambiguity which occur when words are used to signify things (i.e., *dictiones*) as distinct from the types which occur when words are mentioned for the sake of various sorts of analysis *(verba)*.

⁷ See Introduction, p. 6 for use of this passage in the *Libri Carolini*.

⁸ I have not translated *'nomen'* by the more grammatical term 'noun' because, even though it is a noun in our sense of the word, for Latin grammar *'nomen'* included not only our nouns but also adjectives.

⁹ The term does have both meanings, but I do not know the different origins of them.

¹⁰ This list should be compared with the list of kinds of *vicinitas* in VI, 11, 2–8. There are six items in common, one unique to Ch. VI *(per abusionem)*, and three unique to Ch. X *(similitudine, a genere species, a specie genus)*.

¹¹ *'Pluit'* can be either the present or the perfect tense.

¹² Note the contrast between *'fit'* and *'est'* regarding these two words. Though *'homo'* is a name in both uses, it does different things, naming in the first and addressing in the second case. On the other hand, *'doctius'* is different in the two uses, being an adjective in the first instance and adverb in the second, though it does the same thing in both, namely, modifies.

¹³ *'Tu'* is a form of the personal pronoun in Latin and could be confused with τοῦ, a form of the definite article in Greek.

¹⁴ This is a hard sentence to make sense of as it stands. My translation depends partly on the emended version given by the Louvain and the Benedictine editions: Quod genus tamen non omnis novit: non enim unicuique perspicuum est, nisi qui linguas nosset aut qui linguas disputaret (*PL* 32, 1418). Their version of the sentence could be translated as: "But not everyone experiences this kind of ambiguity, for it will not happen to anyone unless he speaks several languages or at least is able to discuss them."

¹⁵ At 19, 3.

¹⁶ Terence, *Andria* III.iii.33, line 565.

¹⁷ If the first syllable is short it is in the present tense, if long, it is in the perfect tense.

¹⁸ Vergil, *Georgica* IV.487. *'Pone'* can be the imperative form of the verb *'pono'* (put, place) or it can be the adverb *'pone'* (behind), as it in fact is in the line from Vergil.

¹⁹ Ch. IX, 16, 10–12.

APPENDIX

Description of the data sets studied in the introduction

Author	Work	Edition	Passages[a]
Augustine, Early Dialogues	*Contra Academicos*	*CSEL* 63	II.iii.7–9
			II.v.12–vi.14
			III.iv.9–v.11
			III.xv.34–xvi.35
	De beata vita	*CSEL* 63	i.5–ii.8
	De ordine	*CSEL* 63	I.i.1–ii.3
			II.vii.21–23
			II.xv.43–xvii.46
	Soliloquiorum	*PL* 32	II.viii.15–x.18
			II.xvii.31–xviii.33
	De quantitate animae	*PL* 32	vii.12–viii.13
			xvi.28–xviii.31
			xxxiv.77–xxxv.79
	De musica	*PL* 32	I.iv.5–7
			I.ix.15–x.17
			I.xii.20–21
			III.i.1–ii.3
			IV.xii.14–15
			IV.xvii.35–V.i.1
			VI.ii.3–iii.4
			VI.x.28–xi.31
	De libero arbitrio I	*CSEL* 74	I.1–9
	De magistro	*CSEL* 77	4–6
			28–30
Augustine, Early Prose	*De immortalitate animae*	*PL* 32	i.1–iii.3
	De moribus eccles. catholicae	*PL* 32	I.v.8–vi.10
			I.xvi.28–xvii.31
			II.ix.14–16
			II.xi.20–23
			II.xvi.41–43
	De Genesi contra Manichaeos	*PL* 34	I.vii.14–ix.16
			II.x.13–xi.15
			II.xx.30–xxi.32
	Epistula	*CSEL* 34	XI.1–3
	De vera religione	*CSEL* 77	xx.38–xi.41
Augustine, Logical Writings	*Contra Academicos*	*CSEL* 63	III.xiii.29
	De ordine	*CSEL* 63	xii.35–xiii.38
	De doctrina christiana	*CC* 32	II.xxxi.48–xxxv.53
	Contra Cresconium	*CSEL* 52	I.xiii.16–xx.25

Author	Work	Edition	Passages[a]
Marius Victorinus	*Ars grammatica*	*GL* 6	II, pp. 69–70 III. pp. 104–105 IV, pp. 158–159
	De definitione	*PL* 64	Col. 893–894
	Explanationum in Ciceronis rhetoricam	*RLM*	I, pp. 155–156 I, pp. 171–172 I, pp. 227–228
Chirius Fortunatianus	*Ars rhetoricae*	*RLM*	I.1–6 I.6–12 I.27–II.5 II.16–23 II.23–31
Ambrose	*De officiis ministrorum*	*PL* 16	II.xvi.77–82 III.vi.42–vii.47
	De virginibus	Cazzaniga	I.vii.37–viii.45
	De fide	*CSEL* 78	II.7.52–8.59 V.4.49–5.58
	De Spiritu Sancto	*CSEL* 79	I.vii.83–88
	De incarnationis Dominicae sacramento	*CSEL* 79	5, 42–6, 47
	De paenitentia	*CSEL* 73	II.viii.66–72
Augustine (?)	*De dialectica*	Crecelius	Complete

[a] By book, chapter, and paragraph as designated in the edition used. My 500 word samples do not include the whole of each passage listed. In most cases the sample begins at the start of the first paragraph given and ends somewhere in the last given. Abbreviations for the editions are the same ones used throughout the book. In addition, *CC* is *Corpus Christianorum, Series Latina*, and *GL* is *Grammatici Latini* (ed. H. Keil).

BIBLIOGRAPHY

I. EDITIONS OF *De dialectica* CONSULTED

Puteolano, Francesco (?), ed. *Dialectica Chirii consulti Fortunatiani*. Printed in two books, both without title, place, printer, or date. The first page of each begins: *Hoc in uolumine aurea haec opuscula continentur*. Venice (?): C. de Pensis (?); J. Tacuinus (?), ca. 1498–1500.

Amerbach, Johannes, ed. *Principia Dialecticae*. In *Prima pars librorum divi Aurelii Augustini quos edidit cathecuminus*. Basel: Amerbach, J. Petri, J. Froben, 1506.

Erasmus, Desiderius, ed. *Principia Dialecticae*. In *D. Aurelii Augustini Hipponensis Episcopi Omnium Operum*, T. I. Basel: J. Froben, 1529. Reissued by Haemer, Jacob, ed., T. I, foll. 56–59. Paris: Claude Chevallon, 1531.

Louvain, Theological Faculty of, eds. *Principia Dialecticae*. In *Opera D. Aurelii Augustini*, T. I, pp. 111–117. Antwerp: Christopher Plantin, 1577.

Benedictines of St. Maur, eds. *Principia Dialecticae*. In *Sancti Aurelii Augustini Hipponensis Episcopi Opera Omnia*, T. I, Appendix, columns 16–22. Paris, 1679. Reprinted in *PL*, 32, cols. 1409–1420.

Crecelius, Wilhelm, ed. *S. Aurelii Augustini De Dialectica Liber*. *Jahresbericht über das Gymnasium zu Elberfeld*: S. Lucas, 1857.

Barreau, M. H., trans. *Principes de Dialectique*. French translation of the Maurist text in *PL* 32, in *Oeuvres Complètes de Saint Augustin*, Vol. IV, pp. 52–68. Paris: Librairie de Louis Vivès, 1873.

II. TEXTS AND TRANSLATIONS

Apuleius (?). *Peri Hermeneias*. Ed. by Paul Thomas. Leipzig: Teubner, 1921.

Aristotle. *The Categories* and *On Interpretation*. Ed. with a trans. by Harold P. Cook. *LCL*. Cambridge and London, 1938.

Aristotle. *Categories* and *De Interpretatione*. Trans. with Notes by J. L. Ackrill. Clarendon Aristotle Series. Oxford, 1963.

Augustine. *Confessiones*. Ed. Pius Knöll. *CSEL*, 33. Vienna, 1886.

Augustine. *De doctrina christiana*. Ed. by Josef Martin. Corpus Christianorum, Series Latina, 32. Turnhout: Brepols, 1962.

Augustine. *On Christian Doctrine*. Tr. by D. W. Robertson, Jr. Indianapolis: The Bobbs-Merrill Company, Inc., 1958.

Augustine (?). *De grammatica*. Ed. by H. Keil in *Grammatici Latini*, Vol. V, pp. 494–524. Leipzig: Teubner, 1923.

Augustine. *De magistro*. Ed. by Guenther Weigl. *CSEL*, 77. Vienna, 1961.

Augustine. *De musica*. Ed. by Benedictines in *PL* 32, cols. 1081–1194. Trans. by Robert C. Taliaferro. New York: Cima Publishing Company, 1947.

Augustine (?). *De rhetorica*. Ed. by Benedictines in *PL* 32, cols. 1439–1443. Ed. by C. Halm in *RLM*, pp. 135–151. Leipzig: Teubner, 1863.

Augustine. *Retractationes*. Ed. by Pius Knöll. *CSEL*, 36. Vienna and Leipzig, 1902.

Augustine. *The Retractations*. Trans. by Mary I. Bogan. Fathers of the Church, Vol. 60. Washington, D. C.: Catholic University of America Press, 1968.

Aulus Gellius. *Attic Nights*. Ed. with a trans. by John C. Rolfe. 3 vols., *LCL*. London and New York, 1927.

Martianus Capella. *De nuptiis Philologiae et Mercurii.* Book IV, *De arte dialectica*, ed. by F. Eyssenhardt, Leipzig: Teubner, 1866. Book V, *De arte rhetorica*, ed. by C. Halm, *RLM*, pp. 449–492.

Cassiodorus Senator. *Institutiones.* Ed. by R. A. B. Mynors. Oxford: At the Clarendon Press, 1937.

Cassiodorus Senator. *An Introduction to Divine and Human Readings.* Trans. by Leslie W. Jones. New York: W. W. Norton, 1969.

Cicero. *De inventione.* Ed. with a trans. by H. M. Hubbell. *LCL.* London and Cambridge, 1949.

Cicero. *De oratore.* Ed. with a trans. by E. W. Sutton and H. Rackham. 2 vols., *LCL.* London and Cambridge, 1942.

Cicero. *Orator.* Ed. with a trans. by H. M. Hubbell. *LCL.* London and Cambridge, 1939.

Diogenes Laertius. *Lives of Eminent Philosophers.* Ed. with a trans. by R. D. Hicks. Vol. II, *LCL.* London and Cambridge, 1925.

Chirius Fortunatianus. *Ars rhetoricae.* Ed. by C. Halm. *RLM*, pp. 81–134.

H. Funaioli, ed. *Grammaticae Romanae Fragmenta*, Vol. I. Leipzig: Teubner, 1907.

Henry of Kirkstede (?). *Catalogus de libris autenticis et apocrifis.* Intro. and trans. by Richard Rouse, unpublished Cornell University dissertation, 2 vols., 1963.

John of Salisbury. *Metalogicon.* Ed. by C. C. I. Webb. Oxford: At the Clarendon Press, 1929.

John of Salisbury. *The Metalogicon of John of Salisbury.* Trans. by Daniel McGarry. Berkeley and Los Angeles: University of California Press, 1955.

Possidius. *Operum S. Augustini Elenchus.* Ed. by A. Wilmart in *Miscellanea Agostiniana*, Vol. II, pp. 149–233. Rome: Tipografia Poliglotta Vaticana, 1936.

Pseudo-Augustine. *Categoriae decem.* Ed. by Benedictines in *PL* 32, cols. 1419–1440. Ed. by L. Minio-Paluello in *Aristoteles Latinus*, Vol. I, pp. 128–175. Paris: Desclée de Brouwer, 1961.

Quintilian. *Institutio oratoria.* Ed. with a trans. by H. E. Butler. 4 vols., *LCL.* London and New York, 1921.

Sextus Empiricus. *Adversus Mathematicos.* Ed. with a trans. by R. G. Bury. Vol. II, *Against the Logicians. LCL.* London and Cambridge, 1935.

Varro. *De Lingua Latina quae supersunt.* Ed. by G. Goetz and F. Schoell. Leipzig: Teubner, 1910.

Varro. *De Lingua Latina.* Ed. with a trans. by Roland G. Kent. 2 vols., *LCL.* London and Cambridge, 1938.

Wilmanns, Augustus, ed. *De M. Terenti Varronis Libris Grammaticis.* Berlin: Weidmann, 1864.

III. SECONDARY LITERATURE

Bandini, A. M. *Catalogus Codicum Latinorum Bibliothecae Mediceae Laurentianae*, Vol. II. Florence, 1775.

Bandini, A. M. *Biblioteca Leopoldina Laurentia seu Catalogus manuscriptorum qui iussi Petri Leopoldi… in Laurentianam translati sunt…*, Vol. I. Florence, 1791.

Barwick, Karl. *Probleme der Stoischen Sprachlehre und Rhetorik* (Abhandlungen der Sächsischen Akademie der Wissenschaften zu Leipzig, Philologisch-historische Klasse, Bd. 49, Hft. 3). Berlin: Akademie-Verlag, 1957.

Becker, Gustav. *Catalogi Bibliothecarum Antiqui.* Bonn: M. Cohen, 1885.

Bibliothèque Nationale. *Catalogue Générale des Manuscrits Latins*, Vol. II. Paris: Bibliothèque Nationale, 1940.

Billanovich, Giuseppe. "Il Petrarca e i Retori Latini Minori," *Italia medioevale e umanistica* V (Padova, 1962), 103–164.

Blumenkranz, Bernhard. "La survie médiévale de saint Augustin à travers ses apocryphes," *Augustinus Magister*, Vol. II, pp. 1003–1018. Paris: Études Augustiniennes, 1954.

Bocheński, I. M. *Ancient Formal Logic*. Amsterdam: North-Holland Publishing Company, 1957.

Bond, W. H., and Faye, C. U. *Supplement to the Census of Medieval and Renaissance Manuscripts in the United States and Canada*. New York: The Biographical Society of America, 1962.

Brinegar, Claude S. "Mark Twain and the Quintus Curtius Snodgrass Letters: A Statistical Test of Authorship," *Journal of the American Statistical Association* **58** (1963), 85–96.

Brown, Peter. *Augustine of Hippo, a Biography*. London: Faber and Faber, 1967.

Catalogue Général des Manuscrits des Bibliothèques Publiques de France. Departments (Octavo Series), Vol. XII. Paris: Libraire Plon, 1889.

Catalogue Général des Manuscrits des Bibliothèques Publiques des Departments (Quarto Series), Vols. II and V. Paris: Imprimerie Nationale, 1855 and 1897.

Catalogus Codicum Manuscriptorum Bibliothecae Regiae, Vol. IV. Paris: Typographia regia, 1744.

Courcelle, Pierre. *Late Latin Writers and Their Greek Sources*. Trans. by Harry E. Wedeck from *Les Lettres Grecques en Occident de Macrobe à Cassiodore*, 2nd edn. (Paris, 1948). Cambridge: Harvard University Press, 1969.

Cousin, Victor. *Ouvrages Inédits d'Abélard*. Paris: Imprimerie Royale, 1836.

De Ghellinck, Joseph. "Une Edition ou une Collection Médiévale des Opera Omnia de Saint Augustin," in *Liber Floridus* (Festschrift for Paul Lehmann), ed. by B. Bischoff and S. Brechter. St. Ottilien: Eos Verlag, 1950.

De Ghellinck, Joseph. *Patristique et Moyen Age*, Vol. III. Paris: Desclée de Brouwer, 1948.

Delatte, L., and Evrard, E. *Sénèque, Consolation à Helvia, Index verborum, Relevés statistiques*. The Hague: Mouton, 1963.

Delatte, L., and Evrard, E. *Sénèque, Consolation à Marcia, Index verborum, Relevés statistiques*. The Hague: Mouton, 1964.

Delatte, L., and Evrard, E. *Sénèque, Consolation à Polybe, Index verborum, Relevés statistiques*. Liège: Laboratoire d'Analyse Statistique des Langues Anciennes, 1962.

Delatte, L., and Evrard, E. *Sénèque, De Constantia Sapientis, Index verborum, Relevés statistiques*. The Hague: Mouton, 1966.

Delisle, Léopold. "Inventaire des Manuscrits Latins de Saint-Germain-des-Prés," *Bibliothèque de l'École des Chartes* **28** (1867), 343–376 and 528–556.

Delisle, Léopold. "Inventaire des Manuscrits Latins de la Sorbonne, conservés a la Bibliothèque Impériale sous les numeros 15176–16718 du Fonds Latins," *Bibliothèque de l'École des Chartes* **31** (1870), 135–161.

Dobiš-Roždestvenskaïa, Olga. *Histoire de l'Atelier Graphique de Corbie de 651 à 830 dans les Corbeienses Leninopolitani*. Leningrad: L'Academie des Sciences de l'URSS, 1934.

Dolezel, Lubomir, and Bailey, Richard W., eds. *Statistics and Style*. New York: American Elsevier, 1969.

Duchrow, Ulrich. *Sprachverständnis und Biblisches Hören bei Augustin*. Tübingen: J. C. B. Mohr, 1965.

Ehrle, Franz. *Historia Bibliothecae Romanorum Pontificum tum Bonifatianae tum Avenionensis*, Vol. I. Rome: Typis Vaticanis, 1890.

Ellegård, Alvar. *A Statistical Method for Determining Authorship: The Junius Letters, 1769–1772*. Goteborg: Acta Universitatis Gothoburgensis, 1962.

Faucon, Maurice. *La Librarie des Papes d'Avignon (1316–1420)*, 2 vols. Paris: Libraire des Écoles Francaises d'Athènes et de Rome, 1886 and 1887.

Fischer, Balduin. *De Augustini Disciplinarum Libro qui est De Dialectica*. Iena: G. Nevenhahn, 1912.

Gillis, John H. *The Coordinating Particles in Saints Hilary, Jerome, Ambrose, and Augustine*. Washington, D. C.: Catholic University of America Press, 1938.

Giornale Storico degli Archivi Toscani, Vol. VI, no. 2. Florence: G. P. Vieusseux, 1862.

Hagen, Hermann. *Catalogus Codicum Bernensium*. Bern: B. F. Haller, 1875.

Hagen, Hermann, ed. *Codex Bernensis 363 phototypice editus. Codices Graeci et Latini*, Vol. III. Leyden: A. W. Sijthoff, 1897.

Hagen, Hermann. "Zur Kritik und Erklärung der Dialektik des Augustinus," *Jahrbücher für Classische Philologie* 18 (1872) or *Neue Jahrbücher für Philologie und Paedagogik* 105 (1872), 757–780.

Hagendahl, Harald. *Augustine and the Latin Classics*, 2 vols. Goteborg: Acta Universitatis Gothoburgensis, 1967.

Hartmann, Alfred, ed. *Die Amerbachkorrespondenz*, Vol. I, *Die Briefe aus der Zeit Johann Amerbachs, 1481–1513*. Basel: Verlag der Universitatsbibliothek, 1942.

Hauréau, B. *Histoire de la Philosophie Scolastique*, Vol. I. Paris: Durand et Pedone-Lauriel, 1872.

Herdan, G. *Quantitative Linguistics*. Washington, D. C.: Butterworths, 1964.

Jackson, B. Darrell. "The Theory of Signs in St. Augustine's *De Doctrina Christiana*," *Revue des Études Augustiniennes* 15 (1969), 9–49.
    Reprinted in *Augustine*, A Collection of Critical Essays, ed. by R. A. Markus. Garden City, N.Y.: Doubleday, 1972, pp. 92–147.

Jaffé, Philipp, and Wattenbach, Wilhelm. *Ecclesiae Metropolitanae Coloniensis Codices Manuscripti*. Berlin: Weidmann, 1874.

James, M. R. *A Descriptive Catalogue of the Manuscripts in the Library of Corpus Christi College, Cambridge*, Vol. I. Cambridge: At the University Press, 1912.

James, M. R. *A Descriptive Catalogue of the Manuscripts in the Library of Eton College*. Cambridge: At the University Press, 1895.

Janson, Tore. "Word, Syllable, and Letter in Latin," *Eranos* 65 (1967), 49–64.

Keil, Heinrich. Review of Crecelius's Edition of Augustine's *De Dialectica* in *Jahrbücher für Classische Philologie* 5 (1859) or *Neue Jahrbücher für Philologie und Paedagogik* 79 (1859), 154–157.

Kenney, James F. *The Sources for the Early History of Ireland*, Vol. I. New York: Columbia University Press, 1929.

Kneale, William and Martha. *The Development of Logic*. 2nd impression, revised. Oxford: At the Clarendon Press, 1962.

Kretzmann, Norman. "History of Semantics," in *Encyclopedia of Philosophy*, Vol. VII, pp. 358–406. New York: The Macmillan Company, 1967.

Lacombe, George, and others. *Aristoteles Latinus, Codices Descripsit*. Vol. I, Rome: La Libreria Dello Stato, 1939. Vol. II, Cambridge: At the University Press, 1955. (See Minio-Paluello.)

Leed, Jacob, ed. *The Computer and Literary Style*. Kent, Ohio: Kent State University Press, 1966.

Lehmann, Paul, ed. *Mittelalterliche Bibliothekskataloge Deutschlands und der Schweiz*, Vol. I. Munich: C. H. Beck, 1918.

Leonardi, C. "I Codici di Marziano Capella," *Aevum* 34 (1960), 43ff. and 474ff.

Levison, M., Morton, A. Q., and Winspear, A. D. "The Seventh Letter of Plato," *Mind* 77 (1968), 309–325.

Lowe, E. A. *Codices Latini Antiquiores*, Pt. IV. Oxford: At the Clarendon Press, 1947. Pt. VIII. Oxford, 1959.

Lowe, E. A. "A List of the Oldest Extant Manuscripts of Saint Augustine," *Miscellanea Agostiniana*, Vol. II. Rome: Tipografia Poliglotta Vaticana, 1931.

Lowe, E. A. "A New List of Beneventan Manuscripts," *Studi e Testi* **220** (1962), 211–244.

Madan, Falconer, and Craster, H. H. E. *A Summary Catalogue of Western Manuscripts in the Bodleian Library at Oxford*, Vol. II, pt. I. Oxford: At the Clarendon Press, 1922.

Manitius, Max. "Handschriften Antiker Autoren in Mittelalterlichen Bibliothekskatalogen," *Zentralblatt für Bibliothekswesen*, Beiheft 67. Leipzig, 1935.

Marrou, Henri-Irénée. *Saint Augustin et la Fin de la Culture Antique*. 4th edn., including the *Retractatio* published in 1949. Paris: Éditions E. De Boccard, 1958.

Martin, Henry. *Catalogue des Manuscrits de la Bibliothèque de l'Arsenal*, Vol. I. Paris: Libraire Plon, 1885.

Mates, Benson. *Stoic Logic*. 2nd printing. Berkeley and Los Angeles: University of California Press, 1961.

Mazzatinti, Giuseppe. *Inventari dei Manoscriti delle Biblioteche d'Italia*, Vol. XXXI, ed. by Albano Sorbelli, Florence: Leo Olschki, 1925.

Meier, Gabriel. *Catalogus Codicum Manuscriptorum qui in Bibliotheca Monasterii Einsidlensis O.S.B.*, Vol. I. Leipzig: O. Harrassowitz, 1899.

Mendenhall, T. C. "The Characteristic Curve of Composition," *Science* **9** (1887), 237–249.

Mendenhall, T. C. "A Mechanical Solution of a Literary Problem," *The Popular Science Monthly* **60** (1901), 97–105.

Milic, Louis T. *A Quantitative Approach to the Style of Jonathan Swift*. The Hague: Mouton and Co., 1967.

Minio-Paluello, Lorenzo. *Aristoteles Latinus, Codices*, Supplement. Paris: Desclée de Brouwer, 1961.

Minio-Paluello, Lorenzo. "The Text of the *Categoriae*: the Latin Tradition," *Classical Quarterly* **39** (1945), 63–74.

Mohrmann, Christine. *Études sur le Latin des Chrétiens*. Rome: Edizioni di Storia e Letteratura, 1958.

Molinier, Auguste. *Catalogue des Manuscrits de la Bibliothèque Mazarine*, Vol. I. Paris: Libraire Plon, 1885.

Morin, Germain. "Le Catalogue des Manuscrits de l'Abbaye de Gorze au XIe Siècle," *Revue Bénédictine* **22** (1905), 1–14.

Morton, Andrew Q., and McLeman, James. *Paul, the Man and the Myth*. New York: Harper and Row, 1966.

Möser-Mersky, G., and Mihaliuk, M., eds. *Mittelalterliche Bibliothekskataloge Österreichs*, Vol. IV. Vienna: Hermann Böhlaus, 1966.

Mosteller, Frederick, and Wallace, David. *Inference and Disputed Authorship:* The Federalist. Reading, Mass.: Addison-Wesley, 1964.

Nogara, Bartholomeus. *Bibliothecae Apostolicae Vaticanae Codices. Codices Vaticani Latini*, Vol. III. Rome: Typis Vaticani, 1912.

Oberleitner, Manfred. *Die Handschriftliche Überlieferung der Werke des Heiligen Augustinus* (Sitzungberichte der Österreichischen Akademie der Wissenschaften, Philosophisch-Historische Klasse, Bd. 263). Vol. I, pt. 2. *Italien. Verzeichnis nach Bibliotheken*. Vienna: Hermann Böhlaus, 1970.

Ogilvy, J. D. A. *Books Known to Anglo-Latin Writers from Aldhelm to Alcuin (670–804)*. 2nd edn. Cambridge: The Medieval Academy of America, 1967.

Palmer, L. R. *The Latin Language*. London: Faber and Faber, 1954.

Pfligersdorffer, Georg. "Zu Boethius, De Interp. Ed. Sec. I, p. 4, 4 sqq. Meiser, nebst Beobachtungen zur Geschichte der Dialektik bei den Römern," *Wiener Studien* **56** (1953), 131–154.

Pinborg, Jan. "Das Sprachdenken der Stoa und Augustins Dialektik," *Classica et Mediaevalia* **23** (1962), 148–177.

Prantl, Carl. *Geschichte der Logik im Abendlande*, Vols. I and II (2nd edn.). Leipzig: Gustav Fock, 1927 (originally published in 1855 and 1885).

Reitzenstein, R. M. *Terentius Varro und Johannes Mauropus von Euchaita.* Leipzig: B. G. Teubner, 1901.

Rose, Valentin. *Verzeichniss der Lateinischen Handschriften der Königlichen Bibliothek zu Berlin*, Vol. I. Berlin: A. Asher, 1893.

Ruf, Paul., ed. *Mittelalterliche Bibliothekskataloge Deutschlands und der Schweiz*, Vol. III. Munich: C. H. Beck, 1932.

Sandys, John Edwin. *A History of Classical Scholarship*, Vol. II. Cambridge: At the University Press, 1908.

Schillmann, Fritz. *Verzeichnis der Lateinischen Handschriften der Preussischen Staatsbibliothek zu Berlin*, Vol. III. Berlin: Behrend, 1919.

Staerk, Antonio. *Les Manuscrits Latins de Ve au XIIIe Siècle conserves à la Bibliothèque Impériale de Saint-Petersbourg*, Vol. I. St. Petersburg: Franz Krois, 1910.

Stanley, Thomas. *The History of Philosophy, The Eighth Part, Containing the Stoick Philosophers.* London: H. Moseley and T. Dring, 1656.

Stornajolo, Cosimus. *Bibliothecae Apostolicae Vaticanae, Codices Urbinates Latini*, Vol. I. Rome: Typis Vaticanis, 1902. Vol. III, 1921.

Van de Vyver, A. "Les Étapes de Dévelopment Philosophique de Haut Moyen-Age," *Revue Belge de Philologie et d'Histoire* **8** (1929), 435–452.

Van den Gheyn, J. *Catalogue des Manuscrits de la Bibliotheque Royale de Belgique*, Vol. II. Brussels: H. Lamertin, 1902.

Vernet, M.-Th. "Notes de Dom André Wilmart sur quelques Manuscrits latins anciens de la Bibliothèque nationale de Paris," *Bulletin d'Information de l'Institut de Recherche et d'Histoire des Textes* **8** (1959), 7–45.

Ullman, B. L. *The Humanism of Coluccio Salutati.* (Medievo e umanesimo 4) Padova, 1963.

Valentinelli, Joseph. *Bibliothecae Manuscripta ad S. Marci Venetiarum*, Vol. IV. Venice, 1871.

Waite, Stephen V. F. "Approaches to the Analysis of Latin Prose, applied to Cato, Sallust and Livy," *Revue de l'Organization Internationale pour l'Étude des Langues Anciennes par Ordinateur*, 1970, no. 2, 91–112.

Weiss, Roberto. *Humanism in England During the Fifteenth Century*, 3rd edn. Oxford: Basil Blackwell, 1967.

Wilmart, André. *Bibliothecae Apostolicae Vaticanae, Codices Reginenses Latini*, Vol. I. Rome: Typis Vaticanis, 1937.

Woodward, William Harrison. *Studies in Education during the Age of the Renaissance, 1400–1600.* New York: Russell and Russell, 1965 (Originally published in 1906).

Woodward, William Harrison. *Vittorino da Feltre and Other Humanist Educators: Essays and Versions.* Cambridge: At the University Press, 1912.

Yule, G. Udny. *The Statistical Study of Literary Vocabulary.* Cambridge: At the University Press, 1944.

Zacour, Norman, and Hirsch, Rudolf. *Catalogue of Manuscripts in the Libraries of the University of Pennsylvania to 1800.* Philadelphia: University of Pennsylvania Press, 1965.

INDEXES

I. INDEX TO THE LATIN TEXT OF *DE DIALECTICA*

The method of reference is the one described above on p. XII. When there is more than one occurrence of a word in a passage designated, the number of occurrences is given in parentheses. Page and line numbers in italics indicate quoted material. For the words chosen, the index of terms (A) is complete. The index of words discussed (B) is of mainly philological interest. The indexes of names (C) and of authors (D) are complete.

vinco   VI 12,8
vincula   VI 11,20
vis   VI 11,19 and 12,8f.
vites   VI 12,1 and 7
voluptas   VI 10,6
vomis   VI 11,15f.
vulnus   VI 11,15f.

C. *Names*

Aeneas   V 8,19f. (2)
Antonius   IX 15,18
Artaxerxes   VII 12,16
Augustinus   VII 13,6f. (2)

Capitolium   X 18,4
Catilina   X 17,20
Cicero   VI 8,27; 9,2; 9,18f. (2)   IX
   15,14; 15,18   X 19,11f. (2)
Cotta   VII 12,19

Ennius   VI 9,12
Euryalus   VII 12,16

Graeci   VI 9,12   X 19,26

Hortensius   IX 15,15–19 (2)

Motta   VII 12,19

Pompeius   VIII 15,8–12 (2)

Scaevola   IX 15,18
Stoici   VI 9,18; 11,12

Terentius   VI 12,2
Tullius   X 17,17–25 (9); 18,1–10 (7);
   19,1; 19,6f. (2)

Vergilius   V 8,18   VI 9,13; 11,5
   VIII 15,9–12 (2)
Vulcanus   V 8,19

D. *Authors Quoted*

Cicero
   De oratore I.x.44   IX 15,18f.
   Hortensius, fr. 99 (Mueller, 1890)
   IX 15,15–17

Ennius
   Fr. L (Vahlen, 1903)   VI 9,12

Sallust
   Bellum Catilinae 14.2   VII 13,10

Terence
   Andria III.iii.33, line 665   X 20,5f.
   Eunuchus IV.iv.21, line 688   VI 12,2

Vergil
   Aeneis V.755   VI 11,5
   Georgica III.223   VI 9,13
   Georgica IV.487   X 20,12f.

II. INDEX TO THE INTRODUCTION, TRANSLATION, AND NOTES

Page numbers in italics indicate topics and names occurring in *De dialectica*.

SYNTHESE HISTORICAL LIBRARY

Texts and Studies
in the History of Logic and Philosophy

Editors:

N. KRETZMANN (Cornell University)
G. NUCHELMANS (University of Leyden)
L. M. DE RIJK (University of Leyden)

SYNTHESE LIBRARY

Monographs on Epistemology, Logic, Methodology,
Philosophy of Science, Sociology of Science and of Knowledge, and on the
Mathematical Methods of Social and Behavioral Sciences

Editors:

ROBERT S. COHEN (Boston University)
DONALD DAVIDSON (The Rockefeller University and Princeton University)
JAAKKO HINTIKKA (Academy of Finland and Stanford University)
GABRIËL NUCHELMANS (University of Leyden)
WESLEY C. SALMON (University of Arizona)

18. ROBERT S. COHEN and MARX W. WARTOFSKY (eds.), *Proceedings of the Boston Colloquium for the Philosophy of Science 1966–1968*, Boston Studies in the Philosophy of Science (ed. by Robert S. Cohen and Marx W. Wartofsky), Volume IV. 1969, VIII + 537 pp.
19. ROBERT S. COHEN and MARX W. WARTOFSKY (eds.), *Proceedings of the Boston Colloquium for the Philosophy of Science 1966–1968*, Boston Studies in the Philosophy of Science (ed. by Robert S. Cohen and Marx W. Wartofsky), Volume V. 1969, VIII + 482 pp.
20. J. W. DAVIS, D. J. HOCKNEY, and W. K. WILSON (eds.), *Philosophical Logic*. 1969, VIII + 277 pp.
21. D. DAVIDSON and J. HINTIKKA (eds.), *Words and Objections: Essays on the Work of W. V. Quine*. 1969, VIII + 366 pp.
22. PATRICK SUPPES, *Studies in the Methodology and Foundations of Science. Selected Papers from 1911 to 1969*, XII + 473 pp.
23. JAAKKO HINTIKKA, *Models for Modalities. Selected Essays*. 1969, IX + 220 pp.
24. NICHOLAS RESCHER *et al.* (eds.), *Essays in Honor of Carl G. Hempel. A Tribute on the Occasion of his Sixty-Fifth Birthday*. 1969, VII + 272 pp.
25. P. V. TAVANEC (ed.), *Problems of the Logic of Scientific Knowledge*. 1969, XII + 429 pp.
26. MARSHALL SWAIN (ed.), *Induction, Acceptance, and Rational Belief*. 1970, VII + 232 pp.
27. ROBERT S. COHEN and RAYMOND J. SEEGER (eds.), *Ernst Mach; Physicist and Philosopher*, Boston Studies in the Philosophy of Science (ed. by Robert S. Cohen and Marx W. Wartofsky), Volume VI. 1970, VIII + 295 pp.
28. JAAKKO HINTIKKA and PATRICK SUPPES, *Information and Inference*. 1970, X + 336 pp.
29. KAREL LAMBERT, *Philosophical Problems in Logic. Some Recent Developments*. 1970, VII + 176 pp.
30. ROLF A. EBERLE, *Nominalistic Systems*. 1970, IX + 217 pp.
31. PAUL WEINGARTNER and GERHARD ZECHA (eds.), *Induction, Physics, and Ethics, Proceedings and Discussions of the 1968 Salzburg Colloquium in the Philosophy of Science*. 1970, X + 382 pp.
32. EVERT W. BETH, *Aspects of Modern Logic*. 1970, XI + 176 pp.
33. RISTO HILPINEN (ed.), *Deontic Logic: Introductory and Systematic Readings*. 1971, VII + 182 pp.
34. JEAN-LOUIS KRIVINE, *Introduction to Axiomatic Set Theory*. 1971, VII + 98 pp.
35. JOSEPH D. SNEED, *The Logical Structure of Mathematical Physics*. 1971, XV + 311 pp.
36. CARL R. KORDIG, *The Justification of Scientific Change*. 1971, XIV + 119 pp.
37. MILIČ ČAPEK, *Bergson and Modern Physics*, Boston Studies in the Philosophy of Science (ed. by Robert S. Cohen and Marx W. Wartofsky), Volume VII. 1971, XV + 414 pp.
38. NORWOOD RUSSELL HANSON, *What I do not Believe, and other Essays*, ed. by Stephen Toulmin and Harry Woolf. 1971, XII + 390 pp.
39. ROGER C. BUCK and ROBERT S. COHEN (eds.), *PSA 1970. In Memory of Rudolf Carnap*, Boston Studies in the Philosophy of Science (ed. by Robert S. Cohen and Marx W. Wartofsky), Volume VIII. 1971, LXVI + 615 pp. Also available as a paperback.
40. DONALD DAVIDSON and GILBERT HARMAN (eds.), *Semantics of Natural Language*. 1972, X + 769 pp. Also available as a paperback.
41. YEHOSHUA BAR-HILLEL (ed.), *Pragmatics of Natural Languages*. 1971, VII + 231 pp.
42. SÖREN STENLUND, *Combinators, λ-Terms and Proof Theory*. 1972, 184 pp.
43. MARTIN STRAUSS, *Modern Physics and Its Philosophy. Selected Papers in the Logic, History, and Philosophy of Science*. 1972, X + 297 pp.

44. MARIO BUNGE, *Method, Model and Matter*. 1973, VII + 196 pp.
45. MARIO BUNGE, *Philosophy of Physics*. 1973, IX + 248 pp.
46. A. A. ZINOV'EV, *Foundations of the Logical Theory of Scientific Knowledge (Complex Logic)*, Boston Studies in the Philosophy of Science (ed. by Robert S. Cohen and Marx W. Wartofsky), Volume IX. Revised and enlarged English edition with an appendix, by G. A. Smirnov, E. A. Sidorenka, A. M. Fedina, and L. A. Bobrova 1973, XXII + 301 pp. Also available as a paperback.
47. LADISLAV TONDL, *Scientific Procedures*, Boston Studies in the Philosophy of Science (ed. by Robert S. Cohen and Marx W. Wartofsky), Volume X. 1973, XII + 268 pp. Also available as a paperback.
48. NORWOOD RUSSELL HANSON, *Constellations and Conjectures*, ed. by Willard C. Humphreys, Jr. 1973, X + 282 pp.
49. K. J. J. HINTIKKA, J. M. E. MORAVCSIK, and P. SUPPES (eds.), *Approaches to Natural Language. Proceedings of the 1970 Stanford Workshop on Grammar and Semantics*. 1973, VIII + 526 pp. Also available as a paperback.
50. MARIO BUNGE (ed.), *Exact Philosophy – Problems, Tools, and Goals*. 1973, X + 214 pp.
51. RADU J. BOGDAN and ILKKA NIINILUOTO (eds.), *Logic, Language, and Probability*. A selection of papers contributed to Sections IV, VI, and XI of the Fourth International Congress for Logic, Methodology, and Philosophy of Science, Bucharest, September 1971. 1973, X + 323 pp.
52. GLENN PEARCE and PATRICK MAYNARD (eds.), *Conceptual Chance*. 1973, XII + 282 pp.
53. ILKKA NIINILUOTO and RAIMO TUOMELA, *Theoretical Concepts and Hypothetico-Inductive Inference*. 1973, VII + 264 pp.
54. ROLAND FRAÏSSÉ, *Course of Mathematical Logic – Volume 1: Relation and Logical Formula*. 1973, XVI + 186 pp. Also available as a paperback.
55. ADOLF GRÜNBAUM, *Philosophical Problems of Space and Time*. Second, enlarged edition, Boston Studies in the Philosophy of Science (ed. by Robert S. Cohen and Marx W. Wartofsky), Volume XII. 1973, XXIII + 884 pp. Also available as a paperback.
56. PATRICK SUPPES (ed.), *Space, Time, and Geometry*. 1973, XI + 424 pp.
57. HANS KELSEN, *Essays in Legal and Moral Philosophy*, selected and introduced by Ota Weinberger. 1973, XXVIII + 300 pp.
58. R. J. SEEGER and ROBERT S. COHEN (eds.), *Philosophical Foundations of Science. Proceedings of an AAAS Program, 1969*. Boston Studies in the Philosophy of Science (ed. by Robert S. Cohen and Marx W. Wartofsky), Volume XI. 1974, X + 545 pp. Also available as paperback.
59. ROBERT S. COHEN and MARX W. WARTOFSKY (eds.), *Logical and Epistemological Studies in Contemporary Physics*, Boston Studies in the Philosophy of Science (ed. by Robert S. Cohen and Marx W. Wartofsky), Volume XIII. 1973, VIII + 462 pp. Also available as paperback.
60. ROBERT S. COHEN and Marx W. WARTOFSKY (eds.), *Methodological and Historical Essays in the Natural and Social Sciences. Proceedings of the Boston Colloquium for the Philosophy of Science, 1969–1972*, Boston Studies in the Philosophy of Science (ed. by Robert S. Cohen and Marx W. Wartofsky), Volume XIV. 1974, VIII + 405 pp. Also available as paperback.
61. ROBERT S. COHEN, J. J. STACHEL and MARX W. WARTOFSKY (eds.), *For Dirk Struik. Scientific, Historical and Political Essays in Honor of Dirk J. Struik*, Boston Studies in the Philosophy of Science (ed. by Robert S. Cohen and Marx W. Wartofsky), Volume XV. 1974, XXVII + 652 pp. Also available as paperback.
62. KAZIMIERZ AJDUKIEWICZ, *Pragmatic Logic*, transl. from the Polish by Olgierd Wojtasiewicz. 1974, XV + 460 pp.

63. Sören Stenlund (ed.), *Logical Theory and Semantic Analysis. Essays Dedicated to Stig Kanger on His Fiftieth Birthday.* 1974, V + 217 pp.

64. Kenneth F. Schaffner and Robert S. Cohen (eds.), *Proceedings of the 1972 Biennial Meeting, Philosophy of Science Association,* Boston Studies in the Philosophy of Science (ed. by Robert S. Cohen and Marx W. Wartofsky), Volume XX. 1974, IX + 444 pp. Also available as paperback.

65. Henry E. Kyburg, Jr., *The Logical Foundations of Statistical Inference.* 1974, IX + 421 pp.

66. Marjorie Grene, *The Understanding of Nature: Essays in the Philosophy of Biology,* Boston Studies in the Philosophy of Science (ed. by Robert S. Cohen and Marx W. Wartofsky), Volume XXIII. 1974, XII + 360 pp. Also available as paperback.

67. Jan M. Broekman, *Structuralism: Moscow, Prague, Paris.* 1974, IX + 117 pp.

68. Norman Geschwind, *Selected Papers on Language and the Brain,* Boston Studies in the Philosophy of Science (ed. by Robert S. Cohen and Marx W. Wartofsky), Volume XVI. 1974, XII + 549 pp. Also available as paperback.

69. Roland Fraïssé, *Course of Mathematical Logic* – Volume II: *Model Theory.* 1974, XIX + 192 pp.

70. Andrzej Grzegorczyk, *An Outline of Mathematical Logic.* Fundamental Results and Notions Explained with All Details. 1974, X + 596 pp.